CRIME AND MON[...]

Crime and Money
Laundering:
The Indian Perspective

JYOTI TREHAN

OXFORD
UNIVERSITY PRESS

OXFORD
UNIVERSITY PRESS

YMCA Library Building, Jai Singh Road, New Delhi 110 001

Oxford University Press is a department of the University of Oxford.
It furthers the University's objective of excellence in research, scholarship,
and education by publishing worldwide in

Oxford New York

Cape Town Dar es Salaam Hong Kong Karachi Kuala Lumpur Madrid
Melbourne Mexico Nairobi New Delhi Toronto Shanghai

With offices in

Argentina Austria Brazil Chile Czech Republic Eire France Greece
Guatemala and Central America Hungary Italy Japan Korea New Zealand
Poland Portugal Singapore Switzerland Taiwan Thailand
Turkey Ukraine Vietnam

Oxford is a registered trade mark of Oxford University Press
in the UK and in certain other countries

Published in India
By Oxford University Press, New Delhi

ISBN 0 19 567306 9

Printed by Roopak Printers, New Delhi 110 032
Published by Manzar Khan, Oxford University Press
YMCA Library Building, Jai Singh Road, New Delhi 110 001

To
my father, Shri R.N. Trehan,
and
my mother, Smt. Sheila Trehan,
who are no more

Contents

Contents

Preface

This book was conceived during the period 2000–2001, when I was a Jawahar Lal Nehru Fellow working on the project 'Proceeds of Crime and Money Laundering: how it impinges on National Security'. In fact, it would be more accurate to say that the foundations of this book were laid as far back as the 1980s when I had my first brush with the subject matter of 'Money Laundering'.

I am by temperament an ambitious man, therefore the canvas on which I proposed to carry out my study and to write this book was so 'broad' from the very outset that a number of friends/doubters wondered if it was possible to carry through such a project in one go and to put it down in a single book. It was as a result of a systematic approach on my part that the project was successfully completed and the book came to be written.

Apart from research by way of reading basic material, other factors that shaped the writing of this book were talks given by me and the articles that I wrote in my capacity as a Jawahar Lal Nehru Fellow. The seminars, symposiums, conferences and working group meetings that I attended, both at the national and international level, also enabled me to interact with experts in the field of money laundering and get to know of the latest developments on a topical subject matter that is dynamic and continually evolving.

Since I am a police officer by profession and training, at the very outset I had decided that my study and the book would not be purely academic or theoretical – I had no desire to generate a lot of hot air. Thus, the basic approach that I adopted was a proactive one; it meant going out into the field and interacting with enforcement officers, professionals such as bankers/chartered accountants/lawyers, captains of trade and industry, bureaucrats dealing with economic affairs/finance, members of regulatory bodies/expert bodies/study groups, politicians of all hues, academics and personnel from relevant international/regional agencies. The net result was that I carried out very extensive field studies both in India and abroad. The time and effort expended on these field studies will be well worth the effort if the readers find that this book has a ring of truth about it.

The book has been divided into six parts. The first deals with 'big crimes – big money'. How money is laundered is dealt with in the second part. In the third part, national security and economic liberalization dimensions vis-à-vis crime and money laundering are considered. Some of the important facets and recent developments related to the subject matter are covered in the fourth part. The laws and the role of international organizations in countering money laundering are the subject matter of the fifth. Part Six is an important addition because it contains the select bibliography, other references and the index. As already stated, the book has been written with a certain sweep; I would be more than happy if the readers also remember it for its pithiness, clarity and simplicity. I also crave the reader's indulgence for any repetitions in the text; they have been kept to a minimum and have been inserted to clarify or highlight a point. The footnotes have also been kept to a minimum and have been given only where they are considered necessary.

During the highs and lows of my fellowship I was once told that a dialogue with the government is like a dialogue with the deaf, but considering the topicality of the subject matter, I hope that the governments of the day will wake up to the dangers posed by crime and money laundering and take timely preventive action. I would also like to add here that this book is meant as much for the professional as for the layman – the basic idea being to sensitize all thinking individuals to the 'lurking threat'.

Jyoti Trehan
Punjab, March 2003

Acknowledgements

I would like to extend my sincere thanks and a deep sense of gratitude to the Jawahar Lal Nehru Memorial Fund for having afforded me an opportunity to write this book as a sequel to the Jawahar Lal Nehru Fellowship that was awarded to me to work on the project 'Proceeds of Crime and Money Laundering in the Indian Context: how it impinges on National Security'.

I would also like to thank all the persons with whom I interacted and all those who helped me in putting the manuscript together; much as I would have preferred to acknowledge them by name, they are so numerous that it is not practicable to do so.

I would also like to acknowledge my debt to my dear friend Professor Barry A.K. Rider, for having introduced me to the very fascinating subject of money laundering in 1985.

Above all, I would like to thank Dr Karan Singh, Vice Chairman of the Jawahar Lal Nehru Memorial Fund, for his constant encouragement during the period of my fellowship.

About the Author

Jyoti Trehan is Inspector General of Police, Indian Police Service, Punjab. Until 2001 he was a Jawahar Lal Nehru Fellow, the project for his fellowship being 'Proceeds of Crime and Money Laundering in the Indian Context: how it impinges on National Security'.

During his distinguished career in Punjab, Mr Trehan has held key assignments and also has the distinction of raising the largest commando force in the world from within the police, which played a critical role in putting an end to terrorism in that state. During his assignment with the Central Bureau of Investigation, a federal agency, he headed the Interpol Wing of India. He therefore has ample experience of dealing with all forms of crime.

Mr Trehan is familiar with money laundering, having worked in the Financial Investigation Unit of the Interpol General Secretariat. He has delivered a number of talks on the subject at international forums and has also contributed articles on matters of professional interest which have been published in a number of prestigious journals. He also serves on the Advisory Board of the *Journal of Money Laundering Control* and is a recipient of the Police Medal for Meritorious Service.

PART I

BIG CRIMES – BIG MONEY

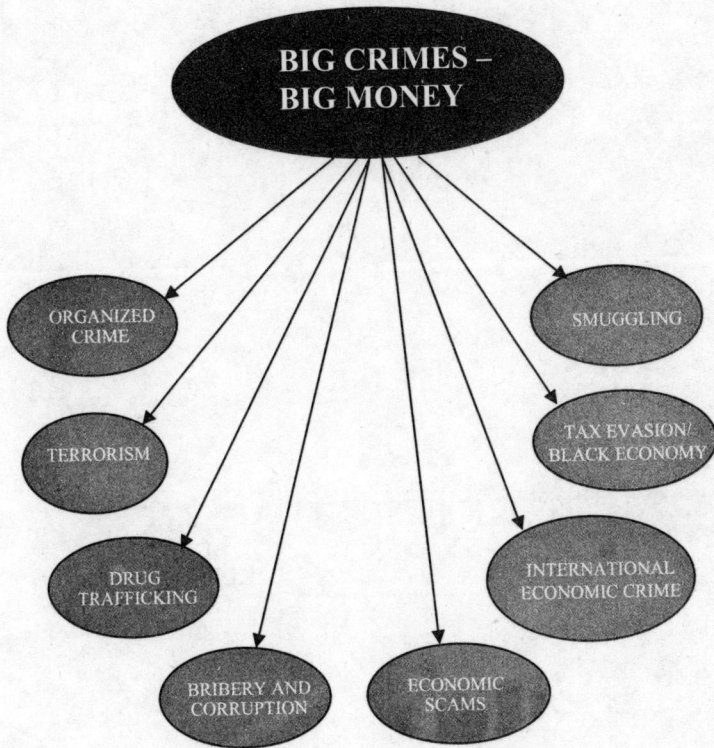

CHAPTER I

CRIME IN GENERAL – A BRIEF SURVEY

In the fast-changing world of today, advances are being made in practically all areas of human activity: it is perhaps axiomatic that these advances are not necessarily confined to beneficial areas. Take crime, for instance, which has increased greatly in the last two decades. While surveying crime in general, I attempt to highlight its characteristics and the environment in which it occurs: such an attempt will hopefully lead to a better understanding of this phenomenon. Proper understanding of the present-day crime scenario should also enable one to devise the most effective strategies to counter this problem.

In today's world, crime can no longer be described as simply an individual aberration, because criminal activities have assumed the dimensions of 'large enterprises'. Crime today is not only 'big' but also has a tendency to become bigger still. The best illustration of this 'bigness' are the organized-crime groups which have surfaced all over the world. Not only has crime become big, but it is also a big money-spinner. It is these large sums of money which act as motivating factors for the criminal enterprises of today, another feature of which is that they are run along business lines – one could even say that they are more or less like corporate entities. To give an idea of the large sums of money involved in crime, drug trafficking worldwide, according to UNDCP estimates, exceeds US$500 billion.

Another peculiar feature of present-day crime is that it is not confined to one country; it spreads across several countries/regions and in some instances its reach is almost global. The nature of present-day crime is thus transnational. The transnational character of crime is one of the principal reasons contributing to its lucrativeness; again, it is primarily because of its transnational character that law enforcement is finding it so difficult to tackle. Because of its global reach, drug trafficking is perhaps the best example of the transnational character of crime today. Terrorism, which has both a global and a regional reach – depending upon the organizations involved – can serve as another example of its transnational character. Organized crime, because of its regional orientation, can also be characterized as transnational.

The main basis for the existence of 'state' is that it ensures a civil society, which can only be ensured by the rule of law. If the law of the land is flouted, it leads to crime. Widespread crime as witnessed today has resulted in social chaos which, in other words, amounts to disruption of civil society. If one surveys the present-day crime scenario, terrorism and organized crime are perhaps the two crimes which seem to pose the maximum threat to a civil society. The extent to which that civil society is threatened or imperilled by crime is the extent to which the state can be characterized as a failed state.

Economic activity is the hub around which a state revolves. Economic well-being of a state is thus an area which must be zealously guarded. However, today widespread criminal activities are posing a threat which can or does tear asunder the economic fabric of the state. Tax evasion and other forms of crime lead to generation of black income, which in turn leads to black economy; if allowed to go unchecked, the black economy emerges as a parallel economy, almost rivalling the national economy. By its sheer size this black economy can throw all macro-economic projections of the state out of gear; if it is accompanied by capital flight, it can cause tremendous damage to the economic fabric of the state. Likewise, economic scams which seem to be occurring with a certain degree of periodicity in most of the countries of the world, and various other forms of economic crime, also pose a very serious threat to the economic well-being of a state.

The crime and criminal enterprises of today also pose a serious threat to the security of the state. This threat has both an external and internal dimension; moreover, this threat to national security can be direct or indirect. Organized crime, which thrives on a nexus between politicians, bureaucrats and criminals, poses an indirect threat to national security by way of internal sabotage. The extent to which organized crime has developed links with terrorists – for instance, in the case of India, where Inter-Services Intelligence of Pakistan has been instrumental in forging such links – poses an external direct threat to national security. Terrorism, a form of low-intensity conflict, generally fomented by hostile neighbours/countries, poses a direct threat to internal security; depending upon the way this form of warfare is carried out, terrorism can have either an internal or an external dimension, or both.

Another trend that has been noticed worldwide is that these criminals are branching out into legitimate commercial activities. With their criminal mindsets and the back-up of a criminal enterprise behind them, they pose a very serious threat to legitimate commerce. It is not uncommon to find criminal enterprises running legitimate businesses to fund their activities; for example, some of the terrorist organizations also run legitimate businesses to finance their activities. Organized crime needs a façade of legitimacy to operate with impunity; it acquires this by entering into legitimate commercial activity. Organized-crime groups are also entering into legitimate commercial activity to maximize their profits. Sometimes this craving for legitimacy can by itself be an overriding reason for criminals to enter into legitimate commerce, in the hope that in three-to-four generations the family will emerge as a 'pure business house'; perhaps it is for this reason that one often comes across the saying, 'behind every fortune there is a crime'.

Since the demise of communism in the early 1990s, most of the erstwhile Communist states have embarked on the path of economic liberalization. Even the developing states, which were tinkering with socialism and planned economies, have taken a similar route. Economic liberalization not only entails the opening up of the economy, but also results in greater integration of a country's financial and banking system with the international financial and banking system. In such a state of transition from one economic system to another, states are particularly vulnerable to the manipulation of criminals. One example is the role played by organized-crime groups in Russia. Disinvestment, which was one of the main planks of economic liberalization in Russia, was so manipulated by the organized-crime groups that what took place was more or less plundering of state-owned assets. Likewise, in many of the developing economies, some sectors of the economy became more active as a result of economic liberalization; in these active sectors, due to lack of vigilance, the criminals have been at work – such as, for instance, in the two scams of major proportions to hit the Indian stock market in the last ten years.

Crime today also has to contend with the revolutionary developments that have marked the emergence of the information technology (IT) sector. The reach, the speed and the ease of communication afforded by the IT sector have blurred the national boundaries; things are so amorphous that it is sometimes almost impossible to identify jurisdictions in cases of cybercrime. New and strange types of crime are also surfacing in the IT sector, because of its newness. Moreover, the IT environment deals with virtual documents produced electronically, and the laws of evidence are not geared to deal with such a situation. The IT sector has led to the emergence of virtual jurisdictions, also known as cyberspace. So long as criminals are operating out of conventional jurisdictions, one can still deal with them, but once they go into cyberspace, they are without traditional forms of control.

Crime also has to be viewed in the context of some of the global trends, also described as globalization. One such trend is the growth of mega-corporations, resulting from mergers of existing multinational corporations; it is anticipated that these mega-corporations could become so powerful that even states would not be able to combat their actions. Another global trend is an attempt to provide 24-hour seamless trading, through the merger of stock exchanges of different countries. Considering the way people travel nowadays – for business or tourism – the world seems like a global village. All of the above global trends, coupled with many others, afford tremendous opportunity to criminals of today – in fact, all forms of transnational criminality could thrive in such an environment.

If physics and chemistry were the great sciences of the twentieth century, then biotechnology and psychology are going to be the great sciences of the twenty-first century. Both of these sciences have the potential to open up a Pandora's Box in the criminal sphere. The opportunities that biotechnology could afford to criminals came across to me in a very stark manner in a film that I saw recently; in this film human clones were used to create a deliberate mix-up of identities in the commission of crimes. At the beginning of the twentieth century, Shri Aurbindo, a great mystic, remarked that we are living in the Stone Age of psychology; since then, tremendous advances have been made in the exploration of the human mind. These advances are likely to produce situations where mind control could be employed by criminals for their illicit ends.

The various types of crime with the attributes described above on which one could focus are organized crime, terrorism, trafficking in small arms, drug trafficking, bribery and corruption, smuggling of gold/diamonds, economic scams, international economic crimes, tax evasion/black economy, trafficking in women/immigrants, antiques/other forms of smuggling, credit-card frauds, counterfeiting of goods and counterfeiting of currency. It is evident that diversification and increased sophistication are two important trends of crime today. The various types of crimes which I propose to deal with in the context of this book are organized crime, terrorism, drug trafficking, bribery and corruption, economic scams, international economic crime, smuggling and tax evasion/black economy.

One of the greatest concerns of criminals today is to legitimize the proceeds of crime – the process also called money laundering. According to World Bank estimates, money laundering today is an US$800 billion to US$1 trillion problem. According to the Managing Director of the International Monetary Fund in his address to the Financial Action Task Force (FATF) in 1989, 'money laundering' constitutes 2 per cent to 5 per cent of the world GDP. In recognition of the gravity of the problem posed by money laundering and in order to deprive the criminals of their illegal proceeds, thereby hitting them where it hurts them most, money laundering has recently been categorized as a crime in the criminal laws of several countries. In the context of this book, the money laundering dimension, along with national security and economic liberalization, is a major dimension and therefore will be dealt with in all of its ramifications.

To combat crimes, states have devised laws – penal codes/special laws – on the basis of which enforcement agencies, based upon their investigations, charge the criminals to face trial. In general, the law enforcement machinery is lagging behind criminals and the crimes they commit, in the sense that criminals not bound by any constraints are generally a step ahead, and the new types of crimes they commit have not been criminalized by the state concerned. Moreover, it has been noted that often the criminals escape with a rap on the knuckles by way of punishment. Inadequate punishments are generally the norm in cases of white-collar crimes and economic crimes, even though they cause much more damage to society than 'conventional' crimes. Another noteworthy feature of the criminal justice system that needs to be highlighted is the cost-benefit analysis of the cost involved in investigation and trial of criminals and the amount confiscated as 'the proceeds of crime'. It is the experience that, whereas the cost of administering justice runs into millions of dollars – especially in cases of money laundering, drug trafficking, terrorism and organized crime – the proceeds confiscated are 'peanuts'. From the above discussion, one inescapable conclusion that emerges is that national responses have not been adequate to deal with modern-day serious crime.

Grave and serious crimes such as terrorism, narcotics trafficking, organized crime and money laundering, which are also transnational in character, have been engaging the attention of the 'comity of nations'. Several international conventions have been promulgated to deal with them. Although conventions to deal with narcotics trafficking and some forms of terrorism, such as hijacking, have existed for some time, the latest in the series of such conventions is the United Nations Convention against Transnational Organized Crime. This covers organized crime, money laundering and corruption, and the protocols annexed to it cover trafficking in arms and in human beings (women and children, and immigrants/labourers). Likewise, at regional and bilateral level, too, similar conventions/agreements have been concluded to deal with serious crime. Although the above conventions/agreements have been able to focus world attention on the issue of serious criminality, their impact in combating the same can once again be termed as inadequate.

Realizing that the criminal justice system has been unable to deal with the problem of present-day crime in an effective manner, intelligence agencies – which are looking for a new role following the demise of communism and the consequent cold war – and law enforcement agencies have concluded that certain disruptive strategies would be a more effective way to deal with the problem of widespread serious crime. Depending upon the nature of the crime, suitable intelligence modules could now easily be worked out for effective disruptive action.

This chapter would be incomplete if it did not touch upon good governance in the context of crime. It is the decline in the standards of governance over the last two or three decades that has resulted in a breakdown of the state machinery in several areas, including that of combating crime. This lack of good governance can be ascribed to greed, corruption, nepotism, erosion of value systems and a general decline in administrative capabilities. To tackle crimes of today effectively, restoration of good governance can be said to be a *sine qua non*.

At this stage, one may well ask what the future portends vis-à-vis the fight against crime. Are the prospects for the future optimistic or bleak? Will it always be a losing battle, and will one always be left to seek solace in the oft-repeated statement that 'at the end of the day it is not always the good guys who win'? Are we to assume that human endeavour is not sufficient to deal with this problem? Do we have to pray for a messiah to come and set things right? I, for one, am a firm believer in the dictum that one should constantly strive to do one's duty in the best possible manner, whether it be in the area of combating crime or other spheres of human activity, and always to hope for the best.

CHAPTER II

ORGANIZED CRIME

Organized crime is generally perceived as a US phenomenon; this image has to a considerable extent been fostered by the media and feature films. Practically every literate person is familiar with the film *The Godfather* and the name of Al Capone, one of the most notorious organized-crime figures on the American scene in the 1930s.

ORGANIZED CRIME GROUPS – EVOLUTION AND GEOGRAPHICAL SPREAD

The United States – la Cosa Nostra

Americans consider organized crime as a formally structured nationwide conspiracy involving thousands of criminals organized to gain control over whole sectors of legal as well as illegal activities. Today, *la Cosa Nostra* families indigenous to the United States constitute the biggest organized-crime groups in that country. The evolution of *la Cosa Nostra* as an offshoot of the Sicilian mafia, within the Italian immigrant community in the United States, originated at the beginning of the twentieth century.

Italy – the Mafia

'Mafia' clans first surfaced in Sicily 700–800 years ago; in their original 'avtar' these were the secret sects formed to overthrow foreign rule – the origins of mafia were thus honourable. Over a period of time, the activities of these mafia clans underwent a change; they began to indulge in illegal activities and ultimately became the organized-crime groups of today. Mafia is a generic term by which all organized-crime groups in Italy are known today: the groups in Italy are the Cosa Nostra in Sicily, the Camorra in Naples, the Ndrangheta in Calabria and the United Holy Crown in Apulia; their areas of operation, the crimes in which they specialize and the level of their sophistication differ to a considerable extent. The number of organized-crime groups/clans based in Italy, belonging to the various regions described above, run into several hundred.

China and Hong Kong – the Triads

Organized crime in China is generally linked with the Triads. According to one school of thought, Triads came into existence in seventeenth-century China to overthrow the alien Manchu dynasty, though according to some others, Triads were formed in the eighteenth century as a means to offer mutual protection to their members; the necessity for this mutual protection was linked to migration patterns and socio-economic

8

conditions in South-East China in the eighteenth century. The Triads evolved into purely criminal organizations after the Ching dynasty was overthrown in China in 1911. With the advent of communism in China, criminal activity was ruthlessly suppressed, and as a result the Triads ceased to exist in mainland China. The Hong Kong branch of the Triads thus became very powerful, exerting a worldwide influence in the context of the Chinese diaspora. According to one estimate made in 1990, there are 160,000 Triad members in Hong Kong; one should not be misled by this very large figure of Triad membership, however, because the majority of these are passive members – only 10 per cent are actively involved in crime.

Japan – the Yakuza

Not much was known about Japanese organized crime a decade or so ago. The image of Japan as a highly ordered and law-abiding society was shattered when it came to light that a very large criminal enterprise by the name of Yakuza exists in Japan. The origin of the Yakuza can be traced to the Samurai traditions of seventeenth-century feudal Japan. The membership of the Yakuza was in the region of 180,000 in 1963; it had reportedly fallen to 80,000 by the 1990s, following a crackdown by the Japanese police.

India – Pindari, Thugs and the Mumbai underworld

Organized crime was widespread in India in the eighteenth century. Following the decline of Marathas, Pindaris as a gang of marauding robbers used to roam the plains of central India – mostly out-of-work mercenaries banded together to form the Pindari gangs.

Thugs were another organized-crime group operating in north India in the eighteenth century; the *modus operandi* of these Thugs was to join a group of travellers as fellow travellers, win their confidence, give them a herbal intoxicant/sedative to put them into a deep sleep and then strangle them with yellow-coloured scarfs while they were asleep. The criminal activities of Thugs were steeped in a religious cult associated with Kali – an incarnation of the mother goddess with primarily violent and destructive attributes. It was Colonel Sleeman who put an end to both the Pindaris and the Thuggi.

At present, India has been afflicted by organized crime to a certain degree. Organized crime in its traditional sense has not only taken firm root in Mumbai, but has also developed a transnational dimension, since quite a few organized-crime gangs of Mumbai also have a presence in South-East Asia and the Middle East. In other metropolitan cities such as Delhi, Chennai and Kolkata, organized crime is still in its formative stage, and if the present trend continues there is every likelihood that it will develop along classic lines.

Another peculiar feature of organized crime in India is that some of the states, like Uttar Pradesh and Bihar,[1] are deeply in its grip; because of the way in which it has

---

[1] India has a federal structure comprising the union and the states.

affected whole states in India, it has ceased to be an urban phenomenon and thereby has followed a pattern quite different from the traditional pattern of organized crime.

Russia and former communist regions

Ever since the demise of communism, the Russian organized-crime groups have become very active, not only in Russia, but practically all over the world, particularly in North America and Europe. Chechens, Armenians, Azerbaijanis, Solntsevos, Dolgoprudnoyes, Tambovs and Malyshevs are the ethnic communities from which the membership of most of the Russian organized criminal gangs is drawn; the total number of such gangs operating in Russia is estimated to be in the region of 3,000. The Russian organized-crime groups have a fairly fluid structure and are very ruthless in their operations. The power of Russian organized crime is such that Russia as a state is virtually in its grip; by corrupting the state machinery it has managed to permeate most spheres of state activity.

The CIS states of the former USSR have also developed their own network of organized-crime groups operating within the country and in countries in the neighbouring regions. A manifestation of this trend is smuggling activities of Uzbek organized-crime groups. Consider, for instance, the case of 'Olga Korbut', in which silk was being smuggled into India on a large scale in complicity with the Indian customs, who had also fallen prey to honey traps primarily set up through couriers.

Since the collapse of communism, the former East-European states have also seen the widespread emergence of organized crime. The East-European crime groups have forged links with the Russian organized-crime groups and other organized-crime groups in the CIS states; they are fairly active in Europe and North America. They specialize in prostitution and immigration rackets, and are also involved in drug trafficking and counterfeiting.

Western Europe

Organized crime in the classic sense, which was unknown in Western Europe two decades ago, has now taken firm root there and continues to spread its tentacles still further. Not only indigenous crime groups primarily amongst immigrants (such as Pakistanis and Indians in the UK, Turks in West Germany, Africans in France) but also Italian, Chinese and Japanese crime groups, which have a global reach, are also fairly active in these countries. Russian organized-crime groups and those from the former communist states of Eastern Europe are also active in Western Europe due to the contiguity and the relative prosperity of this region.

Latin America – Cali and Medallin cartels

Latin American organized-crime groups are deeply involved in cocaine trafficking. Cali and Medallin cartels based in Colombia are the most prominent organized-crime groups in Latin America. The activities of these cartels extend to North America and

Europe. In terms of money these two cartels are perhaps the richest in the world and have forged links with other organized-crime groups in such a way that many of the drug trafficking activities at the wholesale/retail level have been sub-contracted to them.

Africa – Nigerian organized-crime groups

Although many countries in Africa are afflicted by organized crime, it is the Nigerian organized-crime groups that have emerged as a major force on the world scene. They specialize in advance-fee frauds and drug trafficking.

The Caribbean – Jamaican organized-crime groups

The Caribbean-based organized-crime groups, especially those from Jamaica, are also fairly active not only in their own country but also in the countries to which they have migrated, for instance, the UK. Moreover, these Caribbean organized-crime groups have also entrenched themselves very firmly in the state machinery in their country of origin. They are reported to be very violent and in their countries of adoption operate at the level of street crime.

Canada – Hell's Angels

Organized crime is also fairly widespread in Canada. Motorcycle outlaw gangs are very powerful in Canada and are involved in all kinds of illegal activities. Hell's Angels is the most dominant and the largest organized motorcycle gang in Canada. Asian organized-crime groups are also active in Canada in drug trafficking and trafficking in human beings.

Mexican organized-crime groups

Mexican organized-crime groups are also reported to be active in the United States; their main activity is trafficking heroin and human beings – Mexicans constitute a large proportion of illegal residents in the United States.

South-East Asia – Asian organized-crime groups

Vietnam, Thailand, the Philippines and other countries in the South-East Asian region have also witnessed the growth of organized crime. Moreover, quite a large number of people from this region have migrated to other regions of the world – especially the USA, Canada, Western Europe and Australia – and have spawned organized-crime groups in their countries of adoption where they are known by the generic name 'Asian organized-crime groups'. Some of these organized-crime groups are active in crime at street level; some are reported to be extremely violent.

11

One can safely make the statement that organized crime is a worldwide phenomenon and has afflicted practically every country of the world in some form or other.

ORGANIZED CRIME – A QUESTION OF PERSPECTIVE

The problem of organized crime has also been viewed from different perspectives, more so in the context of the United States. According to the law enforcement perspective prevalent there, organized crime is a question of dealing with the Mafia. The law enforcement approach views the Mafia as an organized, structured and alien criminal encroachment.

In contrast, the socio-economic perspective in the United States views organized crime as an adjunct of the political, social and economic life of the nation – a major social evil that can be categorized along with poverty and racism. In the earlier days of immigration, minority groups in the United States tended to be closed groups, because they were widely discriminated against. While seeking a place in society, these minority groups took to crime, which manifested itself as organized crime. These groups were also driven by a desire for upward social mobility, and as such when an opportunity arose they moved into more socially respectable areas. Most minority ethnic groups in the United States have followed this path in their ultimate quest for social acceptance.

Some other social scientists, i.e., economists, consider organized crime as operating like any other enterprise in the United States. Like any other business, organized crime follows the rules of demand and supply – even if it is characterized by illegal activities. Moreover, accumulated proceeds of organized crime are further utilized in maximizing profits through criminal activities or through legitimate commerce. Thus, the socio-economic perspective treats organized crime as indicative of certain perversities prevalent in the society and the economy of the United States.

The law enforcement perspective and the socio-economic perspective of organized crime become all the more important in the context of formulating effective strategies to deal with this problem. If viewed purely as a legal problem, the approach would obviously be based on having more effective laws and strict enforcement of the same. If viewed as a socio-economic problem, perhaps the approach would be to alleviate the socio-economic conditions so that organized crime does not take root and prosper.

DEFINING ORGANIZED CRIME

When it comes to defining organized crime, one is confronted with a peculiar dilemma. In order to deal with this problem, some countries in their laws have tried to adopt an approach which defines organized crime *per se*; other countries, realizing that organized crime *per se* defies attempts to define it, have adopted a different approach, preferring to define organized criminal groups, and by linking their activities to specific crimes they endeavour to deal with the problem in the context of their legal system.

As stated earlier, organized-crime groups operating in the United States were the first to capture the public imagination. As such, it is in the United States that serious attempts have been made to study organized crime and devise strategies to deal with it.

In the United States

Estes Kefauver's Special Committee to Investigate Organized Crime in Interstate Commerce, set up as long ago as 1951, defined it as 'a nationwide crime syndicate known as the "mafia" '. The Presidential Commission on Law Enforcement and Administration of Justice in 1967, in its Task Force report on organized crime, described it as:

> *'a society that seeks to operate outside the control of the American people and their governments. It involves thousands of criminals working within structures as complex as those of any large corporation, subject to laws more tightly enforced than those of legitimate governments. Its actions are not impulsive but rather the result of intricate conspiracies, carried on over many years and aimed at gaining control over whole fields of activity in order to amass huge profits.'*

Since the above definition tends to fit any illegal activity, the Task Force report specifically identifies this society as la Cosa Nostra. The Commission's report further describes organized crime as:

> *'controlled by a nationwide alliance of at least twenty-four tightly knit gangs, or families, whose members are of mainland Italian or Sicilian descent. Each family has a hierarchical structure of position that regulates power in it. The families are linked by a shared set of understandings and agreements and are obedient to a nine-member national commission selected from among the leaders of the various families. The members of these families control (1) all but a tiny part of illegal gambling in the United States; (2) virtually all of the loansharking operations in the United States; (3) the importation of narcotics; and (4) most of Las Vegas, as actual or behind-the-scenes owners. In addition, they have infiltrated labour unions, they control or corrupt politicians and government officials, and they completely dominate a number of legal business enterprises. All of these activities produce huge amounts of money, estimated to reach $50 billion each year, of which at least $15 billion represent profits.'*

In 1968 the US Congress enacted the Omnibus Crime Control and Safe Streets Act. According to this Act:

> *'organized crime includes the unlawful activities of the members of a highly organized, disciplined association engaged in supplying illegal goods and services, including but not limited to gambling, prostitution, loan sharking, narcotics, labour racketeering and other unlawful activities of such associations.'*

The Organized Crime Control Act of 1970 in its preamble further elaborates on what organized crime is. It states:

> *'organized crime in the US is a highly sophisticated, diversified and widespread activity that annually drains billions of dollars from America's economy by unlawful conduct and illegal use of force, fraud and corruption; organized crime derives a major portion of its power through money obtained from such illegal endeavours as syndicated gambling, loan sharking, the theft and fencing of property, the importation and distribution of narcotics and other dangerous drugs, and other forms of social exploitation; this money and power are increasingly used to infiltrate and corrupt our democratic processes; organized crime activities in the US, weaken the stability of the nations' economic system, harms innocent investors and competing organizations, interferes with free competition, seriously burdens interstate and foreign commerce, threatens the domestic security and undermines the general welfare of a nation and its citizens.'*

The approach of tackling organized crime as a continuing criminal enterprise has been incorporated in the Racketeer Influenced and Corrupt Organizations (RICO) Act of 1970, which tries to deal with it by defining racketeering activities as follows:

> *'Racketeering is an act or threat involving murder, kidnapping, gambling, arson, robbery, bribery, extortion or dealing in narcotics or dangerous drugs and other denominated crime.'*

> *'A pattern of racketeering activity requires at least two acts of such activity.'*

There was a lot of resentment among the Italian immigrant community as a whole, since various presidential commissions/task forces/laws, and novels like *The Godfather* – which was also made into a highly successful film – had identified organized crime in the USA with Italian immigrants. The 1976 report of the National Advisory Committee on Criminal Justice Standards and Goals linked organized crime to other ethnic communities as a whole; moreover, in a radical departure, the 1976 Task Force, instead of attempting to define organized crime, elaborated on its features.

In other countries

In Italy, the 'organized-crime group' approach has been adopted. The Italian Penal Code states 'when three or more persons associate for the purpose of committing more than one crime, whoever promotes or constitutes or organizes the association, shall be punished, for that alone, with imprisonment from 3 to 7 years'.

In Japan, a similar approach to defining the organized-crime group has been adopted. The Japanese Law on Prevention of Irregularities by Gangsters states that 'gangs means any organization likely to help its members (including members of affiliated organizations of the said organization) to collectively and habitually commit illegal acts or violence'.

In India

There is no federal or central law to deal with organized crime in India: however, some states have laws with which they can deal with it. Only the state of Maharashtra has enacted a law exclusively to deal with the serious nature of organized crime in Mumbai city; this law is know as the Maharashtra Control of Organized Crime Act 1999, which defines organized crime as:

> *'any continuing unlawful activity by an individual, singly or jointly, either as a member of an organized-crime syndicate or on behalf of such syndicate, by use of violence or threat of violence or intimidation or coercion, or other unlawful means, with the objective of gaining pecuniary benefits, or gaining undue economic or other advantage for himself or any other person or promoting insurgency.'*

The state of Uttar Pradesh strives to tackle organized crime through the Gangsters and Anti-Social Activities (Prevention) Act 1986, which is only applicable in that state. In this Act, 'gang' has been defined as a group of persons who, singly or collectively, indulge in anti-national activities by violence or threat of violence for gaining undue political, economic or physical advantages, etc., and includes offences against the body, bootlegging, forcible possession of immovable property, creating communal disturbances, obstructing public servants in the discharge of their duties, kidnapping for ransom, diverting an aircraft or public transport vehicle from its scheduled path, etc. This Act has a wide canvas and purports to cover large areas of organized criminal activity. However, it is different from laws enacted in other countries in that, apart from criminalizing moneymaking activities of the criminal gangs, it also criminalizes infringement of election laws, causing obstruction or disturbance in the pursuit of lawful trade, business or profession and incitement to violence and disturbance of communal harmony, and so on.

International organizations

ICPO-Interpol

ICPO-Interpol has also made attempts to define organized crime. Interpol's First International Symposium on Organized Crime in May 1988 defined organized crime as:

> *'Any enterprise or group of persons engaged in a continuing illegal activity which has as its primary purpose the generation of profits, irrespective of national boundaries.'*

Italy, Spain and Germany complained that the above definition left out the requirement of an organized command structure. A BKA (German Federal Police) group defined organized crime as:

> *'Any group of people who have consciously and deliberately decided to co-operate in illegal activities over a certain period of time, apportioning tasks among themselves and often using modern infrastructure systems, with the principal aim of amassing substantial profits as quickly as possible.'*

15

Americans and Canadians felt the 1988 Interpol definition left out the requirement of using violence to attain the group's goals. Thus, the new definition now in use by Interpol's Organized Crime unit is:

> *'Any group having a corporate structure whose primary objective is to obtain money through illegal activities, often surviving on fear and corruption.'*

The United Nations

The United Nations Convention against Transnational Organized Crime in defining organized crime has adopted the approach of defining 'structured groups' and relating their activity to 'serious crimes' in order to combat the same. According to this Convention:

(i) 'Organized criminal group' shall mean a structured group of three or more persons, existing for a period of time and acting in concert with the aim of committing one or more serious crimes or offences established in accordance with this Convention, in order to obtain, directly or indirectly, a financial or other material benefit.

(ii) 'Serious crime' shall mean conduct constituting an offence punishable by a maximum deprivation of liberty of at least four years or a more serious penalty.

(iii) 'Structured group' shall mean a group that is not randomly formed for the immediate commission of an offence and that does not need to have formally defined roles for its members, continuity of its membership or a developed structure.

FEATURES OF ORGANIZED CRIME

The problem of defining organized crime becomes much simpler if one lists its main features. Such an approach not only leads to a clearer and more comprehensive understanding of this concept, but is also conducive to drafting an effective law to deal with it. The main features of organized crime are:

- illegal activities in the nature of a continuing criminal enterprise;
- illegal activities which can be in either illegal or legal areas, or both; an example of the illegal area is bootlegging and of the legal area is collection of protection money in the construction industry/business;
- by its very name it is evident that it has an organized structure, which is more or less akin to corporate structure, considering that it is run more or less along business lines;
- an organized-crime group has a head, with a concomitant hierarchy;
- organized-crime groups have a permanent existence; even if their head changes, the group survives;
- organized-crime groups thrive on fear; as such, they resort to violence or the threat of violence to generate the same;
- they follow a strict code of conduct which, above all, entails loyalty to their chief; other elements relating to the code of conduct may differ from gang to gang;
- these groups are generally formed on the basis of ethnicity and close family ties; sometimes shared/common experience can also be a factor in their formation;

– one essential condition for these groups to thrive is corruption amongst public/ government officials; they are thus actively engaged in corrupting public and government officials, because once these officials are compromised, carrying on the enterprise of crime becomes much easier;
– greed, money and power are the principal motivating factors for these groups;
– specialized or support groups such as lawyers and chartered accountants are integral features of these groups; and
– they often acquire a 'Robin Hood' image which acts as a positive public relations factor. This Robin Hood image stems from the social support these groups enjoy because of their philanthropic activities, by way of providing much-needed money or other support to members of their community, or the so-called dispensation of justice they carry out for ethnic groups.

TYPES OF ORGANIZED CRIME

Bootlegging, gambling, loan-sharking, prostitution, drug trafficking, arms trafficking, smuggling, extortions/racketeering activities of all types, kidnapping for ransom, contract killing, trafficking in human beings (women, children, immigrants/labour) and counterfeiting of goods and currency are the types of crimes in which organized-crime gangs generally indulge.

The more sophisticated types of crime in which they are involved are:

(i) Economic scams – for instance, in the stock market or in avoiding excise duties, duping investors through a variety of ingenious but fraudulent investment schemes.
(ii) International economic crimes – involving, for example, invoice manipulations across several countries.
(iii) White-collar crime – namely avoiding taxes, frauds in corporate entities.

An organized-crime group generally specializes in particular crimes, depending upon its evolution, the membership and the area of operation.

ORGANIZED CRIME – ITS TRANSNATIONAL CHARACTER

The organized-crime groups generally start out as street-level gangs. If allowed to operate unchecked, over a period of time they not only become bigger, but also diversify into more sophisticated types of crime; alongside these developments their areas of operation also enlarge, so much so that initially they assume regional/national dimension and in the course of time, international dimension. Organized crime therefore has an inherent tendency to become transnational in character.

Links between organized-crime groups

Organized-crime groups tend to forge links with other such groups whenever their areas of operations overlap or there is convergence of interest. These linkages can also result from a profit motive, in the sense that if a particular crime is yielding high profits (for instance, drug trafficking) the organized-crime groups would tend to form linkages with other groups involved in this crime, even if it means extending their area of operation or playing a subordinate role to another gang.

Links with terrorism

Another sinister trend that has been noted lately is the links that these organized-crime groups have developed or are tending to develop with terrorists. Often these links are forged due to the efforts of intelligence agencies interested in fomenting a particular terrorist activity. They can also develop independently of intelligence agencies, but due to their interest in terrorist activity, the intelligence agencies ultimately become involved in these links and in the course of time take control of it. An illustration of such links are the links of the Cali and Medallin cartels with revolutionary groups in Colombia, Peru and Bolivia and the linking of (Inter-Services Intelligence) (ISI) of Pakistan with the Mumbai underworld (also known as the D Company or Dawood Ibrahim gang). Another trend which has to be taken into account is that of terrorism reducing itself to a purely organized-crime problem over a period of time.

ORGANIZED CRIME AND THE MONEY LAUNDERING DIMENSION

Organized crime generates large sums of money. It is obvious that some of the proceeds need to be legitimized. Money laundering is thus an exercise in which every organized-crime group is involved, be it in a small or a big way. Moreover, some of the organized-crime groups specialize in money laundering, in the sense that they also undertake it for other organized-crime groups. Money laundering is engaging the attention of states and the international community more and more; lately it has been categorized as a crime by many countries; an international convention on transnational crime concluded recently by the United Nations also categorizes money laundering as one of the major crimes and urges member states to enact legislation to deal with it.

ORGANIZED CRIME – SOME OTHER IMPORTANT DIMENSIONS

Organized crime must also be viewed in the context of some other dimensions, such as:

(a) the penetration of legitimate commercial activity by these groups;
(b) the context of erstwhile Communist economies in a state of transition to market economies;
(c) the context of developing economies which profess socialism, but which have now taken to the path of economic liberalization as a means of rapid growth and raising the living standards of their people; and
(d) the context of the national security of states and to what extent it is threatened by organized-crime groups.

PROFILING OF ORGANIZED-CRIME GROUPS

From the perspective of a criminologist, sociologist, law enforcement agent or any other discipline relating to crime and criminals, it is essential to have a profile of the organized-crime groups and the members of the group. Such profiling enables one to have a proper understanding of these groups; with proper understanding one can decide what is the best strategy to deal with a particular organized-crime group. By profiling, one is also able to gather all possible information and intelligence on the organized-crime groups in order to deal with them in a more effective manner in terms of law enforcement (which would entail investigation, prosecution, trial and criminal prosecution/further follow-up after release) and crime prevention (which means keeping a close watch on them and their areas of operation or putting them in preventive detention so that they can not commit crime).

Some of the points to be borne in mind while profiling the organized-crime groups are the following:

(i) Criminal gangs are generally the product of social and economic conditions; they have a distinct cultural milieu; often there is a long history behind their evolution and growth (the Yakuza and the Mafia); at times they can also be inspired by a religious cult (the Thuggi).

(ii) The criminal gangs are mainly connected by family and ethnic ties; sometimes this bonding can cut across the ethnic divide and the bonding factor can be a shared social experience of discrimination and exploitation.

(iii) Criminal gangs are generally known by the head of the gang (Mumbai gangs); sometimes they are also known by the place from where most of the members come (Italian Mafia); at times their names are shrouded in mystery due to cult and secretive factors which led to their evolution.

(iv) The criminal gangs have a hierarchical structure; some gangs have lately been found to be very fluid/loose in their criminal structure, for instance, Russian organized-crime groups.

(v) They generally specialize in certain types of crimes.

(vi) They generally have turfs or areas of operation divided amongst themselves, with the exception of Russian organized-crime groups.

(vii) They have links/understandings with other organized-crime groups regarding their crimes/areas of operation. Sometimes this link can be of a subordinate gang to a larger gang; the Mumbai Mafia is an example of such relationships.

(viii) Sometimes small/organized criminal groups have to pay royalties to the larger group as a form of protection money.

(ix) The profits being generated by criminal gangs and the properties that belong to them also need to be documented; it is when the proceeds of crime are attacked that the criminal groups feel the pinch the most.

(x) The weapons that belong to the criminal groups also need to be known; sometimes these are centrally stored and given out during specific criminal operations – a typical *modus operandi* of some organized-crime groups in Mumbai.

19

(xi) The support/specialist groups that lend support to the gang, e.g. money launderers, underground bankers, expert assassins, lawyers, chartered accountants, etc., also need to be well documented.

In profiling the individual gang members the following points should be borne in mind:

(a) the history of each gang member, including his place in the hierarchy, has to be properly documented, which should also include his family members;
(b) the types of crimes in which he specializes also has to be documented, along with his criminal record;
(c) his involvement even as a suspect in crimes must be documented;
(d) his aliases should be known;
(e) his accomplices/close associates have to be listed;
(f) the types of weapons used or held by him must be known;
(g) the vehicles used by him in a certain crime or which belong to him must also be known;
(h) his telephone numbers and those of his associates/family members must be known;
(i) the property held by or purported to belong to him must be known;
(j) important interrogation statements which contain useful information need to be attached to the dossier; and
(k) the support group/known sympathizers must also be identified.

LAWS TO DEAL WITH ORGANIZED-CRIME GROUPS

In the United States

The country that has been able to target organized-crime groups in the most effective manner is the United States. Effective targeting of organized crime there became almost imperative considering the serious threat which it posed. The Organized Crime Control Act 1970, in conjunction with the Omnibus Crime Control and Safe Streets Act 1968 and the Racketeer Influenced and Corrupt Organizations (RICO) Act 1970, forms the legal basis for law enforcement agencies in the United States to deal with organized crime. The Racketeering Influenced and Corrupt Organizations Act is the centrepiece of the Organized Crime Control Act 1970 in the fight against organized crime.

RICO makes racketeering activity illegal in relation to certain specified offences. Moreover, it defines as illegal any racketeering activity committed within the previous ten years; however, this limitation period of ten years does not apply to murder cases. RICO also provides for certain presumptions against the big Mafia dons of the organized-crime groups based upon circumstantial evidence. The Organized Crime Control Act provides for immunity for organized-crime witnesses and has a clause which provides for 'compulsory testimony of witnesses'. This act also provides for the witness protection programme which is administered by the United States Marshal Services. Electronic surveillance is enabled by the Omnibus Crime Control and Safe Streets Act 1968. In addition, undercover operations are admissible evidence in the United States. RICO has not only a criminal law side, but also a civil law side to it. The criminal law section of RICO provides for prison sentences and forfeiture of property based upon evidence that is 'beyond reasonable doubt'; however the civil law section relies upon 'preponderance of probability' to forfeit criminal assets or place them under trusteeship.

Some of the states in the US also have laws along the same lines as RICO. The state of New York has enacted the Enterprise Corruption Act (also known as ECHO) to deal with organized crime. During my field visit to New York, a representative of the New York District Attorney's Office took me to witness a trial under this Act; the trial pertained to offences in the securities market in the New York Stock Exchange. I was quite surprised to see a jury trial in a case for which a lot of expertise is required and which was quite difficult to comprehend even by normal standards, considering the complicated nature of criminal activity. But, then, that is the way justice is administered in the United States – whether the jury understands a case or not, it has to be there. In this trial even the judge frequently had to call proceedings to a halt in order to confer with the lawyers, in order to comprehend the full implications of the complicated nature of the case.

In India

Some of the states in India have enacted laws to deal with organized crime. The state of Maharashtra has the Maharashtra Control of Organized Crime Act 1999. The salient features of this Act are as follows:

(i) a group of two or more criminals should have committed recognized offences punishable with imprisonment of three years or more;

(ii) more than one charge-sheet should have been filed against the members of the gang;

(iii) the charge-sheet should have been filed in the preceding 10 years;

(iv) the court should have taken cognizance of such offences;

(v) the offences should have been committed with the objective of gaining pecuniary benefits for the members of the gang;

(vi) violence or threats of violence, intimidation or coercion or other unlawful means should have been used by the members of the gang in perpetrating the crimes;

(vii) the minimum punishment provided is imprisonment for five years, which may extend to life. The death penalty can also be awarded under this Act;

(viii) if a criminal gang cannot account for the wealth or properties in its possession, such properties or wealth are liable to be attached or forfeited;

(ix) trial is required to be conducted by special courts;

(x) at the request of a police officer of the rank of superintendent of police, the state government can authorize interception of wire, electronic or oral communications. The evidence collected through such interception would be admissible evidence;

(xi) confession made before a police officer of the rank of superintendent of police is admissible as evidence;

(xii) it provides for protection of witnesses by way of holding in camera trials at the public prosecutor's request;

(xiii) bail provisions have been made stringent inasmuch as no court can grant bail to a criminal arrested under this law without giving an opportunity to the public prosecutor of being heard and also without satisfying itself that *prima facie* there is no case against the person arraigned before it;

(xiv) if the person is convicted under this law, apart from imprisonment, the movable and immovable properties of such accused shall stand forfeited to the state government;

(xv) certain provisions of the Criminal Procedure Code have been amended. It provides for police custody remand for up to 30 days instead of 15 days. If an investigation cannot be completed in 90 days, on the request of the public prosecutor, the court can grant another 90 days for its completion. The accused would not be released on bail after the expiry of the first 90 days.

Initially, there was apprehension about the attitude of the judiciary regarding criminals from the Mumbai underworld prosecuted under this Act, but the judiciary responded very positively to its provisions. In the first judgment to be delivered under the Act, three persons prosecuted were sentenced to death.

The Uttar Pradesh Gangsters and Anti-Social Activities (Prevention) Act 1986 has also been used to deal with organized crime; it has already been alluded to above. The salient features of this Act are as follows:

(i) A gangster is punishable with minimum imprisonment of two years, extendable to 10 years.

(ii) The rules of evidence have been modified and certain statutory presumptions can be raised against the gangsters by the trial court.

(iii) Provision has also been made for the protection of witnesses; the trial may be held in camera at the request of the public prosecutor; the name and address of a witness can be omitted in the court records, if the court so desires.

(iv) The property of the gangster can be attached by the district magistrate if he is satisfied that it was acquired through criminal activity.

Even under the existing penal legislation[2] there are certain provisions whereby the problem of organized crime could be tackled to an extent. Under the Indian Penal Code, the law relating to conspiracy, dacoity and kidnapping for ransom could be used to deal with organized crime. However, a substantive law at the federal level – which would also be applicable to states – on the same lines as the Maharashtra Control of Organized Crime Act 1999 would go a long way in dealing effectively with organized crime in India.

There are several other central statutes which deal with specific facets of organized crime, i.e., the Public Gambling Act 1867; the Explosives Act 1884; the Immoral Traffic (Prevention) Act 1956; the Excise Act 1956; the Arms Act 1959; the Customs Act 1962; the Emigration Act 1983; and the Narcotic Drugs and Psychotropic Substances Act 1985, etc. The state governments have also legislated on subjects such as excise, prohibition and gambling.

---

[2] India has a uniform penal and criminal code.

There are laws in India which deal exclusively with preventive detention. Preventive detention has also been resorted to in the Indian context to deal with organized criminals, because by taking the criminal out of circulation it is sought to put an end to his activities. The preventive detention laws in India are:

(i) The National Security Act 1980, which provides for preventive detention by the Central Government or the State Government. The detention order under this Act is for one year with a view to preventing a person from acting in any manner prejudicial to the defence of India or friendly relations with foreign powers. The expression 'security of India' is open to liberal interpretation and this Act has been used, though sparingly, against anti-national elements and hard-core gangsters. Detention is an executive action and the case does not go to court for trial.

(ii) The Prevention of Illicit Traffic in Narcotic Drugs and Psychotropic Substances Act 1988, which provides for detention of persons involved in drug trafficking – a crime in which the organized-crime groups are heavily involved because of its lucrativeness.

(iii) The Conservation of Foreign Exchange and Prevention of Smuggling Activities Act 1974, which also provides for preventive detention. Under 'Cofeposa' there is no bail, and it has been used very extensively against smugglers – the Mumbai underworld dons, for instance.

In other countries

Several of the developed and developing countries have also enacted legislation to deal exclusively with organized crime. There are notable exceptions. Italy has enacted a fairly comprehensive legislation to deal with organized crime. In the 1990s, the United States–Italy joint endeavour to counter organized-crime groups operating within Italy led to enactment of Italian legislation on organized crime, which was modelled to a large extent on the United States legislation. South Africa is another country that has enacted legislation on organized crime; however, its effectiveness has been blunted to a large extent by constitutional provisions which lay a lot of emphasis on the rights and freedom of individuals. On the other hand, India, a developing country, and the United Kingdom, a developed country, have yet to enact legislation to deal exclusively with organized crime.

International conventions

To combat organized crime, the United Nations Convention against Transnational Organized Crime was adopted by the General Assembly in November 2000. The twin objective of this Convention is to set standards for domestic laws so that they can effectively combat organized crime and to eliminate differences among national legal systems which has blocked mutual assistance in the past. Under this Convention, the states commit themselves to:

(i) criminalizing offences committed by organized-crime groups, including corruption and corporate or company offences;

(ii) cracking down on money laundering and the proceeds of crime;
(iii) speeding up extradition;
(iv) protecting witnesses testifying against criminal groups;
(v) tightening co-operation to seek out and prosecute suspects; and
(vi) boosting prevention of organized crime at the national and international levels.

General crime-fighting measures in the Convention against Transnational Organized Crime are supplemented by a series of protocols targeting specific types of crime. Three such protocols that have been adopted aim to combat the smuggling of migrants, the trafficking and exploitation of persons (particularly women and children), and the illicit manufacture and trade of firearms. A protocol to combat the illicit manufacture and traffic of explosives is also under consideration.

THE PROBLEMS IN ENFORCEMENT

The criminal justice system in most countries is confronted with serious problems relating to enforcement vis-à-vis organized crime. Often an inadequate legal framework or the absence of a substantive law on the subject considerably hampers the enforcement effort. In the absence of a substantive law, enforcement officers often use the existing legislation to somehow target criminals belonging to organized-crime groups; this can be described as a 'piecemeal approach' and amounts to fighting the criminals with one hand tied behind the back. An example of this piecemeal approach is the use today of laws relating to criminal conspiracy and dacoity by the enforcement agencies in India to book such criminals.

Procedural laws steeped in antiquity also hamper enforcement efforts. For instance, a reasonable period of remand of an accused in police custody is necessary to tie up all the ends of a continuing criminal enterprise. In most countries this is not the case: in India a police remand of 15 days is the maximum permissible under law, whereas a police remand of 60 days is the reasonable requirement to get to the bottom of most organized-crime groups. Liberal bail provisions are another aspect of procedural laws that hamper police investigation and need to be curtailed; in India 'Bail and not the jail' was a slogan coined by a Supreme Court judge in a judgment delivered by him some time ago. Another serious lacuna in Indian procedural law is that statements made to the police by witnesses are not required to be signed by them: thus, if a witness resiles in a court of law, this unsigned statement can only be used to contradict his testimony.

Evidentiary laws can sometimes be another major obstacle in the enforcement efforts against organized crime. Distrust of the police, which is inherent in the Indian legal system, makes a confession made to a police officer inadmissible evidence in court. In this age of scientific investigation and forensic science, the accused in India are not legally bound to give a specimen of their handwriting, blood samples or footprints, or intimate or non-intimate body specimens, even if court orders to this effect are produced.

Difficulties in obtaining proof are symptomatic of the collapse of the criminal justice system and blunt the edge in the fight against organized crime; in this scenario, witnesses are not willing to testify against the 'big dons' of the organized-crime groups for fear of reprisals, which can extend to their family members. Even investigating officers and members of the judiciary can be intimidated; officers investigating cases and judges trying cases are sometimes assassinated by the organized-crime groups.

Slow and dogged judicial process also makes the fight against organized crime a losing proposition. In most countries the speed of trial is very slow; the percentage of convictions is also very dismal. The net result is that criminals think that crime is not a hazardous occupation. If justice is not delivered, the people become cynical about the efficacy of the due process of law; sometimes they even take the law into their own hands. Delays can also lead to memory lapses on the part of witnesses, apart from which, the prosecution and judges lose interest in the case. Above all, delays result in a large number of pending cases in courts, a tendency which only results in increasing the backlog. In India 5,660,484 cases under the Indian Penal Code were pending at the beginning of 1998; the seriousness of the problem can be gauged from the fact that only 17 per cent of this large number of cases were disposed of by the courts and the conviction rate was just 38.2 per cent.[3]

Lack of resources is another major factor, more so in developing countries, in the failure to combat organized crime effectively. When resources are scarce, there are not a sufficient number of investigating officers, prosecutors and courts to deal with the problem. Moreover, adequate training cannot be given to the investigating officers, prosecutors and judges due to a resources crunch/absence of training institutes.

Lack of co-ordination at various levels of policing, irrespective of whether the state has a unitary or federal character, is another problem area that affects the fight against organized crime. Such a lack of co-ordination at all levels can happen if the policing happens to be a purely local affair and there is no co-ordinating authority at the national level; in the United Kingdom this situation existed until the National Criminal Intelligence Service (NCIS) and National Crime Squad (NCS) were set up. In India such a situation still obtains, as policing is a state responsibility and the Central Bureau of Investigation has not really developed to the stage of a federal investigating agency at the national level which could also co-ordinate the national crime effort.

The organized-crime groups are able to operate with impunity because they are able to corrupt the government machinery, which includes both bureaucrats and politicians. Due to vagaries inherent in an electoral process, criminals are often elected to legislatures, and there have been instances where they have gone on to occupy positions of power in government, in India and several other countries. With organized-crime groups in power, the fight against organized crime is a virtual non-starter.

COMBATING ORGANIZED CRIME

In order to combat organized-crime effectively, substantive laws need to be enacted and loopholes in procedural and evidentiary laws plugged to deal with this problem. As far

---

[3]   *Crime in India 1999* (National Crime Record Bureau, New Delhi).

as Indian procedural law is concerned, the first thing that needs to be done is to remove distrust of the police. Towards this end, the following amendments to the criminal procedure code are needed:

  (i) Statements made to police officers by witnesses should be required to be signed.
 (ii) The period of police remand should be increased from 15 days to 30 days for a thorough investigation of the accused in organized-crime cases.
(iii) At present if a charge-sheet is not filed within 90 days the accused is released on bail; for a thorough investigation, this period of 90 days should be extended to 180 days.
 (iv) Bail provisions, especially those relating to anticipatory bail, should be made more stringent; and the prosecution viewpoint must always be taken into account in all cases of bail – this will ensure that criminals, once booked, cannot take the law lightly and be at liberty, to tamper with the evidence at will.
  (v) The scope for combined offences should be further increased by making more offences compoundable without the permission of the court; this would also clear up the large number of cases pending in courts.
 (vi) Plea bargaining should be introduced as a way of speedy disposal of cases and also to lighten the burden of courts.
(vii) Approvers granted immunity should be released immediately and not after the trial is over, because the trial can often take up to several years – this would serve as an incentive for criminals to turn approvers.
(viii) Admissibility of documents to be used during a trial should be agreed upon at the outset by all the parties concerned so that witnesses need not be called upon as regards their admissibility. This would also shorten the trial period considerably.
 (ix) A law for witness protection should be enacted along the same lines as the US law. Though these programmes are expensive, they are essential for the successful fight against organized crime. Forty-five federal witnesses were killed by organized-crime groups in the United States until the witness protection programme was introduced; after the introduction of this programme, not a single witness was killed in organized-crime cases there.
  (x) The prosecution agency should once again be brought under the auspices of the police in India so that it is accountable for its conduct; moreover, prosecution would then be better guided with inputs from the police. The way things stand now, the prosecutors are more or less unaccountable to anyone and the police have lost control of accused in trials and their ultimate conviction.
 (xi) In camera trial should be the norm to protect witnesses until such time as a witness protection programme is in place.
(xii) Provisions should be introduced for designated courts to try organized-crime cases for their effective and quick disposal.
(xiii) Confiscation of the proceeds of crime, preferably under an all-encompassing money laundering statute, should be ensured.

Certain amendments also need to be made to the evidentiary laws and new provisions added to make the legal armoury strong enough to fight organized crime. In the Indian law of evidence, the following need to be done; the same changes to some degree or the other may be required in the laws of other countries, too:

(i) Confessions made to police officers should be made valid in a court of law.

(ii) Witnesses should be legally bound to give forensic evidence (as referred to above), which is not the case now.

(iii) Electronic surveillance should be made legal and it should be treated as admissible evidence.

(iv) Undercover operations should also be treated as admissible evidence.

(v) Adverse inferences by courts should be permitted against the accused in cases of a serious nature.

(vi) Reversal of the burden of proof, i.e. shifting the onus onto the accused to prove his innocence, should be introduced in cases of corruption and money laundering: in cases of corruption, which has been and is one of the prime movers behind organized crime, so as to have a salutary effect, and in cases of money laundering because of complicated and intricate investigations involved which are sometimes beyond the capabilities of law enforcement officers.

The quality of investigation under the existing and the proposed laws also needs to be improved. For this to happen, the investigating officers would need to be properly trained, as also a dedicated group of investigating officers would have to be earmarked. In India, investigation is generally a neglected area, because most of the police officers are performing law and order duties. Joint task forces with members from several enforcement agencies could also be constituted for effective investigation and prosecution of cases against organized-crime groups.

Crime is no longer a localized affair, nor should it be treated as such. Within the context of federal or unitary states, co-ordinating units at national level and other levels all the way down to the police station would have to be set up. In the context of co-ordination, reference has also been made to the UK effort and similar efforts in India. Specialized cells at local level/state level, wherever needed, would go a long way in further strengthening the national effort to curb organized crime.

Intelligence is the key to success in the fight against crime, especially organized crime. Intelligence databanks at the national level and local levels are an imperative in the present-day situation; considerable efforts would have to be devoted to develop the databanks, which at present are a neglected area, particularly in the developing countries. Intelligence databanks can be utilized for developing both strategic and tactical intelligence. Strategic intelligence enables one to understand the general crime trends and to chalk out a broad strategy in terms of thrust areas and allocation of resources; tactical intelligence is case-related and can be utilized to unearth various facets of a criminal enterprise.

The judiciary also needs to be sensitized regarding its crucial role in the fight against organized crime. This can be done by way of symposiums and seminars to be attended jointly by various components of the criminal justice system. Training could also be used as a tool to sensitize the judiciary.

Generally, in the fight against organized-crime groups, honest police officers are targeted by such groups by launching a smear campaign against them and hoping for their removal. Protection should be offered to honest police officers by giving them a reasonable tenure of three years.

INTERNATIONAL CO-OPERATION

Considering the transnational character of various types of crimes, international co-operation is essential to putting an end to them. Since international co-operation is a major dimension in the context of all crimes, it has been dealt with in detail at various points in this book.

ROLE OF THE MASS MEDIA

The mass media can play both a positive and a negative role in the fight against organized crime: mass media includes newspapers, magazines, radio, television and feature films. Often the projection of violence and crime in the mass media on a large scale has led to organized crime being romanticized in the same way as some revolutionary movements, a trend which leads to or which has led to its proliferation. The mass media can also play a positive role by building up a campaign against organized crime so that all sections of society co-ordinate in the endeavour to root it out.

CONCLUSION

No one is born a criminal. Poor socio-economic conditions have played a very important role in the evolution of organized crime. Generally, the first-generation organized-crime group leaders are the product of urban slums and ghettos; for instance, Al Capone, Dawood Ibrahim, Chotta Rajan. The slums/ghettos are a continual source for membership of these organized-crime groups. Thus, any effort to contain organized crime must have a poverty alleviation programme as a principal component. From an enforcement angle, it must always be borne in mind that ordinary crime, if allowed to go unchecked, coalesces to form organized crime; the same loose approach can lead to organized crime becoming transnational in character.

Above all, informed public opinion and political commitment are two essential conditions that one should strive for to obtain success in any serious and sustained programmes designed to fight organized crime.

CHAPTER III

TERRORISM

SOME IMPORTANT FACTORS

Terrorism is a new kind of warfare that emerged on the world scene in the 1970s. The most gruesome aspect was first witnessed during the 1972 Munich massacre of Israeli athletes. This one incident, followed by a few spectacular hijackings, brought terrorism to the centre stage of the world. With the reach of the media today, terrorism creates a disproportionate fear in the minds of people; if terrorism is carried on over a period of time in a particular region, terror grips the minds of the people of that region, e.g. the terrorism in Punjab at its height and the terrorism in Kashmir today.

Terrorism also leads to disruption of normal life, which mainly occurs because of fear, referred to above. In regions where terrorists operate, people retire indoors early in the evening; the general gaiety is missing in their normal interactions. Perhaps the most serious manifestation of disruption of normal life occurs in the sphere of economic activity; slowly but surely, over a period of time, most economic activities except those which are essential to sustain life come to a grinding halt – industries cease to function, trade and commerce witness a sharp decline, transportation of goods, which is the most visible indicator of a thriving economy, becomes minimal.

Terrorism in any given situation is perceived by some as an armed struggle to achieve independence, or as the genuine aspirations of the people, whereas others perceive it as a form of insurgency or violent acts purely and simply against the state. These two perceptions have led to much international debate as to what constitutes terrorism. By and large this debate is polemical in nature and has served no useful purpose; so much so that when one talks to so-called experts in the field of international law, they are hard-pressed even to put together a definition of terrorism. It would not be out of place to mention here that whenever a terrorist act occurs, it is perceived as such by everyone, and when one is striving to define terrorism, one is in the realm of paradoxes.

Several states – mostly totalitarian or dictatorial regimes – realizing the potential of this new kind of warfare, have also used it on an extensive scale against perceived enemies. These unscrupulous states have used terrorism as a low-cost option and as a form of low-intensity conflict to wage a kind of proxy war against other states. Democracies are generally more vulnerable to these kinds of low-intensity conflicts; the basic idea of a low-intensity conflict is to keep the war simmering at a certain level without having to face up to the devastating effects of a full-scale war.

Terrorism generally starts with an ideological base or a strong sense of being wronged; sometimes, especially in the initial phases, the terrorists may have the strong support of the masses or a section of the same. Over a period of time the ideological base

29

becomes diluted, or is simply forsaken, and mass support is also lost. In such a scenario the terrorist gangs still continue to operate and the problem then reduces itself to one of combating organized crime.

When terrorism is being practised by certain states/countries, it can also have sympathizers and harbourers in the government or the state apparatus. These sympathizers and harbourers are quite often playing for high stakes, hoping to become ambassadors and ministers, etc., once the new regime is in place.

TACTICS

The tactics of the terrorists are again driven by a single overriding motive – to generate terror. In order to do so, the terrorists target not only political leaders and other important persons, but also innocent civilians. They also target strategic institutions and other vulnerable points to create terror. Since most of the targets are innocent victims, the violence indulged in by terrorists has also been characterized as mindless and barbaric by many thinkers on the subject.

Until recently, terrorists resorted to the use of small-arms and explosives to carry out terrorist attacks. In the execution of their aims and objectives, terrorist organizations have also resorted to the use of suicide squads, depending upon the level of indoctrination of their cadres.

Normally, terrorist groups operate in a given area, but sometimes the acts perpetrated by them may extend across the globe. Terrorist organizations within a country and also worldwide have resorted to networking in order to enhance their capabilities, and also to gain expertise from other groups. Some of the terrorist groups also specialize in certain forms of violent acts; for example, a particular terrorist group might have a good deal of expertise in the use of improvised explosives, whereas another might have expertise in carrying out assassinations of VIPs.

In order to be more effective, terrorist gangs, in some instances, have also managed to secure sanctuaries and training camps abroad. Even the top leadership of the terrorist organizations generally bases itself abroad or operates out of 'safe havens' abroad, in order to function more effectively.

FUNDING OF TERRORISM

As with any other organization or enterprise, at the end of the day it is money that keeps the enterprise or the organization running. For terrorist organizations, too, 'funds' are of paramount importance. Funding of terrorist organizations takes place in a variety of ways. Not constrained by any law, the most common form of funding to which terrorists resort are extortions, kidnappings for ransom and various types of the crimes which would result in large profits, such as bank robberies. Once terrorist organizations become entrenched in a certain region, they even resort to imposing their 'taxes' on the salaries of government servants and others; certain proportions of the government budget are even expropriated by them at gunpoint from drawing and disbursing officers.

The areas under the control of terrorists are also subject to all kinds of racketeering activities, extending from taking cuts from pavement hawkers to truck drivers travelling across certain routes controlled by the terrorists.

Terrorist organizations are also known to run legitimate businesses to generate funds for their activities; earnings from crime are invested by the terrorists in legitimate business to generate profits for the organization. Often the terrorist organizations represent a certain diaspora; such displaced populations are prone to be taken in by the terrorist rhetoric and to give very substantial donations to fund these organizations. Terrorist organizations are also known to play the religious card quite well, and religious institutions also contribute substantial funds of money to their coffers. Another way terrorist organizations obtain money is by way of donations to charitable institutions – these are, in fact, fronts for terrorist organizations. Clandestine movement of money is also resorted to by terrorists, especially in operational areas. Underground or parallel banking channels are used extensively by the terrorists to fund their operations – the money might be coming from legal or illegal sources in such cases. Conventional money laundering techniques are also used by terrorists, because they need to have fronts for operational purposes.

It would be pertinent to point out here that the networking resorted to by terrorist organizations, the advances in technology to which terrorists have access and the large sums of money available to them, act as multipliers in enhancing their capabilities.

TERRORISM IN INDIA

There are several theatres of terrorism in India, namely Jammu and Kashmir, the Punjab, the North East, Central India and Tamil Nadu. There is evidence that terrorism in Jammu and Kashmir is fomented by the ISI of Pakistan, and virtually amounts to a proxy war against India; it costs Pakistan Rs. 250 crores per annum to wage this proxy war against India – a sum which it can well afford and does not mind spending in order to drain the fighting forces and economic strength of India. In the Punjab, too, the ISI of Pakistan waged a proxy war against India during the 1980s and early 1990s, but terrorism in the Punjab was put down with a heavy hand and at present the minuscule number of terrorists surviving are lying low.

Terrorism in the North East has affected several states in that region; at present Manipur is the worst affected; Assam also continues to suffer periodic waves of terrorism. The major terrorist groups in Manipur and Assam are now truncated organized-crime groups; it is estimated that ULFA (United Liberation Front of Asom) in Assam has generated money to the extent of INR 10 billion by way of kidnappings, etc., and it has invested this money all over the world to generate still-larger sums.

In contrast to other areas, the left-wing terrorism in Central India (particularly Andhra Pradesh and, to an extent, Madhya Pradesh) is a poor cousin; it operates on a paltry budget of INR 10 million per annum. However, left-wing terrorism which began in the 1940s has managed to survive until today because it was romanticized to a very larger extent. Terrorism in Tamil Nadu is an offshoot of the activities of the

31

LTTE (Liberation Tigers of Tamil Eelam) of Sri Lanka and continues to pose a threat which cannot be taken lightly.

11 SEPTEMBER 2001 AND AFTERWARDS

On 11 September 2001, four planes were hijacked in the United States, apparently by suicide squads; two of the hijacked planes rammed into the twin towers of the World Trade Center in New York, one of the planes hit the Pentagon building in Washington and another was brought down and crash-landed in Pennsylvania. The casualties resulting from these terrorist attacks are somewhere in the region of 5,000. The terrorist attacks of 11 September 2001 are the most audacious to date. As a result of these attacks, the war by the terrorists has been taken several degrees higher; one can even say that what happened to the USA on 11 September 2001 was almost an act of war.

Some of the features of the terrorist attack of 11 September 2001 need to be highlighted. The first of these is that the tools of terror have undergone a revolutionary change – instead of kalashnikovs, aeroplanes are now being used as projectiles to target vulnerable locations. Considering the sea change in the operational attitude of terrorists, one can even conceive that they might resort to the use of biological weapons. Even a nuclear strike by terrorists cannot be ruled out, considering that the technology exists whereby suitcase nuclear devices can be assembled.

In the context of the attacks of 11 September 2001, the selection of targets is another feature that needs to be highlighted. The terrorists chose to hit at a superpower by striking at its economic might, represented by the World Trade Center, and its military prowess, represented by the Pentagon. Of course, there is no need to add that meticulous organization spread over a considerable period of time must have gone into the planning of the attacks of 11 September 2001.

The world is still contemplating who could be behind the attacks. Although the Taliban regime in Afghanistan and Osama Bin Laden are being projected as the most likely suspects, the terrorists still remain unidentified. This is further reinforced by the fact that no terrorist organization has come forth to claim responsibility for them and even those like Osama Bin Laden who have initially been named have issued disclaimers regarding their involvement. One could even ask another moot question, as to what fundamentalist Muslim terrorist groups were likely to gain most from such an attack, or for that matter, what point they were trying to prove. One cannot seem to find a logical answer to this. It is obvious that this attack was the handiwork of those with expertise, and those likely to gain the most from it. Even the involvement of intelligence agencies cannot be ruled out, because they generally have this kind of expertise. There is even speculation that these attacks could have been engineered by worldwide corporate interests with a certain aim in mind. One could even argue that some nations, wishing to maintain their hegemony, continually plunge the world into a state of war every few years, so that the struggling nations at the bottom of the heap who were trying to climb up, slip back still further.

There has also been a lot of discussion about choking the money supply to terrorist organizations following the 11 September attacks. The words 'money laundering' have been bandied about a good deal in this context. One point which needs to be emphasized here is that money laundering is not an overriding concern for terrorists; it is only a means to camouflage their funds. Money laundering becomes an overriding concern for them once they reduce themselves into organized-crime groups, because then they have a vested interest in obscuring the origins of criminal money and legitimizing the same.

RESPONSES TO TERRORISM

National level

At this point, one may as well ask what the response should be to terrorism or what is the best way to combat it. In the first instance one should strive for a political solution. For a meaningful political solution, alternative leaderships should be available, and one should strive to develop political leaderships along these lines. Apart from a political initiative, the political will of the state should display a hard line towards the terrorist organizations, because it is generally the experience that a soft approach does not work with them; a hard-line approach would also mean no interference in the enforcement effort against the terrorists. Development of intelligence is always a critical input in anti-terrorist operations. Elite commando units have also been found to be very successful in the fight against terrorism; obviously these elite units would have to have the best equipment to overwhelm the terrorists. In a situation where terrorism is fairly widespread, sufficient manpower would also have to be mobilized to guard vulnerable points and vulnerable persons. Adequate anti-terrorist laws would also have to be put into place to effectively counter the terrorists; India has recently enacted the Prevention of Terrorism Act (POTA) to deal effectively with terrorism. There was tremendous opposition to the enactment of this new anti-terrorist law considering the way the Terrorist and Disruptive Activities (Prevention) Act 1987 was misused by some of the states in India, which ultimately led to its repeal. Any fight against terrorism would, of course, entail the formulation of an appropriate and effective strategy to deal with terrorism in its various phases.

International level

Following the terrorist attack of 11 September 2001, world opinion has certainly focused on launching a global war against terrorism. For this global war, a global coalition would have to be built. The United Nations can play a very constructive role in doing this. The next step should be to identify the various theatres of terrorism in order to root out terrorism from these areas: before doing so, a strategy would obviously have to be worked out for each of these theatres. In any effective strategy, pooling of intelligence at international, regional, national and local level would be very necessary. The development of intelligence would have to be along strategic and tactical lines – the strategic intelligence would help in the formulation of strategy, and tactical intelligence, being case-related, would be very helpful in anti-terrorist operations. Pooling of all the expertise from the various coalition partners would also be another important input. As a matter of expediency, the comity of nations should also be prepared to permit elite commando units – to be formed from the best of forces amongst the coalition partners – to operate in the areas most affected by terrorism, and in cases where specific intelligence relating to terrorist attacks is available. Cutting-off of funds to terrorist organizations is another important area which has also to be taken into account, although it might prove to be the most difficult to tackle in the context of the present-day international financial and banking system.

While this global war against terrorism is waged, protectionist measures would need to be taken at various levels and no expense should be considered excessive in ensuring the same. Obviously, the global war against terrorism would have to be fought on the basis of a timetable, a timetable of ten years seeming reasonable: such a timetable would need to have a very specific focus and it should be spelt out in unambiguous terms for the benefit of all of the coalition partners in the fight against terrorism.

Following the 11 September 2001 attacks in the United States, the world economy has been badly shaken up; economic activity is on the decline in practically all areas. It is ironic that the peace dividend which law enforcement ensures is not always apparent to the people at large, and it is only when a tragedy of such gigantic proportions occurs that the need for old-fashioned law enforcement comes to the fore and governments are willing to loosen their purse-strings to ensure the same. The USA today is committing money in the region of $50 billion in the fight against terrorism. It is also committing $15 to $20 billion to prop up its badly hit aviation industry and around $120 billion to pump up the sagging US economy. Proper remedial measures taken in good time should be a lesson for the future.

Note:
1. The structure of terrorist organizations is given at Appendix 1 to help to draw up strategies to counter them effectively.
2. General theatres of terrorism have been listed at Appendix 2.

APPENDIX 1

Structure of terrorist organizations

- they may have one centralized leadership.
- there may be several factions which control the terrorist movement.
- there may be several terrorist groups operating, each owing allegiance to its respective faction/leadership.
- the recruits may be from diverse backgrounds – educated, not so economically well-off and the common criminal element.
- psychologists have observed that although most of the recruits are normal in the psychological sense, they suffer from a feeling of inadequacy.
- terrorist organizations generally have a youth wing.
- they also have a religious front.
- they will have their sympathizers/harbourers.
- they will have safe houses.
- the terrorists will have a decentralized set-up – just as in intelligence organizations; in a given group/circle only some specific individuals know each other; this prevents the terrorist group from causing the collapse of the whole organization if one of its members is caught and provides information. Moreover, if a group is infiltrated the rest of the set-up remains safe.
- there will be training camps for giving training in the use of firearms and explosives; tactics and physical fitness also form a part of this training.
- there will be procurers for weapons and explosives – these are generally specialists in this trade.
- terrorists can operate in large groups or smaller ones; this would depend upon their objective and inherent strength, the reverses suffered or successes achieved and the strategy of enforcement operations launched by the government in power.

APPENDIX 2

Theatres of terrorism in the world

Asia

India: Jammu and Kashmir
    Punjab
    North-eastern states
    Left-wing terrorists in Central India
    Terrorists of LTTE in Tamil Nadu (a state in South India).
Pakistan: Although afflicted by terrorism in some areas, due to the dictatorial and fundamentalist nature of its regime, it has been accused of being a sponsor of terrorism in several parts of the world.
Nepal: Left-wing terrorism (Maoists).

Sri Lanka:	LTTE/Northern part of Sri Lanka.
Myanmar:	Has a totalitarian regime: some terrorist groups have tried to resist it.
Afghanistan:	Despite overthrow of the Taliban, terrorism has still not been rooted out.
Iraq:	With its weapons of mass destruction, a dictatorial regime and a history of attacking neighbours, was a major terrorist threat before the Iraq War of 2003.
Iran:	Has been prone to terrorism under the fundamentalists; the Iran–Contra affair is a case in point.
Middle East:	The Arab–Israeli stand-off and the resultant terrorist attacks.
Central Asian Republics:	Also afflicted by terrorism to some extent – Islamic fundamentalist groups quite active in these countries.
Russia:	The Chechens are the most active: the hostage drama in a Russian theatre is the prime example of Chechen terrorism.
South-East Asia:	Cambodia, Indonesia and the Philippines are afflicted by terrorism.
Vietnam:	A war-ravaged country.
China:	Has been tackling terrorism – very much a reality there.
Japan:	Has witnessed terrorist attacks by the 'Red Army' and pseudo-religious groups.
Africa:	Several countries in Africa are in the grip of internecine warfare, which is being waged primarily by warring terrorist factions.
Europe:	Northern Ireland is a prime example of terrorism simmering for a long period of time. Religious fundamentalist groups, pseudo-religious groups and other ideologically driven groups are responsible for terrorist acts in a number of countries.
North America:	Post-September 11, the fallout in the United States.
Latin America:	This region has a long history of dictatorial military regimes. Revolutions, coups d'etat and terrorism are almost a way of life in some countries of this region.
Note: 1	Religious fundamentalist groups are the most active terrorist groups in the world – for instance, Al-Qaeda, which has a worldwide presence.
Note: 2	Pseudo-religious groups with a worldwide following such as the 'Anand Marg' also indulge in terrorist acts in order to bring about a revolution in the world.
Note: 3	Other ideologically driven groups such as the 'Red Army' are also quite active on the terrorist front.

CHAPTER IV

DRUG TRAFFICKING

A BRIEF HISTORY OF DRUG ABUSE

Though life is multifaceted, it can sometimes also be a drudgery. Since time immemorial man has devised means of overcoming this drudgery; these means have ranged from physical to mental games and sometimes also involved the use of substances that had a direct bearing on the nervous system and the mind.

It is well documented that for periods of time, which can stretch back 2,000 years, several communities the world over have resorted to the use of various herbs as mood-elevators. However, many of these communities managed to 'socialize' the habit of mood-elevating herbs in the same way that the West has managed to socialize the habit of drinking alcoholic beverages, thus these herbs were never the subject of widespread abuse.

The first recorded instance of widespread abuse of narcotic drugs occurred in China in the nineteenth century. The British East India Company imported opium to China, causing widespread addiction among the population. The Company's motive was profit and their activities in retrospect differ little from those of drug traffickers of today. When China resisted and wanted to put an end to the import of opium, this led to the outbreak of the Opium Wars. These had tragic consequences for the Chinese. Following the defeat of the Chinese, the British continued to import opium. Wanting an assured supply of opium for China and finding that the Indian soil and climatic conditions were ideal for opium cultivation, they introduced the cultivation of opium in central parts of India, near Gwalior – this unwittingly led to the growth of what is now the present system of licit cultivation of opium in India with its attendant controls. In order to cater to the medical needs of the world, as of today India and Australia are the two countries where opium is produced legally.

TYPES OF NARCOTIC DRUGS AND PSYCHOTROPIC SUBSTANCES

Narcotic and psychotropic drugs worldwide are basically categorized as follows:
 (i) Opium-based – opium-based narcotic drugs are morphine and heroin. Poppy husk is also used very extensively in India.
 (ii) Coca-based – coca-based narcotic drugs are cocaine and crack; the tribes inhabiting the coca-growing Andean region also chew coca leaves.
 (iii) Cannabis – cannabis herbal and cannabis resin are two forms in which this naturally growing plant is used.

(iv) Psychotropic drugs and substances include:
    (a) Stimulants, such as methamphetamines and amphetamines;
    (b) Depressants, such as methaqualone and benzodiazepines;
    (c) Hallucinogens, such as LSD and Ecstasy;
    (d) Designer drugs and combination drugs. Designer drugs are psychotropic drugs manufactured to suit individual needs – Angel Dust (PCP) in the USA, for instance. Combinations of various narcotic and psychotropic drugs are also quite popular – for instance, the combination of cocaine and methamphetamine.

MEDICAL USE OF DRUGS

Narcotic drugs and psychotropic substances have a role to play in the treatment of pain and certain neuro-psychiatric disorders. Since these same narcotic drugs and psychotropic substances are also subject to abuse, they have to be controlled both domestically and internationally, all the way from their manufacture, to distribution and consumption.

In general, if medical requirements are properly assessed and the supply is properly regulated, the scope for the abuse of these narcotic drugs through diversion from licit channels is limited. Here, governments and international organizations such as the International Narcotics Control Board have a critical role to play. It is the illicit production of narcotic drugs and psychotropic substances which constitute the major source of supply for the ever-increasing market for these drugs, fuelled as it is by increased demand. Apart from the spread of the drug culture, drug syndicates also have a great part in fuelling the demand by ensuring their availability. Since the majority of the narcotic drugs are produced from natural plants, the chemical substances required for their extraction, along with the processing techniques, also assume an added importance for illicit traffickers.

ILLICIT TRAFFICKING IN DRUGS

Illicit drug trafficking trends worldwide can best be understood if one considers the producing/processing regions and the consuming regions; for a proper analysis, narcotic drugs will be considered under the various classifications set out in (iv) above.

Opium and its derivatives

Illicit opium is produced in the South-West Asian region comprising Afghanistan and Pakistan. It is also produced in the South-East Asian region comprising Laos, Thailand and Myanmar. Most laboratories for processing the opium of South-East Asian origin into heroin are also located in the vicinity of the areas of production – heroin produced in this region is of very high quality.

The South-West Asian region accounted for the bulk of opium production until 1999. However, in 2000 the Taliban issued an edict that no opium was to be cultivated in

Afghanistan, and this edict was followed. One point that needs to be emphasized here, however, is that the Taliban issued this edict not because of moral considerations, but in order to attract world attention, which it had been trying to do for quite some time through acts such as the bombing of the Bamiyan Buddhas. Even though there was no opium production in South-West Asia in 2000, there continued to be a very sizeable amount of opium which was held by the Taliban and other traffickers operating under its control; this ready stock of opium, which had accumulated due to bumper harvests over the years, ensured a steady and continual supply of heroin to the world drug market. In the South-West Asian region, the laboratories for processing opium to morphine and heroin are located near the poppy-producing regions, most of them being located on the Afghan side. The drugs trade in Afghanistan is controlled to a very large extent by ISI of Pakistan, which was believed to finance 75 per cent of the Taliban budget, and also support the ailing Pakistan economy to a considerable extent.[1, 2]

Most of the heroin produced in the South-East and South-West Asian regions is injectable heroin. In 1999, in the South-East Asian region 1,029 tons of opium was produced, 895 tons in Myanmar, 8 tons in Thailand, 124 tons in Laos and 2 tons in Vietnam. In the same year in the South-West Asian region 4,574 tons of opium was produced; 4,565 tons in Afghanistan and 9 tons in Pakistan. Going by the yardstick that 10 metric tons of heroin can be produced from 100 metric tons of opium, the amount of injectable heroin available for trafficking from the South-East Asian region was 102 tons and from the South-West Asian region 457 tons. The principal consumption areas for heroin lie in Europe, North America and Australia. Apart from this consumption area, the countries lying along the drug trafficking routes also suffer a spillover effect in terms of consumption.

The trafficking routes for South-East Asian heroin criss-cross countries in South-East Asia and cut across the Pacific. The trafficking routes for South-West Asian heroin stretch across the Central Asian Republics, the Middle East and the Indian subcontinent. The Balkan route is a major trafficking route to Europe. Africa also plays a very important role as a staging point for heroin trafficking, with Nigerian nationals appearing to be actively involved in drug trafficking worldwide. Sri Lanka is also emerging to play a role similar to that of Africa, although in a much smaller way; the LTTE, a terrorist organization, controls this drug trafficking via Sri Lanka. The trafficking of tar heroin from the Mexican region is also posing a serious threat to the United States.

Cocaine

Cocaine is produced from the coca plant, which grows in the Andean region of South America. Countries where the coca plant is grown are Colombia, Peru and Bolivia.

---

[1]   This was the situation before the 11 September 2001 incidents and before aid in large quantities started flowing to Pakistan: see the article by B. Raman on 'Heroinisation of the Pakistan Economy'.

[2]   Post-11 September 2001, following the overthrow of the Taliban regime in Afghanistan, poppy cultivation has been resumed, and in 2002 was estimated at 3,400 tons.

The process of extracting cocaine from the coca plant is a very intricate one, involving several physical processes and chemical reactions. Most of the cocaine-manufacturing units are located in the riverine tracts in the Andean mountains, the reason being the large requirement of water required in the extraction process. Thus, cocaine production has also adversely affected the ecology of the Andean region, as many chemical pollutants used in it are ultimately dumped in local rivers. In 1999 the area under coca cultivation in Colombia was 128,500 hectares, in Peru 38,200 hectares and in Bolivia 28,800 hectares. The amount of cocaine that can be extracted from the amount of coca leaves indicated above works out at 765 tons.

The consumption areas for cocaine are again countries in North America, Western Europe and Australia. Countries that lie along the trafficking routes also suffer from the spillover effect of consumption. This can range from that of a non-serious threat of drug abuse to a serious threat of drug addiction amongst the local population.

The trafficking of cocaine is controlled by the drug cartels – mainly the Cali and Medallin cartels of Colombia. The cocaine trafficking route to North America lies across the Central South American countries and also along the countries in the Caribbean; both sea and the land routes are used for trafficking. The cocaine trafficking routes to Europe once again cut across Central South American countries and islands in the Caribbean, which act as staging points: container cargo, and also air cargo, is extensively used to traffic cocaine. Various ingenious *modi operandi* for trafficking cocaine have also come to light; for instance, moulds of a suitcase were actually made of cocaine paste. Cocaine is also trafficked to Europe and Australia with Africa as the staging point; once again it appears that Nigerian nationals are involved in this trafficking. Cocaine trafficking has also spread to other parts of the world. It has the potential of being almost universal in its consumption pattern if pushed very hard.

Cannabis – herbal and resin

Cannabis in its herbal form and as a resin is extracted from a plant commonly known as Indian hemp. Both cannabis herbal and cannabis resin can be smoked by mixing them with tobacco. Originally, these cannabis plants used to grow wild, but they can now be grown on a commercial scale in greenhouses. Exotic varieties of cannabis have also been developed for growth in indoor as well as outdoor environments.

Cannabis is the most widely abused drug. It is grown in all parts of the world, although some strains of it, especially cannabis resin from certain regions, are still preferred. Major cannabis-producing countries of the world are Colombia, Mexico, Nigeria and South Africa for cannabis herbal, Morocco, Afghanistan and Pakistan for cannabis resin: there are 67 source countries for cannabis, according to seizures reported to ICPO-Interpol. The estimated production of cannabis in the world varies by a factor of 30; it has been estimated as from 10,000 tons to 300,000 tons – however by taking production and consumption estimates worldwide, cannabis production was estimated at 30,000 tons in 1999. This drug is also treated as a soft drug by some countries and a lenient attitude is adopted towards its abuse, for example, in the Netherlands.

Psychotropic substances

Stimulants

Methamphetamine and amphetamine are the stimulants most widely abused in the world. In earlier times their abuse was confined to countries in the ASEAN region and Japan. However, lately they have been abused on a very large scale in Western Europe and North America. Abuse of 'Ice', also known as crystalline methamphetamine, is extensive in Japan; this drug is smoked and one dose is generally enough to make a person an addict. Stimulants are illicitly manufactured by the diversion of chemicals and tend to be produced and trafficked within countries, although some regional trafficking patterns can be discerned.

Ecstasy

Ecstasy is also known as MDMA. Its abuse was initially confined to Europe. Its production is still concentrated in the Netherlands, with Germany and Belgium also producing it in sizeable quantities. Production of Ecstasy has also begun in Eastern Europe. Ecstasy abuse is no longer confined to Europe and has spread to North America, South Africa, Australia and New Zealand. Countries in the ASEAN region have also fallen prey to its abuse. One major point that needs to be borne in mind is that the bulk of Ecstasy is still produced and trafficked in Europe. Inter-regional trafficking trends can be discerned so far as Ecstasy is concerned, although the volume trafficked continues to be small.

Depressants

Methaqualone continues to be a drug that is widely abused in the African continent. Illicit manufacture of methaqualone takes place in India for trafficking to the African continent. One interesting aspect of the trafficking of methaqualone to the African continent is the emergence of a barter trade. This trade has quite often taken the shape of gemstones being exchanged for methaqualone powder.

Hallucinogenic drugs and designer drugs

LSD is a hallucinogenic drug which is being abused in several parts of the world. Abuse of designer drugs such as Angel Dust (PCP) is also not uncommon. These designer drugs are produced on demand for the very rich.

   In conclusion, it should be stated that drug abuse is a global phenomenon. The most widely abused drug is cannabis; three-quarters of all countries report abuse of heroin and two-thirds abuse of cocaine. Amongst the narcotic drugs, the abuse of stimulants such as amphetamine and depressants such as benzodiazepines has increased.

THE POSITION WITH REGARD TO INDIA: ILLICIT TRAFFICKING

India lies between two major drug-producing regions, i.e. the 'golden crescent' in South-West Asia (comprising Afghanistan and Pakistan) and the 'golden triangle' in South-East

41

Asia (comprising Myanmar, Laos, Vietnam and Thailand). Most of the heroin from the golden triangle region is trafficked along the South-East Asian network. However, as regards India, in the border state of Manipur heroin trafficking has assumed serious dimensions; in 2000, it was estimated that one ton of injectable heroin was being trafficked to Manipur to cater to an addict population of 40,000 Manipuri youth. In retail terms, the price of one ton of heroin in Manipur works out at INR 400 million.

Heroin originating from the South-West Asian region was trafficked through India in the 1980s. However, with the breakup of the USSR, new trafficking routes have emerged through the CIS countries. Moreover, Pakistan, the Middle East and Africa are also important staging points in trafficking heroin into Europe, and to some extent North America. The Balkan route, which has been reactivated, is being used extensively to traffic heroin into Europe.

The heroin seizures of both South-West-Asian and South-East-Asian origin are negligible in India. This is primarily due to lack of co-ordination in the enforcement effort and also lack of resources available to the Narcotics Control Bureau, which is supposed to co-ordinate this effort.

Smuggling of hashish into India from Nepal is another serious problem; hashish from the Himalayan foothills is much sought after. Most of this hashish is consumed in India and some of it is also trafficked outside. The illicit manufacture of methaqualone for trafficking to Africa is another problem facing Indian drug authorities.

One major point that needs to be highlighted as far as India is concerned is that it is the largest producer of legal opium in the world (Australia is another country which is a legal producer of opium). Although opium is produced legally in India under a system of controls established for over 100 years, since the 1990s these controls have more or less broken down and at present the leakages from licit production of opium are estimated to be in the region of 40 per cent. The licit production of opium in India was 1,800 tons in 2000; therefore, the shortfall from this translates into 70 tons of heroin. In fact laboratories have sprung up along riverine tracts in and around Gwalior, and heroin is being trafficked by trucks through the vicinity of Mumbai to Tuticourin in Tamil Nadu, from where it is taken to Sri Lanka, which is the staging point for onward trafficking into Europe and other parts of the world. It is a highly organized pattern of drug trafficking emanating from Central India and is dominated by Sri Lankan Tamils belonging to the LTTE. In fact, heroin trafficking is emerging as a major source of funding for the activities of the LTTE. Since the price of heroin rises exponentially from source areas to consuming regions, the amount involved in shortfalls from licit production works out at INR 25 billion in some parts of India, to INR 100 billion in Europe and the USA.

Another problem which is closely connected to the licit production of opium in India is that of trafficking of poppy straw/poppy husk, which are leftovers of the poppy plant after opium has been extracted. According to the data available, 20,000 tons of poppy husk is being trafficked within the country every year; the trafficking of poppy husk poses a serious health hazard because it has resulted in a very large section of the rural population becoming addicts. There is an economic reason behind abuse of poppy husk – the agricultural landlords give poppy husk to their farm labourers so that they can work for longer hours; after consuming poppy husk for two seasons, these farm labourers cannot live without it and become addicts.

THE MAGNITUDE OF THE PROBLEM IN TERMS OF QUANTITIES AND MONEY

In 1999 the amounts of heroin, cocaine and cannabis available for trafficking worldwide were estimated to be in the region of 578 tons,[3] 765 tons and 30,000 tons, respectively. Of the psychotropic drugs, abuse of stimulants such as amphetamines, Ecstasy and depressants such as benzodiazepines witnessed a sharp increase.

According to UNDCP estimates trafficking in narcotic drugs and psychotropic substances translates itself in monetary terms into US$500–800 billion. The profits from this trafficking are spread across producing regions to consuming regions. Moreover, narcotics trafficking worldwide is being controlled by highly organized criminal groups/gangs/cartels. These gangs have also developed links with other forms of transnational criminal groups dabbling in organized crime, terrorism, trafficking in arms, trafficking in human beings, etc. The links between the drug traffickers and transnational criminal gangs have made their activities more sinister.

It is estimated that US$300 billion-worth of narcotics money is laundered worldwide. All of this laundered money is available to criminal drug syndicates worldwide to be redeployed in an unencumbered way. Such large amounts of laundered money from drug trafficking also has serious macro-economic implications for the national economies of several countries.

AN EFFECTIVE STRATEGY TO COUNTER DRUG TRAFFICKING

Any effective strategy to counter drug trafficking would have to cover the production of drugs, the enforcement effort, the education and rehabilitation of drug addicts and, above all, the proceeds of drug trafficking, which are the single biggest motivating factor propelling this traffic.

Production of drugs

The majority of the drugs worldwide are extracted from natural plants: thus, a major plank of the strategy to put an end to trafficking should be aimed at ceasing the cultivation of such plants. Obviously, those cultivating such plants would have to be given an alternative livelihood. What is being emphasized nowadays is comprehensive alternative development of the cultivators of narcotic plants which involves giving them not only different crops for cultivation or subsidies for non-cultivation, but also covers issues relating to their health, education, environment and the quality of life that they lead.

---

[3] This figure also includes heroin produced in 1999 – in Latin America (14 tons) and other Asian countries (6 tons) that do not form part of the golden triangle.

Enforcement

Of course, enforcement worldwide both at the national level and at the international level, in terms of co-operation amongst countries, needs to be further tightened. Considering that enormous resources are available to the drug traffickers to bribe, and thereby blunt the enforcement effort, extra vigilance is required worldwide to tighten the enforcement agencies. Reasonable pay scales coupled with proper training and good motivation should go a long way in strengthening the enforcement effort worldwide.

Rehabilitation

Rehabilitation of drug addicts by putting them on various rehabilitation programmes, reviving them with occupational therapies so that they once again become useful citizens, is another important area in the fight against drug trafficking. With rapid advances being made in the area of molecular biology and genetics it is quite possible that very effective drugs might be developed in the future to wean the drug addicts away from narcotic drugs; it is also possible that one could even engineer the genetic code so that people start abhorring narcotic drugs in the future.

Proceeds of drug trafficking

It is the experience that the most effective way to render any activity unattractive is to take the economic benefit out of it. This dictum applies all the more to drug trafficking, considering the enormous profits involved. Thus, the countries of the world are trying to attack the proceeds of crime by bringing in suitable anti-money-laundering legislation and by extending co-operation in this sphere through international conventions and other bilateral arrangements.

INTERNATIONAL CONVENTIONS

There are three international conventions dealing with narcotics trafficking. The first is the 1961 Single Convention on Narcotic Drugs, which was further amended by the 1972 Protocol. The 1961 Convention codified all of the existing multilateral treaties in the area of narcotic trafficking. It also simplified and streamlined the control machinery and extended the international control system to include cultivation of plants that were the raw material for narcotic drugs. The 1972 Protocol further emphasized the necessity of preventing illicit production of trafficking in and use of narcotic drugs; this Protocol also strengthened the role of the International Narcotics Control Board (INCB) so that it could maintain a proper balance between supply and demand of narcotic drugs for medical and scientific purposes.

Until 1971, only plant-based drugs had been subject to international control. As a result of the 1971 Convention on Psychotropic Substances, international drug control also extended to the areas of amphetamine-type stimulants and hallucinogens, etc.

The 1971 Convention has more or less the same objectives as the 1961 Single Convention on Narcotic Drugs.

The United Nations Convention against Illicit Traffic in Narcotic Drugs and Psychotropic Substances, adopted in 1988, deals with illicit activities, in contrast to both the 1961 and 1971 Conventions, which focus primarily on the licit activity with regard to markets of controlled substances. The 1988 Convention also attacks the proceeds of crime, has provisions for mutual legal assistance and strives for speedy extradition of drug traffickers.

Note: In this chapter, the figures regarding narcotics have been taken from the *World Drug Report 2000* and *The Opium Economy in Afghanistan – 2003* published by the United Nations Office for Drug Control and Crime Prevention.

CHAPTER V

BRIBERY AND CORRUPTION

DEFINING CORRUPTION

The *Oxford Concise Dictionary* describes corruption as 'dishonest or illegal behaviour of people especially those in authority'; according to the World Bank, corruption is 'abuse of public office for private gains'; 'Corruption is any cause of action or failure to act by individuals or organizations public or private, in violation of law or trust for profit or gain' as per the definition adopted in 1999 by the International Criminal Police Organization. Transparency International[1] defines corruption as 'misuse of entrusted power for private gain'. In 1999 the Council of Europe agreed on a working definition of corruption, which states:

'Corruption is bribery and any other behaviour in relation to persons-entrusted with responsibility in the private and public sector which violates their duties that follow from their status as public officials, private employee, independent agent or other relationship of that kind and is aimed at obtaining undue advantages of any kind for themselves or for others.'

Though some of the above definitions have the advantage of being clear, focused and concise, some feel that they are not comprehensive enough; they even argue that definitions tend to be restrictive and coercive and therefore an impediment to free inquiry. To finally clinch the argument against definitions, it is further stated that corruption is something which is easier to identify than to define. Nevertheless, a definition is still a useful starting point for probing further a phenomenon as complex as corruption.

A BRIEF HISTORY

Corruption has been in the news for the past two decades. Historically, it has existed from the dawn of civilization. From the ancient Indian Kingdoms, to the Mughals and down to British rule, corruption was a part and parcel of the polity in India; only the degree of corruption might have differed. Likewise, the Greeks, the kingdoms of medieval Europe and the revolutionary/democratic regimes which emerged following the French Revolution were also afflicted by this malady. Every civilization, be it the Chinese,

---

[1]   Transparency International is a non-governmental organization that is active in the fight against corruption on a global scale.

Egyptian, or the Incas had its share of corruption. In his famous treatise on the polity and economy of the state, Chankaya has stated in *Arthashasttra*:

> *'Just as it is impossible not to taste the honey or the poison that finds itself at the tip of the tongue, so it is impossible for a government servant not to eat up, at least a bit of the king's revenue. Just as fish moving under water cannot possibly be found out either as drinking or not drinking water, so the government servants employed in the government work cannot be found out [while] taking money.'*

Corruption even finds mention in the ancient mythological texts of most religions. This resulted from the perception that gods and goddesses, like their human counterparts, are also prone to baser instincts which in turn breed corruption. Eve, by partaking the forbidden fruit, and Indra, by tempting seers immersed in deep meditation with the most beautiful maidens, both indulged in corrupt behaviour.

A MULTIFACETED PHENOMENON

Corruption can be many faceted. It might be highly personal, and may involve a steep fall from certain lofty value systems, e.g., from being honest to becoming utterly dishonest. It could be interpersonal and could imply use of underhand methods such as intrigue and deception in violation of accepted ethical and moral codes. One even encounters 'intellectual corruption', wherein thinkers freely plagiarize ideas and pass them off as their own. For many, religion is a convenient tool to deprive the gullible of their wealth. However, the main form of corruption which is the subject of our concern in the context of this book is in relation to public dealings; so-called 'public servants' and 'corporate managers' resort to this type of corruption. Though corruption generally involves a decline of value systems and erosion of the moral code, the driving force behind it is greed.

The extent and level of corruption in a society depends to a very large extent on the social, moral and cultural ethos of that society. Social mores and the cultural ethos of a society are an extension of its value system and are ultimately reflected in its organizational set-up and general attitude towards life. For instance Hindus, having a benign attitude towards wealth, are considered to be more tolerant of its pursuit, even if it is acquired by corrupt means. On the contrary, the Judaeo-Christian tradition treats wealth as a source of evil. Despite these attitudes towards wealth, the irony is that the East is presumed to be spiritual, whereas the West is presumed to be materialistic. Thus, it would be a great distortion to view a phenomenon as complex as corruption in terms of a single attitude. In effect, several attitudes prevalent in society tend to act upon each other to produce a resultant behaviour such as corruption, which again is modified to a considerable extent by the ethical, moral or religious codes of that society.

From the above discussion, it follows that one can have a society which is highly corrupt with a high tolerance level, and a society where corruption is negligible with a zero-tolerance level. Not only are several permutations and combinations on corruption levels and tolerance limits discernible around the world, but as stated by Shri S.S. Gill,[2] 'corruption also has a tendency to acquire a distinct national flavour'; for example, corruption in Mexico, India and Nigeria, though not differing in its basics, can be unique to each country.

ROOT CAUSES OF CORRUPTION

If history, social mores and culture provide the backdrop for understanding corruption, its root causes can be traced to the administrative structure and the legal system which govern the society. An administrative structure might lead to the emergence of monopolies/oligopolies which by their very nature breed corruption; for instance, monopolies can lead to overcharging, and also to low-quality work. Discretionary powers in the hands of few individuals is another administrative trait which leads to corruption; such power can easily be abused to provide unlawful gains. Secrecy and red-tapism, which are generally the hallmark of any bureaucratic system, are the biggest contributory factor leading to corruption; to have even the simplest of things done, often one has to pay to cut across the bureaucratic maze.

Archaic laws and exceedingly slow and time-consuming judicial processes are also a major source of corruption. In most of the developing world which comprises the former colonies, an outdated legal system – which at times is a century and a half old – is still in operation and responsible for rampant corruption, even though it might be totally out of synchronization with the needs of a developing society.

In a similar vein as the outdated laws, the United Nations treats corruption as the result of several asymmetries, which in effect are dysjunctions or discrepancies amongst the various segments of the society; examples of such asymmetries, at the national level, are the creation of illegal markets operating in collusion with the authorities, and, at the global level, the banking and tax regimes of different countries which again are a fertile ground for corruption.

Apart from structures, the role of individuals as leaders of state has been seen to be a critical factor in fostering corruption; for instance, General Abuja in Nigeria, Marcos in the Philippines, Tanaka in Japan, Suharto in Indonesia, and Benazir Bhutto[3] and Nawaz Sharif in Pakistan as heads of state, have been accused of amassing fortunes through corruption, and also for the perpetuation of highly corrupt regimes in their respective countries.

FORMS OF CORRUPTION

There are various forms of corruption. There is grand corruption, such as that indulged in by heads of state who amass fortunes through their corrupt practices. Then there is retail corruption which operates at the cutting edge of administration; it is generally of the

---

[2] Shri S.S. Gill, *Pathology of Corruption* (Harper and Collins, India, 1998) p. 3.
[3] As a result of his corrupt practices, Mrs Bhutto's husband was known as 'Mr Ten Per-cent'.

petty kind and affects the day-to-day life of ordinary people: this type of corruption can be a source of harassment because one encounters it so often. In between grand and retail corruption one can also categorize corruption involving substantial sums of money and indulged in by those vested with great authority. Transparency International also draws a distinction between 'for the rule' and 'against the rule' corruption; in 'for the rule form of corruption' money is taken for applying the norms in force, whereas in 'against the rule form of corruption', rules are bent or misinterpreted in order to take money.

Corruption in its various forms can also be viewed in terms of bribes, speed money, extortion, outright fraud, embezzlement, misappropriation of assets, and operation of vested interests. Bribery is offering of money/other advantages by a private person to a public official in order to influence the decisions of public official in his favour. Speed money is basically a 'bribe' which hastens the decision-making process – those offering speed money justify it in terms of expediency. Extortion is a form of corruption when a public official demands an advantage for doing a thing in a legal or illegal manner. The difference between bribery and extortion can often be quite subtle: for instance, outright fraud might entail using forged documents to gain an advantage. Embezzlement and misappropriation of assets, which also involves breach of trust, is indulged in by those with custody of such assets. Vested interests can be a large motivating factor in corruption: for instance, a public official or his relatives might have an interest in a company which has bid for a project, and the vested interest can sway the decision in the direction of corruption.

Another way to view forms of corruption can be that which involves defrauding the government/exchequer or that which entails taking the money out the of pocket of individuals. An illustration of defrauding the government is the act of an income tax official in under-taxing an assessee for wrongful gain; even though this form of corruption is treated as imperceptible because government is generally regarded as an abstraction, it causes much damage to society. An illustration of taking money out of the pocket of an individual is the act of a policeman making a lorry driver pay for crossing a traffic checkpoint.

TYPES OF CORRUPTION

Bureaucratic

There are basically three types of corruption – bureaucratic, corporate and political. Bureaucratic corruption generally flows from faulty structures, misuse of official position or abuse of power; its incidence increases if the bureaucracy pays low salaries to its employees. Bureaucracy can also be a great facilitator for both corporate and political corruption. Bureaucratic corruption generally involves just sitting on a decision, misrepresentation, bending of rules or even downright fraudulent behaviour. In most of the developing countries, bureaucracies are often corrupt. In fact, a number of bureaucratic systems nowadays function on the basis of percentages; in any public work contract in India, 30–40 per cent of the sanctioned budget is expected to be siphoned off to the coffers of the corrupt. Thus, an index on the level of corruption for bureaucratic departments can also be drawn up; in India it is the revenue-generating departments which are the most corrupt.

Corporate

Corporate corruption is generally on a grand scale, unlike bureaucratic corruption, which can be both big and small. In countries where there is a very large public sector, as in the case of India, such a large public sector is considered to be a convenient and highly profitable milch cow for the corrupt. There are several ingenious ways in which corruption operates in the public sector. It can start from the fudging of muster rolls, to awarding of contracts leading to substandard infrastructure, to retailing products in an unrenumerative manner in order to benefit the corrupt. Corruption in public-sector banks is sequential to non-performing assets; perhaps banking is one sector that would rank very high on the corruption index in most developing countries. In controlled or partially controlled economies the private sector, by manipulation of controls extending over several spheres of economic activities, indulges in large-scale corruption. Any number of subsidies that are devised are also a very lucrative source of corruption for the corporate sector.

The examples that have been given regarding types of corporate corruption are by no means exhaustive; perhaps a monumental work will have to be written to portray the full scope of corporate corruption.

Political

Political corruption is another type of corruption that has been in the limelight. Following the process of decolonization, the political class in the newly independent countries realized that the profits were being taken mostly by the bureaucrats and the corporate world. Soon the political class wanted its share, and it went about it with great gusto. Both democratic and totalitarian regimes fell prey to it. In dictatorial or totalitarian regimes, since the political process was weak, the proceeds of corruption could be easily collected; only its magnitude differed, depending upon the rapaciousness of the corrupt leader. In democratic regimes, politicians had to be more ingenious in order to make money by corrupt means.

In order to make money in a democracy, the politician first of all has to ensure his continuation in politics as a leader, and the role played by money to ensure the same has increased over a period of time. The way the politicians raise money for the electoral process is by way of donations from the corporate world or wealthy individuals, who do so for a consideration, termed as corruption. To stay in power, the politicians also bribe the voters, hire musclemen to intimidate them, indulge in booth capturing (a very typical Indian phenomenon), generally in collusion with the local authorities, buy adversaries so that they deliberately lose, make false promises and indulge in propaganda instead of performance. Patronage is also used by the politicians in an unabashed and shameless manner to ensure their 'vote bank'. Moreover, once in power the politicians, by virtue of heading the executive, have perfected the art of making money. In a recent case of political corruption in India involving Shri Sukh Ram, a Union Minister, INR 25 million was seized during a search of his residential premises. In terms of sheer vulgarity, it has been said that the corruption of Jayalalitha as Chief Minister of Tamil Nadu during her first term would put even Imelda Marcos to shame. Corruption by politicians has also been described by Americans as 'machine politics', in other words 'the commercialization of politics in order to maximize gains'.

ESTIMATE OF AMOUNTS INVOLVED

It is very difficult to arrive at an estimate of the proceeds of corruption. However, since corruption is the lubricant which makes all forms of crime, including economic crime and fiscal crime, tick, then by making certain projections relating to these crimes, one could say that corruption by itself adds up to substantial amounts. According to United Nations estimates, earnings from organized crime are US$1.1 trillion per year, the narcotics trade being a US$500–800 billion enterprise (which is 8 to 10 per cent of international trade). The World Bank has estimated that the amounts involved in money laundering are in the region of US$800 billion–US$1 trillion, and according to the International Monetary Fund, money laundering constitutes 2 to 5 per cent of the world GDP. The Euro-dollar market, running into trillions of dollars, is fuelled not only by petro-dollars but also narco-dollars. Capital flight from India is estimated at US$100 billion according to some estimates. In Russia, following the demise of communism, capital flight and money laundering are reported to be in the region of US$100–400 billion. The parallel black economy almost rivals GDP in many of the developing countries: in India it is estimated to be in the region of 50 per cent of GDP.

From the above figures, it is quite obvious that the share of corruption in terms of money would run into hundreds of billions of dollars. If one were to add grand corruption indulged in by several heads of state, the estimate of corruption is bound to increase substantially.

Another point to be borne in mind while estimating corruption is that in developing economies it tends to be more in the area of economic development and trade, while in the developed countries it is generally a by-product of crime; the figures given in the previous paragraphs would amply substantiate this conjecture. However, out of interest I would like to mention that during my visit to New York the organized crime unit of the New York City Police reported that for every bottle of milk sold in New York, one cent went to the 'Mafiosi'.

IN THE CONTEXT OF GLOBALIZATION AND ECONOMIC LIBERALIZATION

While discussing the international dimension, liberalization and globalization must be considered as inherent traits, and corruption needs to be examined in this context.

Today most countries of the world have embarked on economic liberalization – free trade is the new mantra for economic development and, in the course of time, social equity. Globalization has been fuelled by rapid advances in electronics, telecommunications, location of industries based on cost inputs, travel and a host of other factors. Integration of the financial and banking sectors is also considered an integral part of economic liberalization. In the international scenario described above, multinationals, which in turn are becoming bigger as a result of mega-mergers, are having a field day. Multinationals, which are predominantly from the developed world, have cast their net far and wide in the developing world; such an expansion of the operations of multinationals has inevitably entailed corruption on a fairly large and widespread scale. When the developed world gives bribes, it has also been claiming tax deduction on these bribes by terming them business expenses; of course, the situation has changed considerably now, as a result of exposure by non-governmental groups like Transparency International. The proceeds of corruption and other forms of crimes can also be moved around very easily in the integrated financial system of the world; such movement would imply capital flight in the case of economic crises or plain and simple hiding of wealth, i.e., money laundering to disguise its origin.

The international dimension of corruption would not be complete without a discussion of corruption in defence deals, due to the intense competition amongst the developed countries for such contracts. Considering the vast sums involved in armaments, which is the biggest industry in the world today, commissions or bribes are believed to be offered as a matter of course to the people in authority in the developing world; the bribes in defence contracts can run into billions of dollars and quite a few of the most talked-about corruption scandals have pertained to the defence industry.

It has already been mentioned that corruption is the lubricant or oil that makes all other forms of crime tick. How does such a thing happen? Organized-crime groups have to influence law enforcement agencies, the judiciary and their political masters to carry out their highly profitable illegal enterprises without any hindrance. Likewise drugs, terrorism, tax evasion, black money, economic crime (including those having an international dimension), economic scams and smuggling activities of all sorts are crimes which in order to operate successfully have to corrupt all the levels in their illegal operations. Lately there has also been much talk about the political-bureaucratic-criminal nexus which is posing a great threat to the security of nations.

CORRUPTION IN INDIA: A SHORT SURVEY

To document the history of corruption in various countries of the world is something which is beyond the scope of this book. However, a case study of corruption in India has been attempted and lessons could be drawn from it.

India attained its independence as a result of a non-violent freedom struggle launched by Mohandas Karamchand (Mahatma) Gandhi; it was a unique experiment in the history of the world and was copied successfully by many other countries to achieve their salvation from oppression. Gandhi was essentially a 'votary' of truth and for him there was no difference between means and ends – according to him without the right means, the end could never be reached. Thus, the Indian freedom struggle launched India onto the world scene on a platform of highly desirable and noble value systems; corruption had no place in it. Following independence Nehru, who was the heir to the legacy of Gandhi, attempted to achieve economic growth with social justice within the framework of a democratic polity; such an approach had never been attempted before and, according to Shri S.S. Gill, was doomed to failure because of certain immanent contradictions within it. However, Nehru's achievements in the economic field and the polity were considerable; he built up the basic infrastructure for development through the public sector, fostered the private sector by encouragement and incentive and managed to keep the democratic processes alive in the country, in stark contrast to the newly independent colonies which were falling prey to dictatorships. However, Nehru was a man in a hurry, because he felt India had to achieve a lot in a short span of time to catch up with the rest of world; as the result of such an approach on Nehru's part, he began to tolerate corruption amongst some of his colleagues.

With the passing of Nehru, there was a short interregnum, when Lal Bahadur Shashtri was the Prime Minister. He was an honest man, and was followed by Indira Gandhi, who though personally honourable, introduced the licence, permit, or quota raj to build up her war chest in order to hold sway in the political arena. Rajiv Gandhi, her son and successor, although essentially a man of great charm and with an image (initially) of being Mr Clean, was accused of being directly involved in kickbacks in the 'Bofors' deal. The next full-time successor to Rajiv Gandhi, Narasimha Rao, though he served his full term as Prime Minister, is facing trial in three cases on corruption charges.

Thus expediency, coupled with erosion of the moral fabric of the leadership, had a great part to play in fostering corruption in India. Soon it percolated to all sectors of society, economy and polity; so much so that it has become endemic and can almost be likened to a chronic disease. It is in the context of this depressing scenario in India, which is also the fate of most of the developing world, that ways and means to combat corruption have to be found.

ADVERSE IMPACTS OF CORRUPTION

At this stage, it is in order to examine the damage corruption can do, especially in developing economies. Corruption undermines good governance; it promotes a culture where nothing moves without money: according to Alatas, it leads to negligence in all aspects of administration. It fundamentally distorts public policies; for instance, plans for economic development are unable to achieve their objectives, because resource allocation, particularly in the public sector, is manipulated in favour of the corrupt. Furthermore, it leads to misallocation of resources in the private sector, because large amounts of corrupt money gives a fillip to a consumerist culture for luxury goods, with the result that priority areas such as roads, ports and hospitals are neglected. Thus, in the ultimate analysis corruption is harmful for the private sector and its development. Corruption hurts the poor particularly; it enables the rich to become richer by achieving their ends, whereas the poor are often left behind: as a result it also widens the gap between the rich and the poor. Moreover, widespread corruption leads to a value system which is rotten at the core and certainly not one of the desirable goals for society. This rotten core can undermine and ultimately lead to the destruction of polity, economy and the culture of any society: perhaps this is what prompted Edward Gibbon to state that 'corruption' is one word in which the decline of the Roman Empire can be summed up.

This discussion on the harmful effects of corruption would not be complete without also examining the flip side. According to some American economists, who could be termed 'cloistered sophists', corruption is not opposed to economic development; they even argue that it acts like a lubricant to economic growth. Shri S.S. Gill has beautifully summed up the various arguments advanced by these economists regarding the positive role of corruption; in his summing up he states: 'Corruption seems to be a panacea for all the ills of developing countries; it performs a host of social functions, satisfies unfulfilled needs, regulates the market, helps the system make better economic choices, aids economic growth, removes social tensions, and it is such a powerful tool of reform that it may avert impending revolutions.'[4] The most serious objection to the argument advanced by these economists is that it does not take into account the moral implications for society; at another level these economists are totally oblivious of the fate of the vast majority of economically deprived people in developing countries who are in no position to share the positive gains of corruption.

COMBATING CORRUPTION

In a society where corruption has become endemic and is affecting practically all spheres of human activity, combating it becomes a priority because of its evil nature and potential for damage. Corruption can be opposed at two levels. One level is on the wider canvas of society, wherein it is treated as being systemic in nature; another level is that of enforcement on a case-by-case basis.

Systemic solutions

In any systemic scheme, institutions and value systems play a vital role, and their erosion is a major contributory factor leading to corruption. Thus, institutional building and restoration of the value system, though arduous and time-consuming tasks, must be undertaken. Transparency in public and private dealings is another critical factor at systemic level to curb corruption. Unless one is accountable for one's conduct, one can be capricious in one's acts; thus, holding people in authority accountable for their actions is another discouragement to corruption. Responsiveness to the needs of the people, which is an essential requirement of a democratic polity, would also go a long way in combating corruption; in most democracies, it is generally feudal attitudes which are still predominant

---

[4]   Gill, M. 1 above, p. 265.

and these are hardly conducive to ushering in a society in which the barometer of corruption is low. Economic prosperity by itself, given that the other parameters are sound, can also lead to a decline in corruption. Several thinkers and institutions feel that empowerment of the people, which in turn would lead to transparency and the desired institutional framework, would be the most powerful tool to fight the systemic nature of corruption.

Enforcement

In combating corruption through enforcement, the first requirement is appropriate legislation. Anti-corruption laws should contain provisions regarding misuse of official positions, disproportionate assets and reversal of the burden of proof in cases of disproportionate assets. Moreover, the law should not have provisions that hinder enforcement, such as the requirement for the mandatory sanction of the head of the department before the accused can be prosecuted in a court of law, even if the evidence against him is overwhelming. Considering the seriousness of the problem, provisions in law enabling electronic surveillance and wire tapping as admissible evidence should also be in place. In view of the international dimension of corruption, the bribing of officials in foreign lands should be made an offence.

To be effective in curbing corruption, enforcement agencies should be given a certain degree of independence. The Central Bureau of Investigation (CBI) in India and the Independent Commission against Corruption (ICAC) in Hong Kong are two agencies that were conceived to combat corruption. Whereas the CBI has been kept on such a tight leash that it is ineffective, the ICAC has been given a degree of independence, enbaling it to make a dent in the fight against corruption. Moreover, it should always be borne in mind that vigilant enforcement agencies should always be staffed by agents from various other wings of the government so that vested interests, which in turn breed corruption, do not develop over a period time. In India, which has a federal polity, the provincial vigilance bureaux are the agencies tackling corruption at the province/state level. Since India has a very large public sector, it has been reasoned that enforcement action in such a large sphere of economic activity is not practicable and therefore public-sector units and departments of government should have internal vigilance systems to combat corruption. However, the track record of enforcement agencies at the union level, state level and internal vigilance organizations has been poor.

Other initiatives

Some novel ideas, like the institution of the Ombudsman in Scandinavian countries, can be used to combat political corruption. This idea of the Ombudsman was adopted in India in the form of the 'Lokpal', but what has finally emerged are toothless Lokpals who do nothing to combat political corruption. Lokpals consider their posts to be sinecures for political loyalty of a questionable nature.

Some countries also have vigilance commissioners, who are constitutional authorities set up to oversee the investigation of corruption. These vigilance commissions again need to be strengthened and their recommendations should be treated with more respect instead of being tabled before legislative bodies without follow-up action thereon; it should be mandatory that corrective suggestions by the vigilance commissions are acted upon.

The role of the judiciary can often be critical in the fight against corruption. Lately in India the judiciary, especially the Supreme Court, has been proactive in indicting the corrupt. It has often *suo moto* taken up some of the important cases of corruption in high places, especially against politicians: for instance, in the Jain hawala case, a former Prime Minister has been charged with corruption. It has even imposed hefty fines as penalties, e.g., in the case of Satish Sharma who was fined INR 6 million by the Supreme Court in the case relating to allotment of petrol pumps. The Supreme Court of India is playing a very positive and leading role, by taking up several public-interest litigations, quite a few of which relate to corruption charges.

In conclusion, one can say that even though corruption is rampant all over the world, particularly in developing countries, there is increasing awareness amongst the people at large that it has to be fought in order to ensure that the core of society does not become rotten.

Note: Transparency International also publishes a Corruption Perception Index on an annual basis. This lists countries according to the degree of corruption prevalent in that country. The last Corruption Perception Index published in 2002 is presented as Appendix 1 to this chapter. A low score means a country is more prone to corruption.

Transparency International also publishes a Bribe Payers Index on an annual basis. It lists countries according to the propensity to pay bribes in the developing countries. The Bribe Payers Index for the year 2002 is presented as Appendix 2. A low score means that a country has a greater propensity to offer bribes. According to BPI – 2002, domestic companies bribe more than foreign countries.

APPENDIX 1

Transparency International Corruption Perception Index – 2002

Country	Country rank	CPI 2002 score	Country	Country rank	CPI 2002 score
Finland	1	9.7	South Korea	43	4.5
Denmark	2	9.5	Greece	44	4.2
New Zealand	3	9.5	Brazil	45	4.0
Iceland	4	9.4	Bulgaria	46	4.0
Singapore	5	9.3	Jamaica	47	4.0
Sweden	6	9.3	Peru	48	4.0
Canada	7	9.0	Poland	49	4.0
Luxembourg	8	9.0	Ghana	50	3.9
Netherlands	9	9.0	Croatia	51	3.8
United Kingdom	10	8.7	Czech Republic	52	3.7
Australia	11	8.6	Latvia	53	3.7
Norway	12	8.5	Morocco	54	3.7
Switzerland	13	8.5	Slovak Republic	55	3.7
Hong Kong	14	8.2	Sri Lanka	56	3.7
Austria	15	7.8	Colombia	57	3.6
USA	16	7.7	Mexico	58	3.6
Chile	17	7.5	China	59	3.5
Germany	18	7.3	Dominican Rep.	60	3.5
Israel	19	7.3	Ethiopia	61	3.5
Belgium	20	7.1	Egypt	62	3.5
Japan	21	7.1	El Salvador	63	3.4
Spain	22	7.1	Thailand	64	3.2
Ireland	23	6.9	Turkey	65	3.2
Botswana	24	6.4	Senegal	66	3.1
France	25	6.3	Panama	67	3.0
Portugal	26	6.3	Malawi	68	2.9
Slovenia	27	6.0	Uzbekistan	69	2.9
Namibia	28	5.7	Argentina	70	2.8
Estonia	29	5.6	Côte d'Ivoire	71	2.7
Taiwan	30	5.6	Honduras	72	2.7
Italy	31	5.2	India	73	2.7
Uruguay	32	5.1	Russia	74	2.7
Hungary	33	4.9	Tanzania	75	2.7
Malaysia	34	4.9	Zimbabwe	76	2.7
Trinidad & Tobago	35	4.9	Pakistan	77	2.6
Belarus	36	4.8	Philippines	78	2.6
Lithuania	37	4.8	Romania	79	2.6
South Africa	38	4.8	Zambia	80	2.6
Tunisia	39	4.8	Albania	81	2.5
Costa Rica	40	4.5	Guatemala	82	2.5
Jordan	41	4.5	Nicaragua	83	2.5
Mauritius	42	4.5	Venezuela	84	2.5

Continued

APPENDIX 1 (Continued)

Country	Country rank	CPI 2002 score	Country	Country rank	CPI 2002 score
Georgia	85	2.4	Uganda	94	2.1
Ukraine	86	2.4	Azerbaijan	95	2.0
Vietnam	87	2.4	Indonesia	96	1.9
Kazakhstan	88	2.3	Kenya	97	1.9
Bolivia	89	2.2	Angola	98	1.7
Cameroon	90	2.2	Madagascar	99	1.7
Ecuador	91	2.2	Paraguay	100	1.7
Haiti	92	2.2	Nigeria	101	1.6
Moldova	93	2.1	Bangladesh	102	1.2

APPENDIX 2

Transparency International Bribe Payers Index – 2002

Country	Rank	Score
Australia	1	8.5
Sweden	2	8.4
Switzerland	3	8.4
Austria	4	8.2
Canada	5	8.1
Netherlands	6	7.8
Belgium	7	7.8
United Kingdom	8	6.9
Singapore	9	6.3
Germany	10	6.3
Spain	11	5.8
France	12	5.5
USA	13	5.3
Japan	14	5.3
Malaysia	15	4.3
Hong Kong	16	4.3
Italy	17	4.1
South Korea	18	3.9
Taiwan	19	3.8
People's Republic of China	20	3.5
Russia	21	3.2
Domestic companies		1.9

CHAPTER VI

ECONOMIC SCAMS

WHAT ARE SCAMS?

A scam can be defined as a clever and dishonest way to make money and can occur in practically any area of human activity. Viewed in strictly legal terms, scams are generally offshoots of crimes. Scams are classified depending upon the nature of the crime (for instance, cheating, fraud, violation of fiscal laws).

Scams have several traits which put them in a distinct class vis-à-vis other crimes: especially in the economic sphere scams generally involve manipulation of the system. Often they can go undetected for long periods of time; it is also possible that quite a few scams that have been perpetrated are never discovered. Since scams involve manipulation of the system, collusion of the regulatory authorities has generally been observed in the majority of them. Moreover scams, in order to qualify as such, entail widespread complicity and large sums of money.

Previously, scams surfaced in 'closed economies', activated by the principle of 'self-reliance', and countless instances of such scams can be cited. In India the licence, quota, or permit raj, which was prevalent for many years, spawned the maximum number of scams in the 'closed economic set-up'. Now that economic liberalization is the mantra, a soft attitude coupled with increased economic activity has also created a potential for the occurrence of scams.

MOST LIKELY AREAS FOR SCAMS

Banking

The most likely place for scams to occur is the area where there is money. Today, banking – particularly public-sector banking – is a major area for scams in India. There has been exponential growth in banking activities, and an indicator of this is the number of bank branches (8,867 in 1969, which had increased to 67,525 in 2001). Such a large network of banking in the public sector was undertaken in order to improve the economic lot of a large number of deprived people in India by way of providing them with subsidies, soft loans, grants of various sorts, etc., but it is in this area of developmental activities that some of the biggest scams have occurred in the banking sector: benefits do not reach the people concerned and are generally siphoned-off by politicians, power brokers, and influential and well-off people, mostly in complicity with the bankers. To top it all, corporate India has also been taking banks for a ride – it borrows from banks and then defaults on the repayment of loans through various ingenuous ways, some of these bordering on outright fraud; here again, the complicity of bankers with the corporate world is well documented. According to the latest figures available, in 2002 the non-performing assets of public-sector banks, which in effect is another name for bad debts, were estimated to be in the region of INR 820–1000 billion.[1] Thus, in overall terms, borrowing from banks and then defaulting on loans or siphoning-off of the same is one of the biggest scams in India.

Stock markets

India's stock market was rocked by a scam of major proportions in 1992 – the sums involved have been estimated by the Tarapore Committee at INR 30 billion. Another scam hit the Indian stock market in 2001. In both these stock market scams, large-scale funds were available from banks and financial institutions to the bulls in question i.e., Harshad Mehta (1992 scam) and Ketan Parikh (2001 scam) as a result of which they were able to play the stock market and take certain stocks and the stock market index to unrealistic heights. However, when these fraudsters fell into the bear trap, they defaulted on the payments to the banks/financial institutions and also on their commitments in the stock market. These defaults led to the exposure of the scams.

Apart from the financial institutions which suffered financial 'hits' in these scams, a very sizeable number of investors – considering the large turnover in the stock markets – also lost considerable sums of money. These scams eroded the credibility of the stock market to a significant extent and had a cascade effect on the economy in general.

Collective Investment Schemes

Another type of scam which has surfaced is the plantation companies scams. Such plantation companies take deposits from investors promising interest of up to 40 per cent per annum; to reassure the investor they pledge land to them. The scam is that the same land is pledged to several investors, often at an inflated price. A few of the investors might receive the promised return in the initial phase, but later most of these plantation companies simply vanish with the proceeds, which is the hard-earned money of small investors.

In another variant of scams involving plantation companies, deposits are taken against promises to deliver certain quantities of, for example, teakwood, after twenty years. The teakwood promised generally runs into a value which is twenty times the amount invested; here again, the scam is that there is no plantation, or if there is, it is only a front to defraud the depositor. The plantation companies in these instances also decamp with the proceeds.

The biggest instance of a plantation company scam is the Golden Forests Company, based in Lalru in the Patiala district of Punjab State. This company has managed to collect deposits in excess of INR 10 billion.

---

[1]   Reserve Bank of India estimates and a special investigation report on non-performing assets of banks in *Indian Express*, a leading Indian daily newspaper.

Non-banking financial companies

Non-banking financial companies (NBFCs), which at one point numbered 20,000 in India, were also notorious for committing economic scams. Once again these companies took deposits from investors, promising high returns. Only a few investors were paid the high returns promised and since it is not possible to sustain such high returns, these NBFCs vanished with the proceeds, leaving the poor investors high and dry. According to Reserve Bank of India (RBI) estimates, unsecured deposits of INR 700 billion were lying with the NBFCs prior to 1997.

In 1997 the RBI Act was amended to supervise non-banking financial companies. This supervision entailed NBFCs obtaining a certificate of registration and also permission before accepting deposits. Due to tight supervision by the RBI, the number of NBFCs that can accept deposits has been reduced to 1,005 and the total deposits with them were INR 193.42 billion at the end of March 2000.

Government treasuries

There are also treasury scams in India that result from the sheer administrative incompetence of the states. Treasuries in states become flush with development funds, if the governments of the day are unable to spend them. The funds lying idle in the treasuries became a source of great temptation for politicians, bureaucrats and suppliers/agents, to misappropriate through ingenious ways – the animal husbandry/fodder scam in Bihar being a classic example. The *modus operandi* in this scam was the presentation of forged bills, false intimations of receipt of the supply, having the bills passed by the treasury and depositing the amounts in question in a bank. The fodder scam, with widespread complicity extending over a very large part of Bihar, had a successful run for almost a decade; it was so widespread that even the Chief Minister of the state was involved. This scam was not insubstantial – amounts involved ran into INR 10 billion.

Several other treasury scams with similar *modi operandi* have taken place in Bihar – for example, the health department scam and the bitumen scam. According to Shri S.S. Gill,[2] the principal reason for the occurrence of these scams in Bihar was the total financial chaos prevailing in the state, because 'treasury accounts in the State had not been closed since 1991 thus making it impossible for the CAG to conduct routine audit'. Shri Gill bemoans the fact that only in the scams in Bihar could ridiculous bills like 40 kg of chickenfeed per fowl per day be passed.

Taxation of all sorts

Taxation by the state is another area where numerous scams take place. Some of the fertile areas for scams in the taxation sector are customs and excise duties, income and

---

[2]   Shri S.S. Gill, *Pathology of Corruption* (HarperCollins, India, 1998).

corporate taxes, sales tax and octroi. Scams in relation to customs duties will be discussed in the chapter on international economic crime, while scams pertaining to income tax and corporate tax will be dealt with in the chapter on tax evasion/the black economy.

Excise duty is the tax levied on manufactured goods prior to their leaving the factory. In excise duty scams, the goods are taken out surreptitiously in order to evade paying tax – generally there is complicity by the excise officers in the surreptitious movements of goods. It has also been pointed out by quite a few thinkers that excise duties on the high side is one of the principal reasons for scams in this area of taxation.

As an illustration of the excise scam the case of the Indian Tobacco Company (ITC) is revealing in many respects. This company, which is the 'bluest of blue chip companies', entered into widespread complicity with its dealers that the product would be sold at a price higher than the listed price; apart from claiming the differential in price from dealers, the ITC also evaded excise duty on a very large scale, because it was levied on the lower listed price; evasion of the excise duty in this particular case has been computed in the region of INR 8 billion.

State governments[3] are generally short of funds. To shore up their incomes they resort to imposition of sales tax on various goods. To further boost its revenue, central government also imposes central sales tax on a variety of goods. There is generally a differential in the sales tax imposed by the state and that imposed by the centre – the essential difference between the two being that the central sales tax is applicable on inter-state sales and the state sales tax is applicable on sales within the state. Recently, a diesel scam relating to sales tax was unearthed in Gujarat. In this scam, fictitious sales of diesel were shown by the oil companies outside the state so that the lower central sales tax was applicable, whereas in practice the diesel was given to the local dealers to further hawk it to retailers by way of imposing higher sales tax in Gujarat. The difference between the low central sales tax paid and the actual amount collected by way of sales tax was shared equally by oil companies and oil dealers. The diesel scam, running into INR 10 billion, is currently under investigation by the Central Bureau of Investigation.

Municipalities, which are responsible for some areas of local administration in India, are extremely poor. Their principal source of revenue is the octroi. Octroi are taxes imposed by the municipality on all goods entering the city for manufacture/consumption. Another feature of octroi is that it is a form of taxation where harassment is in-built because a goods lorry travelling to several towns has to contend with octroi in each of them. It has even been proposed that states abolish octroi for more effective commerce and trade, and municipalities would be compensated by the state/central governments by giving them a share from other sources of revenue. In octroi scams, generally what happens is that alternative routes to enter the town, whereby the checkpoints are avoided, are used by the goods lorries so that they do not have to pay a single penny as octroi. Another *modus operandi* is that octroi officials undercharge the octroi for a certain consideration.

---

[3] India has a federal structure comprising several states; there is central government at federal level and state governments at the state level.

In the big cities the total sum involved in octroi scams would run into hundreds of crores of rupees, considering that octroi collection is over thousands of crores of rupees.

Subsidies

India is also a land of subsidies, especially in the agricultural sector, which constitutes 50 to 60 per cent of GDP. Since 80 per cent of India's population lives in villages, the welfare of the rural population assumes great importance. Help in several ways is given to villagers engaged in farming – one of the most obvious is the fertilizer subsidy to the tune of INR 100 billion, provided annually to farmers, most of which is siphoned-off by politicians, power-brokers and the distributive channels. The government also compensates the farmers by buying all their crops at a fixed minimum price, which is known as the support price. The government procurement runs into massive figures – in 2001, 60 million tons of food grains were lying in the buffer stock and just a little fudging of figures, such as weight, wastage or price of sacks, can lead to scams which can run into billions of INR; these scams are at present part and parcel of the Food Corporation of India and other state procurement agencies. In the agricultural sector, which has always been treated benignly, power thefts have always been treated as transmission losses, a scam running into billions of INR, but some of the states, by giving a free power supply to the farmers, have reduced it to a blatant political scam to buy out the vote banks.

Land reforms

When India gained independence it embarked upon a socialist pattern of society. Integral to the achievement of an egalitarian society was to impose a ceiling on land holdings for big landlords and to distribute the surplus land made available to landless labourers or the actual cultivators. The whole process of land reforms was reduced to a sham in most of the states because of the influence wielded at all levels by the big landlords. Non-implementation of land reforms is one of the biggest scams – there have even been instances of benami ownership of land in names like 'Maj Kaur' which translated literally into English means 'Mrs Cow'.

Other areas

Human nature is not particularly characterized by nobility: on the contrary, human beings are prone to material pursuits and can often stoop to fairly low levels of conduct, thus, occurrence of a scam cannot be ruled out in any area of human activity. Insurance scams in which the turnover of money is enormous are quite common all over the world. In rural India, the primary education sector is another area prone to the most shameful scam, wherein while teacher absenteeism is the norm, teachers are claiming salaries; sometimes primary school teachers have even sub-contracted their jobs to all kinds of unqualified personnel.

Scams in the construction industry, in which substandard buildings are constructed, in the manufacturing sector, where the Bureau of Standard's norms are not adhered to and substandard goods are provided to the customers, and scams by way of counterfeiting of goods, are quite common in most of the developing countries of the world.

REGIONS/STATES IN INDIA PARTICULARLY PRONE TO SCAMS

There are certain regions particularly prone to scams in India. For instance, the North East[4] is known as the land of scams. These states are plagued by ethnicity and insurgency. To integrate the North East in every sense with the rest of the country, the Government of India has pumped in money in excess of INR 600 billion since Independence by way of development funds, with very few results to show on the ground. Most of this money has found its way into the pockets of politicians, bureaucrats, power-brokers, and other wheeler-dealers such as contractors and suppliers. On the basis of a study on the North East conducted by Arun Shourie, if, instead of pumping so much money into the region, the government had created a fixed deposit, it would have been possible to give every person in the region a monthly income of INR 1,500 for the rest of his or her life.[5]

Some of the states in India, such as Bihar, Madhya Pradesh, Uttar Pradesh and Rajasthan, are also particularly prone to scams due to administrative inefficiency and a culture of maladministration; these states are also known as Bimaru states, which translated into English means 'sick states'. Mumbai, one of the biggest metropolises in India, where 70 per cent of India's capital is locked up, is also prone to scams. Other metropolitan cities like New Delhi, Kolkata, Chennai, Hyderabad and Bangalore also have their share of scams, albeit on a smaller scale. One could say that no state in India is free from scams. Something unique about these scams in India is that they occur with a high degree of regularity. Practically every other day one reads about a scam in one part of the country or another.

SOME FAMOUS SCAMS: ESTIMATED SUMS INVOLVED

Some of the well-known scams in India are the CRB scam, the Indian Bank scam, the Mesco Group of Companies scam, the Rupee–Rouble scam and the Home-Trade scam. Some of the well-known scams that have occurred abroad are the Enron scam, the World.Com scam, and the South-East Asian economic crisis – countries indulging in scams, the Nick Leeson case, the Hunt Brothers' case involving an attempt to corner the world silver supply, and the Sethia case. Although it is very difficult to quantify the sums involved in scams, they must be huge, considering the fact that scams permeate

---

[4]   The North East comprises seven states, namely: Assam, Nagaland, Arunachal Pradesh, Manipur, Meghalya, Tripura and Mizoram.
[5]   It must also be borne in mind that the North East is sparsely populated, the density of population being 123 persons per square km compared to the Indian average of 273 persons per square km.

practically every area of human activity. Several hundred billion dollars would be the estimate regarding the sums involved in scams, on the basis of extrapolation.

PREVENTION OF SCAMS AND DEALING WITH SCAMSTERS

Scams are best prevented by having a system of checks and balances and periodic audits. However, salutary punishment of scamsters charged with the crime can go a long way in reducing its incidence. The attitude of society is also a great determinant in the occurrence/ non-occurrence of scams. A decline of moral value systems, a high tolerance level borne out of cynicism that 'evil deeds are handsomely rewarded' and increasing participation in scams by several key players of society, are some of the features which would have to be reversed in order to prevent scams.

There are several ways in which governments of the day have tried to deal with scams. Depending upon their gravity, judicial commissions might be appointed, and probes by parliamentary committees might be in order. However, at the end of the day, good old-fashioned investigation by enforcement agencies has to be undertaken to bring scamsters to book. Judicial commissions and parliamentary probes can certainly ensure that adequate laws are put in place for effective prosecution of scamsters. Coming back to investigation, often a high degree of expertise is involved; a multi-disciplinary approach/joint task forces, as well as the services of experts on a retainership basis often result in excellent investigations which are a *sine qua non* for successful prosecutions. Special courts presided over by special judges are also an essential requirement in dealing effectively with scams; these special courts can result in speedy trials and convictions, which in turn influence the attitude of society towards scams and scamsters.

Treatment meted out to scamsters is another area that has to be taken into account before concluding this chapter. Generally, scamsters are treated with 'kid-gloves' and there appears to be a different set of standards for scamsters and 'ordinary criminals'. To top it all, when there is a public outcry over the occurrence of a scam, instead of owning up to responsibility and taking remedial steps, the governments of the day portray these scams as 'systemic failures'.

CHAPTER VII

INTERNATIONAL ECONOMIC CRIME

USE OF THE TERM

The reader might wonder why I have decided to call this chapter 'International Economic Crime' and not just 'Economic Crime'. The main reason for this is that economic crimes within the national context have been described at some length in the previous chapters, albeit under different categories. 'International Economic Crime' tends to stand out for several reasons; these are that it cuts across national boundaries, that cases of international economic crime are complicated (both in terms of detection and investigation) and that they generate large sums of illegal money. The various types of economic crimes that I shall be discussing are those relating to invoice manipulation, frauds in export incentive schemes, maritime frauds, violation of foreign exchange control regulations (where such regulations exist), credit-card frauds, advance fee frauds, and frauds in the financial/securities markets, the banking sector and the commodities markets.

In the past, and prior to the worldwide trend towards economic liberalization, the developing countries generally had numerous financial and fiscal rules and regulations to give a certain direction to their economies. For instance, these developing countries would discourage imports of non-essential consumer items such as Scotch whisky, cigarettes and perfumes; the priority for the developing countries was to encourage import of heavy-duty machinery at affordable rates in order to manufacture other machines which in turn would provide a fillip to the medium- and small-scale industries. To bring this about, customs duty on such heavy-duty machinery import would generally be considerably less than on other goods. Since the trend worldwide is now towards economic liberalization, this in turn has implied a gradual lowering of customs duty and also the abolition of restrictions on the import of most items, including consumer goods; however, developing countries have to be vigilant and cannot afford to embrace total liberalization because of internal economic compulsions. Since customs duty constitutes a major source of revenue for the governments of developing countries, this is another reason that they cannot go the 'whole hog' for liberalization in external trade.

INVOICE MANIPULATION

It is in this scenario that external trade in developing countries has to be examined. On the import side, where custom duties are levied, it has been observed that invoice manipulation on the price of commodities is commonly practised and is a serious crime considering the economic damage that it causes to these developing economies. Invoice manipulation can be of two types. One is under-invoicing of imports so as to pay a lesser amount of customs duty; the extent to which the import is under-invoiced is paid through foreign exchange available to unscrupulous importers by using underground banking channels and a number of other methods. The other type of invoice manipulation in which importers are involved is over-invoicing of imports so that excess foreign exchange released by the developing countries is retained abroad, which in turn leads to a strain on its already fragile foreign-exchange reserves. The excess foreign exchange released as a result of over-invoicing of imports is retained abroad either in the form of capital flight or to pay for the under-invoiced imports and other illegal activities.

Although it has been widely held that reduction in customs duties will bring down the incidence of under-invoicing, intelligence gathered and cases detected in India indicate that even when duty differentials are quite low, unscrupulous elements tend to resort to invoice manipulation for improving profit margins. Further, certain countries, such as China, have acquired a general reputation of supplying goods at unbeatable prices; unscrupulous importers are known to take advantage of this fact by misdeclaring goods to be of Chinese origin in order to justify lower invoice prices.

In the context of India, the extent of invoice manipulation both on under- and over-invoicing of imports is enormous. India's imports are reported to be in the region of US$50.5 billion in the year 2001–02. According to various studies carried out on invoice manipulation on imports, the drain of foreign exchange from India is in the range of US$2.5–5 billion, which works out at 5–10 per cent of imports. If one adds the avoidance of customs duty on under-invoiced imports, which is reported to be in the region of US$2 billion, the damage to India's economy by way of loss of revenue is also considerable.

In order to take a worldwide view of the effect of invoice manipulation in the external trade of countries, the following figures assume relevance. Total world trade is estimated to be in the region of US$15 trillion. The share of the Third World in this works out at US$4 trillion, which is roughly 30 per cent of world trade. Another parameter of relevance in analysing damage caused to economies as a result of invoice manipulation is the GDP of countries. The GDP of the Third World is US$6 trillion, as compared to US$24 trillion of the developed world; translated into percentages, this means that the GDP of the developed and developing world are 25 per cent and 75 per cent respectively.[1] Considering their dismal share in world trade, the low percentage of GDP vis-à-vis the developed world and inadequate growth rates, damage to the economies of the developing countries as result of invoice manipulation is devastating.

EXPORT-RELATED ECONOMIC CRIME

On the export side of external trade, developing countries generally have a trade deficit, in the sense that imports are in excess of exports. The consequence of this trade

---

[1]   GDP of the G-7 countries is 67 per cent of world GDP.

deficit is that the balance of payments position of developing countries is generally precarious – often they do not have sufficient foreign exchange to pay for essential imports and have to rely very heavily on subsidies from international organizations/ developed countries, which generally come with strings attached. The developing countries are therefore constantly striving to increase their exports in order to wipe out their trade deficit and be in a comfortable position to pay for imports: according to economists, nine months of foreign exchange reserve for payment of imports is an economically viable and comfortable position for countries.

India is also a trade-deficit country in terms of its exports and imports in its external trade. In the early 1990s, when India was a closed economy, foreign exchange reserves were down to a level that would pay for just 15 days of imports; to overcome this precarious position, the central bank of the Government of India had to sell gold in the international market to shore-up its foreign exchange reserve. Since India embarked on the path of economic liberalization in 1991, things have improved considerably as regards foreign exchange reserves. Today, India has foreign exchange reserves of $72 billion, which can more than pay for 15 months of imports; but this holding has been built up as a result of Non-Resident Indian (NRI) remittances and investment by foreign institutional investors. If the feel-good factor in the Indian economy disappears, then this sizeable amount of foreign exchange reserve could very easily move out of the country. However, to give a sufficient boost to exports and to wipe out the trade deficit and be comfortable in a real sense, the Indian government has given many incentives to exporters to enable them to be competitive in the international market. These incentives in the Indian context are now considered.

DEEC scheme

The Duty Exemption Entitlement Certificate (DEEC) scheme entails import of goods without payment of duty with the proviso that all manufactures from these imported goods are channelled to exports. However, in several instances there has been outright diversion of duty-free imported goods without fulfilment of export obligations. Even exported goods are reported to be vastly over-invoiced under this scheme and the duty-free licences thus available are being traded through open-market operation. The exported commodities prone to be over-invoiced under this scheme include ready-made garments, pharmaceuticals, articles of ferrous and non-ferrous metals, and marble.

EPCG scheme

According to the Export Promotion Capital Goods (EPCG) scheme, capital goods are allowed to be imported free of duty to enable the manufacture of goods for export. Frauds detected under this scheme have ranged from outright diversion of duty-free capital goods and sale of the same in the local market without fulfilment of any export obligations.

100-per-cent EOU scheme

The 100-per-cent Export Oriented Unit (EOU) scheme, which operates in special zones, allows the manufacturing unit duty-free imports of capital goods and raw materials, only for the purposes of export. This scheme has also been misused; the standard *modus operandi* is diversion of duty-free imported material to the local market, discharge of export obligations by exporting either inferior quality or over-invoiced goods, and use of forged documents to show the fulfilment of a non-existent export obligation.

DEPB scheme

The Duty Entitlement Pass Book Credit (DEPB) scheme is also intended to boost exports. This scheme has been misused by exporters by way of vastly over-invoiced prices for exported goods in order to gain more credits; as the DEPB scheme does not relate to any inputs or outputs, DEPB frauds are more prevalent in the area of software exports.

Duty Drawback schemes

The government of India generally gives a certain amount of duty drawback to exporters on goods exported. This duty drawback is generally the reimbursement of a total of various duties that have been levied in the country on the final exported goods. By giving duty drawbacks, the government is offering an incentive to exporters because it makes their goods cheaper and more competitive in the international market. Under the Duty Drawback scheme, over-invoicing and misdeclaration of the description and quantity of exported goods is the most common *modus operandi* for claiming duty drawback in a fraudulent manner. Under this scheme, it has often also come to notice that the foreign exchange component of the exported goods has also not been repatriated.

In most of the cases of export incentive schemes, there is considerable over-invoicing of exports in order to claim benefits through fraudulent means. At present (2001–02), the total revenue from customs stands at INR 475.42 billion. Under the various export incentive schemes INR 216.58 billion was given to the exporters; considering the frauds in such schemes are in the region of 50 per cent, at a conservative estimate INR 100 billion is the extent of loss to the government as a result of frauds perpetrated under these export-oriented schemes. To have a better control over frauds in the export-oriented incentive schemes, the government of India is now planning to introduce a single all-embracing scheme.

Another point that needs to be emphasized in the context of fraud in these export-oriented incentive schemes is that free ports like Singapore, Hong Kong and Dubai are the focal points for the facilitation of such frauds.

One of the greatest incentives that was previously given to exporters was that all income from exports was free of income tax. This was misused not only to avoid payment of income tax, but also to launder money – this becomes clear in the chapter relating to money laundering. However, in a phased manner, over the next five years, the total income from exports will become taxable. With effect from 2001–02, 20 per cent of export income is proposed to be taxed; the export income subject to income tax will increase by 20 per cent every year, so that over a five-year period, the total amount becomes taxable.

MARITIME FRAUD

Another form of international economic crime that is a matter of great concern is maritime fraud, of which there are several types. The first of these can be termed documentary fraud. In order to facilitate international trade, bills of lading and letters of credits of various types are essential, because buyers and sellers are in different countries/continents and delivery of cargoes has to take place on the basis of these documents. They result not only in the release of commodities to the buyer, but also the release of payment to the seller. This system of cargo shipping and handling is obviously based on trust. However, it has been recognized that often the bills of lading, letters of credit and other forms of certification have been forged in order to enable the seller to realize the money without any cargo, or a lesser amount of or substandard cargo, having been despatched to the buyer. Several variations of these documentary frauds have come to notice; because of constraints of space it is not possible to deal with all of them.

Charter fraud is another type of maritime fraud that is fairly prevalent; in this type of fraud, a ship is taken on charter from the shipowner by payment of a sum of money, the charterer then vanishing from the scene. Charter frauds are generally accompanied by scuttling of ships. Before scuttling the ship, the cargo is also sold clandestinely for more illegal profits. In the scuttling of ships, another feature that has been noted is that the ship would reappear after some time with a totally different identity. In several cases of scuttling of ships, the crew, by assuming different identities, have also settled in other countries. This *modus operandi* with regard to charter frauds was popular off the coast of Lebanon in the 1970s and is used extensively in the Far East.

Container theft is an other form of maritime fraud that is fairly common. Container theft in the maritime context occurs by way of outright theft by way of forged documents, manipulation of the system, substitution, etc.

In most cases of maritime fraud, it is the insurance companies who are ripped off. Moreover, the existence of several claimants is another feature of these frauds, because quite often the same cargo has been sold to different persons. For an idea of the extent of maritime fraud, the insurance claims settled by Lloyds of London, the biggest insurer in the shipping industry, would be a good starting point.

ADVANCE FEE FRAUD

Advance fee fraud is another form of international economic crime to which both developed and developing countries are vulnerable. Advance fee frauds could be described as a Nigerian speciality. Nigerian oil is probably of the best quality in the world and is highly sought after; the Nigerians, through a set of false documentation and front companies, sell off non-existent cargoes to gullible customers, and, after taking a sum of money as an advance fee for processing and other administrative charges, simply vanish from the scene; of course, the understanding in most of these frauds is that full payment would be made on delivery, which in fact never takes place. Amounts involved in these advance fee fraud cases range from US$100,000 to US$1 million. However, in some cases the entire amount has been paid without actual shipment of goods taking place; the classic example of this is the Urea scam in India, wherein INR 1.35 billion were released for import of urea through a Turkish company. In such cases, political clout of the highest order often comes into play.

It is difficult to estimate the amounts involved in advance fee fraud, but they must run into several billion dollars, considering that there are a number of fraudsters at work all over the world and there is no lack of gullible persons.

CREDIT-CARD FRAUD

Credit-card fraud is an other form of international economic crime which is big business. Although credit-card companies have incorporated a number of security features in their cards to prevent such frauds, a cost-benefit analysis is generally carried out by credit-card companies regarding security features; this cost-benefit analysis becomes all the more necessary because of advances in technology; e.g., biothermics enables the fingerprint of an individual to be incorporated as a security feature in the credit cards.

As of today, losses due to credit-card frauds and counterfeiting of the same must run into tens of billions of dollars. Credit-card frauds undermine confidence in the banking systems and are highly damaging to the international retail trade.

AIRLINE TICKET THEFTS

Theft and counterfeiting of airline tickets is another form of international economic crime which is big business. In 1990, the estimated losses due to such thefts were US$500 million; now, of course, these run into a couple of billion dollars.

FRAUDS IN THE SECURITIES MARKET, THE BANKING SECTOR AND THE COMMODITIES MARKET

The securities market today has acquired an international dimension. Considering its turnover and the fact that considerable numbers of securities are traded internationally, the securities market is vulnerable to frauds by way of false documentation and manipulation of virtual securities. Insider trading in the securities market from outside the country is also a fairly serious trend that has been noted. The most daring example of fraud in the securities market is that perpetrated by Nick Leeson, the Singapore-based representative of Barings Bank, which ultimately led to its collapse and liquidation.

Nick Leeson perpetrated this fraud by trading in derivatives, which are a highly complicated form of monetary trading instruments.

International banking worldwide has also become more integrated following economic liberalization and this has also led to an alarming increase in the number of banking frauds; frauds in the banking sector are often fairly difficult to prosecute because of late detection.

Trading of commodities futures and other commodities-related contracts is a growth industry in many countries. This growth, particularly in futures trading, has been accompanied by vast commodity investment frauds; the most high-profile example is that of London-based trader Hamanaka of the Japanese Sumitomo Corporation, who ran up losses of US$1.8 billion in futures trading in copper.

Once again, the developing countries are more vulnerable to these types of international frauds in securities market, in the banking sector and in the commodities market. The damage which these frauds do to their fragile economies is also enormous. Estimates of these three categories of frauds can be made only in hundreds of billions of dollars, considering that the turnovers involved in the international securities market, international banking and trading in commodities will be in trillions of dollars.

EXCHANGE CONTROL VIOLATIONS

Prior to economic liberalization, most developing countries had exchange controls in order to manage their external trade in a prudent manner. However, the trend now is to dismantle most of these exchange controls or to retain them in a highly diluted manner. In the case of India, the Foreign Exchange Control Act, violation of which was a criminal offence, has been replaced by the Foreign Exchange Management Act under which foreign exchange violations are civil offences attracting penalties in the form of fines. In most of the cases of international economic crimes discussed above, exchange control violations, wherever such controls exist, also take place. Thus, violation of exchange controls is another form of an all-pervasive international economic crime. An idea of the sums of money involved in exchange control violations can be reached by extrapolation of sums involved in other international economic crime. The figures would obviously again be hundreds of billions of dollars.

SOME UNDESIRABLE EFFECTS OF THESE CRIMES

Most international economic crime is a major contributory factor to a number of illegal and undesirable activities which cause damage not only to the economies of the countries but also to international trade and commerce. For instance, invoice manipulation is one of the biggest contributory factors to the underground and parallel banking systems, which in turn facilitates capital flight, thereby causing tremendous damage by making productive assets unproductive. Many of these international economic crimes or their resultant effects are also great facilitators in the process of money laundering and enable unscrupulous elements to avoid paying income tax. The money generated by international economic crime is also used to finance smuggling activities. The mechanics of activities related to or associated with international economic crime described above are explained in detail in the chapter relating to money laundering.

Another aspect of international economic crime that needs to be constantly borne in mind is that it can give a 'highly distorted view of the national economy. For instance, invoice manipulation and several other of the crimes described above can lead to an artificial trade deficit in term of imports and exports. In the case of India, invoice manipulation (on both the import and export side), which by itself amounts to US$5–10 billion according to various estimates, has created an artificial trade deficit. This deficit not only hampers healthy economic development, but also leads to distorted policy formulations regarding the country's external trade.

How Best to Tackle these Crimes

Having discussed various types of international economic crimes and their ramifications, one is now confronted with the question of how to tackle them. The first requirement of tackling such crimes is to provide proper training for the investigators. The second requirement would be to adopt a multi-disciplinary approach in investigations; for instance, joint task forces of police officers, customs officers, income tax officers plus others, depending upon the nature of the case, could be formed. Chartered accountants'/auditors' services are often required: if the government is not able to employ them on a full-time basis, they can be hired on a retainership basis in necessary cases.

Since one is dealing with highly sophisticated criminals, using ingenious methods to commit crime and avoid detection, it is necessary to put in place intelligence machinery which could monitor cases of international economic crimes – in India the Directorate of Revenue Intelligence and Economic Intelligence Bureau performs these functions.

Of course, it need not be emphasized that adequate laws without any loopholes also have to be enacted to tackle international economic criminals. In framing laws, countries could draw upon each other's experience, and also the experience in their own country over a long period of time. Special judges/courts would also be needed to successfully prosecute these highly sophisticated criminals without undue delays. However, the main problems with regard to tackling international economic crime are in the arena of international co-operation.

The first problem with which countries are confronted is that of dual criminality; violation of financial and fiscal rules and regulations which may be a serious offence in developing countries may not be treated as an offence in a developed country. The requirement of dual criminality could be overcome by incorporating a dual criminality waiver in bilateral and multilateral co-operation treaties. Since these crimes also involve investigation in foreign countries, these treaties should have provisions for examination of witnesses, searches and seizure of documents abroad and the admissibility of the same in the country where the crime has been committed. Extradition is another sticky area when it comes to prosecuting the perpetrators of international economic crime. Extradition procedures should be streamlined to avoid unnecessary delay; in fact, wherever possible, deportation of criminals should be carried out, as it is a much speedier process.

In cases of international economic crime, often the managers and chiefs of enforcement agencies have to take difficult decisions based upon the costs and resources involved in the investigation and prosecution of these crimes. Compared to these crimes, other criminal cases are low-cost options, are easy to prosecute and require considerably less resources. Confronted with the dilemma of delivering overall satisfactory results with respect to all crimes, international economic crimes are quite often put on the back burner. The budgetary constraints faced by the enforcement agencies are acute; when it comes to international economic crime, a single case from detection to investigation to prosecution to trial can cost upwards of US$1 million and could involve 100 or more enforcement/prosecuting officers and experts.

The only answer for dealing effectively with such a scenario in relation to international economic crime is to have highly specialized agencies that are adequately staffed and have sufficient budgets. Here, one is tempted to ask what the chances of success are in this fragmented, fast-moving world of economic groupings and mega-mergers which also swears by economic liberalization and free trade. Though the task of tackling international economic crime appears to be daunting, it should not lead to despair, and adequate resources and manpower should be allocated by each country to tackle it effectively in a true spirit of international co-operation.

CHAPTER VIII

TAX EVASION AND THE BLACK ECONOMY

'Black Economy' and Related Terms

The black economy tends to be loosely defined due to certain preconceived notions and is therefore a concept not properly understood. People often use the terms black money, black income, black wealth and underground economy in an interchangeable manner, because in their minds these terms are interchangeable and contain the notion of something hidden or illegal. Thus, at the very outset what black money is, what its constituents are and what the various other terms associated with it mean should be clarified.

The black economy can be simply defined as the underground or unreported part of the gross national product of the country. Gross domestic product is generally defined as the sum total of goods and services produced in a country. The unreported gross domestic product or black economy can be ascribed to three principal constituents: legal income on which tax has been evaded; illegal income on which tax has been evaded, and that illegal income which falls below the taxable limit; and legal and illegal incomes which escape measurement due to imperfect accounting methods. For the lay reader, it is necessary to emphasize that the tax authorities do not make a distinction when it comes to taxing incomes – income, whether obtained legally or illegally, is liable to taxation, and of course the illegal income could also attract other provisions of the criminal law which would depend upon the kind of illegal act involved.

The legal income from legitimate sources and legal activities generally flows from industry (medium and small-scale), multinationals, stock markets, commercial establishments engaged in land/real estate, shopkeepers both big and small, street vendors and the salaried class. The illegal income from illegitimate and illegal activities comes from gambling, bootlegging/illicit distillation, prostitution, organized crime, terrorism, drugs trafficking, funds obtained from bribery and corruption, economic scams, frauds in the import and export trade, smuggling of gold/diamond/textiles, etc. and, in the context of some countries, the illegal labour force.

The legal and illegal activities described above attract a host of taxes which can be described as direct and indirect. Direct taxes are those which tax the individual, such as income tax, wealth tax, gift tax, and corporations by way of corporation tax. Indirect taxes are those which tax commodities by way of excise duty, sales tax, octroi, customs duty, etc. Illegal activities, especially crimes, would generally attract income tax, because by negation of their existence under the law, other taxes would not normally be applicable. Although tax evasion/avoidance is discussed in other chapters relating to proceeds of crime, in this chapter it is considered in a focused manner.

75

So far we have discussed the elements that constitute a black economy. The other related concepts that need to be dealt with in the context of the black economy are those of black income, black wealth and black money. Black income can be defined as tax-evaded income – it is a measure of quantity. Black wealth is a measure of stock and is the total of illegal goods and illegal cash accumulated over a period of time. The illegal cash component of black wealth is known as black money.

THE BLACK ECONOMY IN DIFFERENT COUNTRIES

The black economy exists in practically every country, in both market economies and the socialist economies. It even existed in the former Communist economies. Developed economies, developing economies and export-oriented economies are all afflicted by this malady, which is known by different names in different countries. In the UK it is called the black economy, in Germany the *Schattenwirtschaft* or 'shadow economy', in Russia the 'second economy', in South Africa the 'unrecorded sector', in Israel the *kalkala schora*, in Italy the *economia summersa* or 'submerged economy', and in the USA the 'underground' or 'subterranean economy'.

Various estimates have been made as to the magnitude of the black economy in terms of the gross national product of a country. Table VIII.1 shows details for the years 1970–82.

Table VIII.1. Estimated magnitude of the black economy as a proportion of GNP in selected countries, 1970–82[1]

Country	Percentage of GDP
Australia	11
Austria	8
Belgium	10–14
Canada	5–20
Denmark	5–8
Finland	7
France	8
Germany	5–7
India	9–49
Ireland	6
Italy	10–15
Japan	3
Norway	2–5
Spain	5

Continued

---

[1]   See Vito Tanzi, "The Underground Economy", *Finance and Development*, Vol. 20, No. 4, Dec. 1983, 13.

Table VIII.1. (Continued)

Country	Percentage of GDP
Sweden	3–12
Switzerland	4
United Kingdom	2–6
United States	5–21
USSR	10

Note: These show ranges of estimates made for countries at different times. They should not be relied upon as precise.

ESTIMATES OF THE BLACK ECONOMY: METHODS USED

The various ways to estimate the underground economy are the fiscal/taxation approach, the national accounts method approach, the labour participation rate approach and the monetary approach. In the fiscal/taxation approach, independent estimates of taxable income arrived at are compared with the income reported in tax returns, the difference in the estimated and reported income constituting the black economy. In the national accounts method approach, on the basis of special surveys, total income and total expenditure are estimated; the discrepancy between total income and total expenditure is an indication of the magnitude of the black economy. In the labour participation rate approach, the usual labour force is computed on the basis of historical experience; if the estimated participation rate is lower than usual, that is the indicator of labour employed in the black economy.

The monetary approach adopts two methods, namely, Peter Gutmann's method, based on the ratio of currency in circulation to deposits – also called the transaction approach – and that developed by Edgar Feige which uses Fisher's equation of the quantity theory of money to compute the underground economy. It has been observed that estimates arrived at by using the monetary approach are generally on the high side; in the USA they were higher by almost 20 per cent compared to other methods. However, the monetary approach when applied in the Indian context led to totally ridiculous results, i.e., the lowest possible estimates or negation of the black economy.

THE BLACK ECONOMY IN OPERATION

The black economy operates like any other economy. It produces goods and services and creates employment leading to incomes, which in turn are linked to prices. Moreover, the black economy does not operate in isolation and most of the time it and the white economy commingle and intersect at various points, especially if the black economy component in the national economy is high. In such a scenario, it is quite common to find black money being converted to white money and white money being converted to black money to facilitate business operations. Several economists have also pointed out the positive role of the black economy, because it provides the incentive for economic growth in a regime of high taxes. In fact, the black economy in the Indian context, where it is running as high as 50 per cent of GDP,[2] has become the lifeblood of the economy as well as a cancer within it which will ultimately lead to its destruction. According to other economists, the black economy leads to economic growth because it stimulates consumption.

However, despite the economic growth argument advanced in favour of the black economy, it needs to be emphasized that it does tremendous damage to the overall economic effort of the country. The most pernicious effect of the black economy is that it tends to distort or subvert the national economic effort; for instance, in certain economies, basic infrastructure such as roads, power and telecommunications might be needed, but the underground economy might divert the scarce resources to production of goods and services such as luxury items which do not in the long run contribute much to furthering the national economic effort.

The underground economy can also lead to capital flight in the country: this can be considerable, as has been the experience of several countries in the grip of an economic crisis. Capital flight also means direct loss to the productive capacity of a nation.

The black economy not only tends to lock up investment in non-productive assets, but also has a tendency to generate more and more black income. Smuggling is another activity that is fuelled to a considerable extent by the black economy. The black economy, which implies loss of tax revenue, also imposes a greater burden on the honest taxpayers and thus increases disparities in income. It also leads to bribery and corruption. All of these factors lead in turn to loss of confidence in the government.

Another disturbing factor that has been noted in most countries is that the black economy has increased at a rate faster than GDP. This in turn means more money in the hands of unscrupulous elements to play havoc with the economy of the country.

When one is talking about the black economy, some ethical issues are also raised; tax-evaded income on legal activities is not considered to be as bad as income coming from criminal activities – such income has increased considerably. Writers on the subject tend to make a distinction between bad money and not-so-bad money by classifying the tax-evaded income as 'grey income' and income arising from criminal activities as 'black income'. Often there is an overlap of legal and illegal income, as stated earlier.

REASONS FOR THE INCREASING LEVEL OF THE BLACK ECONOMY

There are several reasons which have led to the growth of the black economy. At the individual level, it can be ascribed to the element of greed, the desire to maximize one's wealth, etc. Structurally, high tax rates and government controls are the major contributory factors leading to the emergence and growth of the black economy. The prevalence of crime,

---

[2]   For the year 2000–01, 50 per cent of the GDP of India works out at INR 10,401.5 billion.

which is generally linked to poverty, is an another major contributor to the black economy. Sociologists, psychologists and anthropologists have all tried to explain the prevalence of the black economy in their own way. An economist describes it as a conscious rational decision based upon marginal cost and marginal benefit in the context of illegal economy.

WAYS TO COMBAT THE BLACK ECONOMY

Some of the ways to curb the underground economy are to lower taxes, to loosen government control and to ensure stringent enforcement action. Building up a national value system would be a major contributory factor to reducing the extent of the underground economy.

Several governments, on several occasions, have also made special efforts to unearth this black economy, so that by coming into the open, this segment of the economy becomes part of the national productive effort and leads to attainment of priorities considered to be for the good of the country. Among the methods used by the government are amnesty schemes, whereby those declaring their black incomes and black wealth are given amnesty from prosecution, on payment of certain taxes. Another feature of these amnesty schemes is that no questions are asked about the source of the money. These amnesty schemes have often been criticized because they have not unearthed the expected amount of black money or wealth, and because, according to some, they reward the unscrupulous and penalize the just. Some have even described these amnesty schemes as money laundering schemes run by the government.

Demonetization, i.e., taking certain denominations of a currency out of circulation, is another method which has been employed by governments in the past to tackle the underground economy. The success rate of demonetization in tackling the underground economy has also not been very satisfactory, because people are able to devise methods to explain the demonetized currency notes when it comes to exchanging them.

In a country where the majority of people do not pay taxes and earn handsome incomes even as street vendors, a concept of presumptive tax also needs to be introduced. Presumptive tax computation is again based upon certain factors such as rentals, daily average sales and profit margins.

CHAPTER IX

SMUGGLING

Smuggling can be described as circumventing of legal trade barriers in a clandestine manner. It is a form of crime that is all-pervasive. Smugglers have to cross land or sea borders, and also use aerial routes or resort to smuggling goods in containers meant for legal cargoes. As with all crimes, smuggling is motivated by greed. Scarcity and unavailability of goods in demand are conditions utilized by unscrupulous elements to indulge in smuggling. High customs duties or a ban on the import of certain items can lead to smuggling being a highly lucrative crime.

TRENDS

The form and content of smuggling varies from country to country and region to region in the world – for instance, smuggling of cigarettes into the UK, smuggling of liquor into Pakistan, or smuggling of gold, diamonds and silver into India might be highly profitable activities in the context of smuggling in these countries. During the course of this chapter, smuggling of various goods/commodities worldwide are discussed briefly, and as regards India, in greater detail.

ROUTES/*MODI OPERANDI*

India is a country that is highly vulnerable to smuggling due to its extensive land border, extending to over 15,000 km, and its sea border, extending to over 7,000 km. The countries bordering India are Pakistan, Nepal, China, Burma (Myanmar) and Bangladesh. India and Sri Lanka are separated by a small stretch of sea known as the Palk Strait. To have a better idea of smuggling routes, the extent of borders with neighbouring countries and the stretch of eastern, western and southern coastline are also relevant. The Indo-Pakistan border extends to 2,896 km, the Indo-Nepal border to 1,800 km, the Indo-Myanmar border to 2,965 km and the Indo-Bangladesh border to 2,965 km. The western coastline adjacent to the states of Gujarat, Maharashtra, Goa, Karnataka and Kerala extends to 3,300 km, the eastern coastline adjacent to the states of West Bengal, Orissa, Andhra Pradesh and Tamil Nadu is also fairly extensive and the stretch of sea separating the tip of India from northern Sri Lanka adjacent to Kerala and Tamil Nadu stretches to 930 km. Inland container depots have also been set up in India to facilitate external trade; these are dotted all over the country are also used by the smugglers. International airports prone to smuggling are Delhi and Mumbai.

The west coast of India was formerly the preferred route of the smugglers. However, due to tightening of vigilance along that coast following disclosures that explosives used in the serial bomb blasts in Mumbai in March 1993 were smuggled along it, the smugglers have to a considerable extent abandoned the western coastline. The Indo-Nepal border is now the preferred route because of non-restrictions on movement of persons of Indian and Nepalese origin along it: both the aerial route and land route from Nepal are being used extensively to smuggle goods into the country. Apart from the above two general trends in smuggling routes to India, the trends of smuggling along other sectors of land and maritime borders of India are dictated by cross-border fighting between Pakistan and India, and by drug trafficking.

A Big Money-Spinner

Smuggling is obviously big business. An estimate of smuggling worldwide would call for very detailed surveys which are beyond the scope of this study due to constraints of time, resources and the fact that one was ploughing a lonely furrow; however, estimates regarding particular items being smuggled into India have been made and are taken as significant indicators as to how big a criminal enterprise smuggling is worldwide. In terms of sums of money involved the figure would perhaps run into hundred of billions of dollars (excluding drug smuggling and smuggling in arms and explosives).

Items Favoured by Smugglers

Gold (in the context of India)

In India, gold smuggling was a highly lucrative activity following the enactment of the Gold Control Order of 1968. This Order stipulated that gold could be imported into the country by the Reserve Bank of India and distributed to licensed gold dealers, who in turn were to utilize the gold for having ornaments made by licensed goldsmiths. Provisions were also incorporated in this Gold Control Order to keep track of its consumption. The net result of the order was that officially only an insignificant amount of gold was imported, which made the then Finance Minister, Morarji Desai, very happy, because according to him gold was to be shunned, being a totally unproductive asset. However, by imposing restrictions on the import of gold by way of the Gold Control Order, a fillip was given to gold smuggling. This incentive to smuggle was primarily due to the insatiable demand for gold for which Indians are famous, and rising amounts of black money in the country which were used to pay for the smuggled gold. So long as the Gold Control Order was in operation, the estimated amount of gold smuggled into the country was in the region of 700 tons annually; this estimate is based on the seizure figures and the assumption that only 10 per cent of the smuggled gold was impounded. On the heels of economic liberalization, the Gold Control Order was finally abolished in 1993, but it is estimated on a conservative basis that by this time the gold stockpiled in the country was somewhere in the region of 10,000 tons.

The *modus operandi* of the gold smugglers in the heyday of gold smuggling was to use speedboats to smuggle gold from free ports like Dubai and Singapore and convenient outlets like Phuket in Thailand; this is evident from the fact that most of these ports were importing gold far in excess of their requirements. Dubai was importing 200 tons of gold annually, whereas its domestic requirement was only five to ten tons annually, the rest of the gold was presumably meant to be smuggled into India. Since the hub of the gold trade is London, from where export/import of gold was never a criminal activity, most of the controllers of gold smuggling were based there. The controllers kept in touch with smugglers carrying gold in speedboats via satellite telephone. In the case of hot pursuit by enforcement authorities, smugglers in the speedboats had no authority to decide whether or not to dump the gold into the sea; it was only on receipt of instructions via satellite telephone from controllers in London that the speedboats would dump the gold in order to avoid arrest and seizure. In fact, in 1990, during an interaction with the Directorate General Revenue Intelligence, I was informed that a number of private companies had approached the government of India with proposals to retrieve the gold, which was intended to be smuggled into the country and was buried along the Indian coast, on a shared basis. Although this proposal was under the active consideration of the government for some time, wiser counsel finally prevailed and the government decided not to have any dealings with the companies specializing in retrieving gold, because they were merely fronts for the gold smugglers.

As already mentioned, the Gold Control Order of 1968 was finally abrogated in 1993; in the era of economic liberalization, decriminalization was thought to be a better method for dealing with an activity like gold smuggling. Thus, after 1993, on payment of a token customs duty, gold could be imported into the country by non-resident Indians; any non-resident Indian (NRI) (a person settled outside India for a minimum period of six months) could bring 10 kgs of gold into the country on payment of a token duty of Rs. 250/- per 10 grams. However, there was still a premium on gold in the country compared to international prices; thus, any NRI bringing gold into the country after payment of duty could still make a profit of Rs. 400,000–500,000 per consignment of 10 kgs. Here again, smuggling syndicates seized an opportunity and hired people working as labourers in places such as Dubai, and turned them into couriers to import, or in effect smuggle, gold into the country; for creating a profit of Rs. 500,000 per consignment, a courier was given a return ticket by the gold smugglers in their new 'avatar'. Of course, to pay for gold being carried by the courier, money was sent out through underground banking channels by the smugglers. Even when the Gold Control Order was in force, 90 per cent of gold smuggling payments were settled through hawala/underground banking channels.

In the late 1990s, the government increased customs duty on gold to Rs. 450/- per 10 grams, which has resulted in an increase in outright smuggling, as profits on the gold imported legally have decreased; this may also be described as the balloon effect, wherein if the balloon is pressed at one end, the other end inflates. One of the reasons which prompted the government to raise the customs duty on the import of gold was the fact that it was proving to be a drain on foreign exchange reserves, because the amount of gold imported accounted for 12 per cent of total imports – $6 billion at a rough estimate. Since gold had been put on the open general licences (OGL) list and special import licences also provided for it, 90 per cent of the gold is now imported under OGL and it contributes somewhere in the region of INR 12 billion by way of customs revenue. According to the Directorate of Revenue Intelligence reports:

> 'smuggling of gold into India is a result of complex interplay of factors that deter-
> mine net profitability coupled with risk assessment; the factors that influence the
> profitability are fluctuation in domestic demand, international supply price, customs
> duty, hawala conversion rate and local levies. The fact that most of the smuggling is
> occurring in small quantities now through concealments on air routes reflects rela-
> tive risk assessment and consequent preference.'

Recently there has been a trend worldwide for central banks to offload their gold reserves in the open market. Initially this resulted in reducing the international price of gold, but recently the trend has been that gold prices are firming up worldwide; a contributory factor to this is the 11 September 2001 terrorist attacks in the USA and the resultant disturbed conditions in several parts of the world.

Another point which needs to be mentioned in the context of gold smuggling is that apart from Indians, there is also a great demand for gold amongst the Chinese community, which is spread over all South-East Asia and in small or large numbers in practically every country of the world. The Chinese prefer gold of 24-carat purity (i.e., 99.9 per cent purity) compared to Indians, who prefer gold of 22-carat purity. In fact, Chinese and Indians worldwide hold the majority of gold at present. This trend can only be ascribed to what value to place on your money: it appears that Indians and Chinese do not have much faith in the dollar or the 'floating exchange rate based on a basket of currencies'. In fact, it has been the endeavour of many an economist and entrepreneur to somehow mobilize India's stockpile of gold into a productive asset; with this end in view, the government of India has also come up with several gold bond schemes, under which gold deposited with the government on certain profitable conditions would be sold in the world market, and through its sale proceeds the vast sums of capital raised would be utilized for rapid economic development. None of the schemes to mobilize the stockpile of gold for production purposes have been successful.

Diamonds

The importation of diamonds into India and dummy smuggling of diamonds in the country is also a very fascinating activity to study. I discuss this at length in the chapter on the underground and parallel banking system. However, a few points regarding diamond smuggling need to be mentioned here. The diamond trade in the context of India is an INR 400 billion business, in which raw diamonds are imported and after polishing are supposed to be exported. Since there is no duty on import of raw diamonds, though it continues to be a controlled activity, one wonders why raw diamonds should be smuggled into India. Most of the cutting and polishing of diamonds takes place in Surat in Gujarat and in India this trade is dominated by the Gujarati community. Four focal points of the diamond trade in the world are South Africa for import of raw diamonds, Surat for cutting and polishing of raw diamonds, and Brussels and New York for trade in cut and polished diamonds. The diamond trade is also extensively used to launder money, for which underground and parallel banking channels come in very useful. The diamond trade can also be useful for avoiding income tax. The flip side of the trade in diamonds dominated by smuggling is that it reverses capital flight, and the diamonds remain in the country.

Silver

Although it was formerly fairly extensive, silver smuggling in India is now no longer a lucrative activity and is therefore practically non-existent. However, it may be of interest to readers to know that India has the largest stockpile of silver in the world, and historically the world market in silver has been influenced a great deal by Indian bullion dealers.

I shall give a few interesting anecdotes relating to silver here. According to recorded history two attempts have been made to corner the silver supply of the world. These attempts were made in order to issue a currency backed by silver, a currency that would be stable and not subject to fluctuations caused by the attendant gains and losses incurred by persons engaged in international trade. The first attempt was made in 1909 by Chuni Lal Suraya of India Specie Bank, who in a major operation cornered 26 million ounces of silver by 1913: when the bank ran out of money to buy more silver, Mr Suraya shot himself.

The Hunt brothers, who had inherited a large oil fortune, made the second attempt to corner the silver supply in 1970–80. The brothers managed to corner a major chunk of silver in the world; the result of this cornering operation was that international silver prices jumped phenomenally. This jump in prices at that point of time led to a reverse flow of silver from India, as silver which was earlier being smuggled into the country was now being smuggled out of it in order to be sold at highly lucrative international prices. However, the attempt of the Hunt brothers to corner the world silver supply and to issue silver-backed bonds failed because of various unforeseen circumstances, such as Mexico unloading a major portion of its silver in the world market, which the brothers were unable to buy because of the cash crunch. Thus the net result of the Hunt brothers' foray into the silver market was that they become bankrupt following the crash in the price of silver worldwide from its artificial high.[1]

Antiques

In the context of India, as also many other countries with ancient cultural traditions, smuggling of antiques out of the country is a sizeable and highly lucrative activity, the unfortunate aspect of which is that most of the countries such as India that are prone to

---

[1]   L.J. Davis, *Bad Money* (St. Martin's Press, New York, 1982). This story has been very well documented in the article 'Silver Thursday'

this smuggling do not have sufficient resources to prevent it. Even when it has been brought to light that precious Indian antiques are lying in various airports of the world after they have been seized by the customs authorities of those countries, no attempts have been made to retrieve these 'priceless' items, because the money that would be involved in such operations is simply not available to government agencies charged with the task of preventing antique smuggling.

Another highly undesirable aspect that has been noted is that prestigious auction houses have been involved in the auction of these stolen antiques to a fairly large extent. One case that comes to mind immediately is that of the sale of gold mohurs of Mughal times which were put on sale in Geneva in the mid-1980s. These belonged to the time of Jehangir and were almost the size of modern-day plates. In the days of the Mughals, these large gold mohurs were given as presents to kings of other friendly countries. In the auction in Geneva, the reserve price set by the auction house was several million dollars. These gold mohurs were stolen from the Trust of the Nizam of Hyderabad by one of his descendants and clandestinely sold to the auction house. It was only on the intervention of the Indian government that the sale of these gold mohurs could be delayed on the grounds that they had been stolen in the first instance. They have still not been retrieved. Since they were a part of our rich national heritage, the then Director of the National Museum was so keen to get them back that he even suggested that India should buy them back in the auction, even if it meant spending a couple of million dollars. The smuggling of antiques is dealt with generally under the Antiquities Act enacted in pursuance of guidelines issued by UNESCO to prevent smuggling of antiques.

Commodities

Smuggling of a particular commodity can acquire primacy at a point in time depending on its demand, the international price differential and the customs duties imposed. For instance, smuggling of synthetics into India was big business in the 1970s, the extent of which was estimated at INR 30 billion per year at its peak. Smuggling of drugs, precursor chemicals, arms and explosives into India is also big business, and this has been dealt with in earlier chapters relating to those crimes.

Large numbers of electronic goods/computer parts, pharmaceutical chemicals, ball bearings, silk yarn, spices, betel nuts and incredibly cheap Chinese goods are also smuggled into India. The preferred route for smuggling these goods is via Nepal: it imports a number of the goods in excess of its requirements, the excess goods being either diverted into India while on their way to Nepal from Kolkata or smuggled out of Nepal into India via the land borders.

Foreign currencies

Foreign currency is another item that is being smuggled out of India extensively. Following liberalization of the Indian economy, rules relating to foreign exchange were also relaxed; under the Foreign Travel Scheme for Tourists, one can now take $5,000 annually and under the Business Travel Quota Scheme $25,000 annually out of the country. Both of these schemes have been excessively abused and through fraudulent documents, such as a genuine passport with forged visas, forged passports with forged visas, counterfeit airline tickets or genuine airline tickets which were subsequently cancelled, unscrupulous elements have managed to obtain millions of dollars released in foreign exchange. Since dollars have a premium at free ports like Dubai, Singapore and Hong Kong, the foreign exchange released through fraudulent means is smuggled out of India to these free ports, centres for invoice manipulation and smuggling of goods, to several other countries, including India. Smuggling of foreign currency is resorted to because it brings down the costs considerably vis-à-vis the use of the underground banking system.

Counterfeit goods and currency

Counterfeiting of goods and currency is another form of transnational crime prevalent on a large scale. Counterfeiting of goods is a copyright/patents offence; these are civil offences. Counterfeiting of currency, on the other hand, is regarded as a serious criminal offence. Both counterfeit goods and counterfeit currency are smuggled on an extensive scale, even though counterfeit goods may be marketed within the country and the counterfeit currency manufactured locally might also be used within the country.

There are professional syndicates that are engaged in counterfeiting of goods. These counterfeit goods, whether they are sold within the country or to other countries, cause damage to the national economies of the countries concerned. Although counterfeit goods are generally substandard, it has sometimes been observed that they have been better than the originals. Counterfeiting nowadays also extends to video tapes. Video piracy is big business today, running into several million dollars. Counterfeiting of goods which can range from the simplest of commodities, like a pen, to electronic gadgets, is obviously big business, running somewhere in the region of tens of billions of dollars on a conservative estimate. In fact, some sections/regions of national economies in several developing countries could be termed counterfeit economies.

Counterfeiting of currency is often resorted to against a country by hostile neighbours in order to undermine the economy of the country. In the context of India, Pakistan has been accused of currency counterfeiting of INR 500 denomination notes. A number of counterfeit notes have been seized in terrorist-infested areas of Jammu and Kashmir and the North East by several enforcement agencies.

While on the subject of counterfeit currency, it is also worth looking into the counterfeiting of US dollars, the currency most prone to this form of crime. Although the world abandoned the gold standard, then adopted the dollar standard and is now on a floating exchange rate comprised of a basket of currencies (of which the dollar is the most important component), it might come as a surprise to readers to know that the US dollar is the currency which is the easiest to counterfeit. Even basic security features have not been incorporated in it; in fact, the US dollar continues more or less in its original form of the last century and has only 16 elementary security features. One might wonder why the

United States, which is the most technically advanced country in the world, is continuing with an antiquated currency, whereas even developing countries such as India have currencies which incorporate the latest technology in terms of security features. The only answer to this seems to be that the US government is very conscious of the high costs involved in withdrawing dollars from circulation and reissuing new dollars incorporating the latest security features. In fact, for the US government the counterfeiting of US currency is preferable to facing the prohibitive cost involved in this changeover of currency. It is estimated that there are US$500 billion (in currency notes) in circulation and the counterfeiting of these, going by the rule of thumb of 10 per cent, works out at US$50 billion. It also seems rather strange that the US Secret Service, which is charged with the security of the President of the United States, is also charged with the task of dealing with counterfeit dollars. Surely this job could be better handled by an enforcement agency like the Federal Bureau of Investigation or some enforcement agency specifically created for the purpose, considering the magnitude of the problem.

EFFECTIVE WAYS TO DEAL WITH SMUGGLING

One now comes to the question of how to deal with the problem of smuggling. One of the most effective ways is to rationalize customs duties and to reduce them to acceptable levels. Rationalization of customs duties means that only two to three levels of duties at reasonable rates should be applicable, rather than different customs duties on different items, which can often run into hundreds. In India, the customs duties have now been rationalized and at present we have three levels of duties, viz., 30 per cent, 20 per cent and 10 per cent. It is further proposed to reduce these levels to two, and further reduce the customs duty to 20 per cent and 10 per cent. However, as a note of caution, one should add that as long as there are profits in smuggling, even though they may be marginal, smugglers and smuggling will always be there, albeit on a reduced scale.

Another way to reduce the extent of smuggling is to adopt free trade, which means lifting of restrictions/duties on imports of certain commodities altogether. Of course, strict enforcement is a time-honoured tool for checking and curbing smuggling; to ensure good enforcement, proper supervision of enforcement agencies would have to be ensured. In India, preventive detention laws such as the Conservation of Foreign Exchange and Prevention of Smuggling Activities Act (COFEPOSA), which provides for prevention and detention of known smugglers without trial, has been used to curb smuggling; there is no bail under COFEPOSA and taking the known smugglers out of circulation can be a highly effective tool for curbing the menace of widespread and extremely harmful forms of smuggling. However, even COFEPOSA has been misused by corrupt politicians, bureaucrats and enforcement officers, who now extract their percentages from known smugglers, in return for not charging them under COFEPOSA. Decriminalization of an activity is another way of tackling smuggling, for instance, by abrogation of the Gold Control Order, the government sought to put an end to gold smuggling.

International co-operation is, of course, an essential requirement to curb smuggling. For effective international co-operation, intelligence databanks, both at national and international level, are a must. Moreover, co-operation during investigations between countries is another essential requirement for effective international co-operation. In fact, proactive investigations and intelligence-led investigations are the most effective ways to tackle the menace of smuggling. Co-operation between countries during prosecution and trials of smugglers is also vital; this co-operation would entail production of documentary evidence and ensuring that witnesses are available for examination by the trial courts.

PART II

HOW MONEY IS LAUNDERED

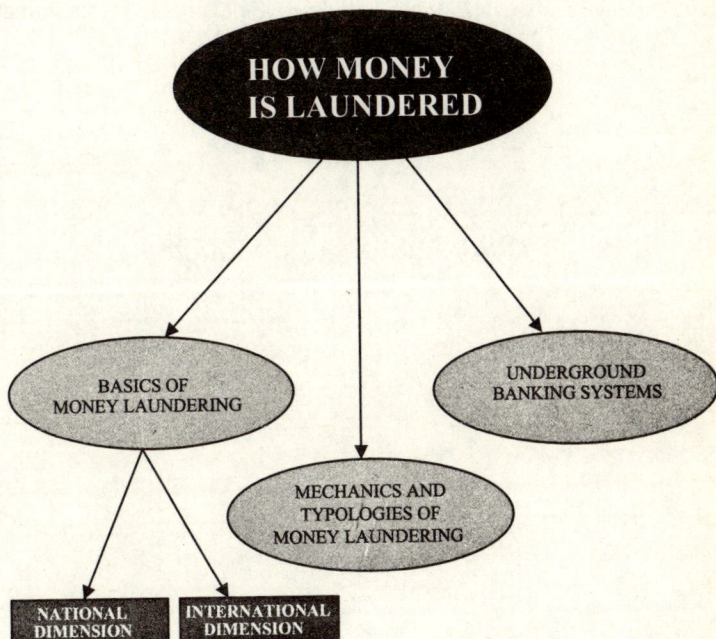

CHAPTER X

THE BASICS OF MONEY LAUNDERING

CRIMINALS: WHY THEY WANT TO LAUNDER MONEY

In earlier chapters we have seen that the proceeds of major crimes run into not just hundreds of billions of dollars, but possibly a few trillion dollars. Considering the sums involved in the proceeds of crime, it is quite logical to ask the question of how these are managed. A substantial portion of the proceeds is required for the running expenses for the criminal enterprises; a large proportion of the proceeds of crime are spent in an open manner with all the attendant risks of being caught; then there are several criminals who like to hide their wealth or secrete it away in secure hiding places. However, the overriding concern of many criminals is to make their proceeds appear legitimate.

Money laundering can be described as a process which is aimed at legitimizing the proceeds of crime. The term 'money laundering' has connotations of washing something which is dirty. The term was first used in the context of Mafia gangs operating in the USA in the 1930s. These gangs, which made huge profits through the illicit manufacture and sale of liquor during Prohibition in the 1930s, had to account for this wealth. Thus, the Mafia gangs opened launderettes or dry-cleaning shops which were very useful in explaining the proceeds of crime in terms of their retail business, even though there was very little actual dry-cleaning taking place.

Criminals want to launder their money or make it appear legitimate for several reasons. First of all, legitimacy enables the criminals to enjoy the fruits of crime in an unencumbered way. These illegal proceeds can also be utilized by criminals to create truly legitimate enterprises. On the basis of these legitimate enterprises, the criminal families can become highly respectable within a couple of generations, because their criminal past generally becomes blurred. Thus, the descendants of these criminals can go on to lead normal and respectable lives as members of society.

DIMENSIONS OF MONEY LAUNDERING: NATIONAL AND INTERNATIONAL

How is money laundered, or, in other words, what are the mechanics and typologies for laundering money? Before one begins to discuss the mechanics of money laundering, one must understand that there is a national dimension and an international dimension to it. The national dimension of money laundering is more easily understood by the residents of a country, because they are familiar with the socio-economic and cultural milieu of that country. The international dimension of money laundering calls for an understanding of international finance and banking which, like high finance, seems very complicated to the general public. This international dimension is becoming more and more important with the march of most countries of the world towards economic liberalization, wherein 'free market' is the new mantra.

Since money laundering is generally not easily comprehensible, the basic idea in this chapter, and indeed the object of the book as a whole, is to demystify the subject. The best way to do this is to have a clear understanding of the fundamentals of the subject. Once the fundamentals are clearly understood the subject becomes very simple.

CONCEPTS, PRACTICES, TRENDS AND ENTITIES THAT ENABLE IT

Money laundering first calls for an understanding of some concepts, practices, trends and entities both in their national and international dimensions. In the context of the national dimension these are:

  (i) Banking and instruments of commercial banking such as drafts, bankers' cheques, cashier cheques and personal cheques.
 (ii) Foreign exchange bureaux or brokerage houses.
(iii) Money transmission agents such as Western Union, and the services offered by them.
 (iv) Correspondent banking as an integral part of national and international banking.
  (v) Money orders issued by post offices.
 (vi) The securities market/stock exchanges.
(vii) Commodities markets/commodity exchanges.
(viii) Retail/wholesale trade involving high volume and high-end products.
 (ix) The gold, diamonds and precious stones market – how these are traded nationally and internationally.
  (x) Insurance companies, both life insurance and general insurance.
 (xi) The role of untaxed sectors in the national economy – for instance, agricultural income and export income in India.
(xii) An understanding of subsidies to certain sectors of the national economy.
(xiii) Casinos and other forms of gambling, including lotteries.
(xiv) A general idea of different economic systems, viz., systems where only the private sector exists and systems where there is mix of public and private sector.
 (xv) A general understanding of trade and commerce.
(xvi) The information technology sector which includes hardware and software, and also an understanding of cyberspace and cybercrimes.
(xvii) Fiscal structure and financial rules and regulations in a given country. This would include customs and excise and other forms of indirect taxes, and also direct taxes such as income tax, wealth tax and gift tax.
(xviii) Conduct of international trade and the instruments that facilitate such trade, including letters of credit, bills of lading and other forms of certification.
(xix) Invoice manipulation in the context of the import/export trade.
 (xx) Subsidies in the export sector.

(xxi) Schemes to channel black money or illegally acquired proceeds into the national economy for more productive utilization.

(xxii) Amnesty schemes for tax-evaded income/illegally acquired proceeds.

(xxiii) Existence and absence of foreign exchange controls.

(xxiv) The barter trade in gems for guns or drugs, and gold for drugs.

Most of the concepts, practices, trends and entities in the national dimension listed above are well known; those that are not will become clear in the next chapter. It must also be borne in mind that although money laundering can have an exclusively national dimension, often there is an overlap between the national and the international dimension. It must also be clearly understood that the international dimension can only exist in the context of the national dimension.

A COMPREHENSIVE PROJECTION OF THE INTERNATIONAL MONEY LAUNDERING DIMENSION IN OPERATION

For a proper understanding and comprehension of the international dimension of money laundering, the following entities and practices relating to international banking and finance need to be explained at length.

Offshore jurisdictions

Legally speaking, offshore jurisdictions are those jurisdictions which exist in other countries and operate bank accounts for foreign nationals in currency other than that prevalent in the offshore jurisdiction. All matters of banking and finance pertaining to foreign nationals in these jurisdictions are termed offshore banking and offshore finance. Historically these jurisdictions have existed in the international financial sector since the early 1950s. It was after the Hungarian crisis of 1956, when Russian dollar accounts in the USA were frozen, that the Dnerdoni Bank of Russia asked a London bank with which it had a correspondent relationship to open a dollar-denominated account in which dollars would not be converted to local currency. Russia made this request in order to facilitate its transactions and obligations in the world of international finance. The dollars held for the Russian bank in the London correspondent bank came to be known as Euro-dollars.

There are other ways in which these offshore jurisdictions have been defined and classified. According to other definitions, offshore jurisdictions are those which are conveniently located (often islands dotted around various parts of the world) and are often set up by poor countries, to raise revenue. The classification of offshore jurisdictions in the world is not limited to poor jurisdictions; some of the offshore jurisdictions are countries which are very rich and politically very stable, e.g., Switzerland.

Offshore jurisdictions not only involve correspondent banking, but also entail setting up bank branches or incorporation of banks in their respective jurisdictions. These offshore jurisdictions not only cater to the needs of genuine businesses and persons with legal and legitimate demands, but are also a useful refuge for criminal enterprises to move their illicit funds and launder the same. There is a great debate going on at present regarding offshore and onshore jurisdictions; this debate has been dealt with at length later in the book.

Tax havens

One of the major benefits offered by offshore jurisdictions is that they are zero-tax jurisdictions or impose a nominal amount of tax – hence they are also known as tax havens. Several multinationals have their holding companies in these tax havens in order to avoid paying heavy taxes in countries where they are conducting the major part of their business activities. For criminals the tax aspect is only an incidental advantage, because money laundering by itself is an exercise that calls for particular expenses.

Banking secrecy

Another service that offshore jurisdictions offer is banking secrecy. The banking secrecy offered by them is of various types, ranging from numbered accounts, to corporate accounts, to attorney-operated accounts, to nominee-operated accounts, in most of which the information regarding the owner is known only to the top echelons of the banks. Some of the accounts are so structured that the real identity of the beneficiary is not known even to the banks – such accounts exist in Austrian banks. The local laws in the offshore jurisdictions also make the violation of banking secrecy a serious criminal or civil offence.

While on the issue of banking secrecy, it should be stated that it also performs legitimate functions; certain business enterprises may like to keep some of their operations secret in order to outmanoeuvre their competitors. Banking secrecy is also very useful to protect the money of persons fleeing from oppressive jurisdictions; for example, the Jews fleeing Germany during the Second World War opened bank accounts in Switzerland because the Swiss banks provided secrecy. Banking secrecy also comes in useful for persons trying to evade taxes or criminals who wish to launder the proceeds of their crimes.

Shell companies

Another feature of offshore jurisdictions is the shell companies that can easily be formed with the minimum of fuss. These are companies in name only and they do not transact any business. There are a number of shell companies that have been formed by professionals specializing in this field; these shell companies are for sale for nominal amounts of money: if one reads the *International Herald Tribune*, *Newsweek* or *Time* magazine, one will find advertisements for the sale of shell companies in offshore jurisdictions for prices ranging from US$100 to US$200.

These shell companies serve as a very convenient medium to move funds in a complex web which may ultimately become a part of the international money laundering cycle for legitimizing the proceeds of crime.

Shell corporations

Like shell companies, shell corporations are another feature of offshore jurisdictions. Once again, these shell corporations are utilized by criminals for money laundering purposes. The added advantage of shell corporations is the corporate veil which comes into operation in business transactions; this corporate veil provides another layer of secrecy.

These shell corporations are also advertised, like shell companies, and can be purchased off the shelf for nominal amounts in offshore jurisdictions.

Shell banks

Shell banks are another integral feature of offshore jurisdictions. These shell banks, which are banks in name only, can also be bought off the shelf in the offshore jurisdictions. They do not conduct any legitimate banking activity and are generally unregulated in a majority of the offshore jurisdictions. Shell banks may be useful for criminals to introduce money into the international financial circuit before such money is laundered.

Trusts

Offshore trusts are another financial vehicle that is a unique feature of jurisdictions which follow the common law. A trust enables its settlor to transfer his assets to an offshore jurisdiction; the beneficiary can be located in another jurisdiction. For a better understanding of trusts, the reader must appreciate that they involve separation of the legal and beneficial ownership of property.

There are legitimate uses of offshore trusts, such as making financial provisions for relatives, multinational companies transferring their assets from politically unstable jurisdictions to prevent their expropriation, or transferring assets to members of a family who would otherwise not be eligible to inherit property and thereby defeating discriminatory inheritance laws.

Offshore trusts have also become a popular money laundering tool. In fact, some of the offshore trusts have a 'flee clause' incorporated in them; according to this flee clause, the moment an investigation into the affairs of a trust is initiated, it automatically moves to another jurisdiction. The flee clause is useful for enabling criminals to frustrate investigations. Apart from the flee clause, by their very construction the trusts and the laws governing them have in-built secrecy to thwart investigations.

Facilitators

The services of a number of experts and professionals are also required in offshore jurisdictions to operate the financial entities which are a part and parcel of them, for both legitimate and illegitimate purposes. Lawyers, professionals from the financial world who specialize in forming companies, corporations and banks, and chartered accountants/ auditors who act as advisers so as to enable structuring of the financial transactions in the most beneficial manner, play a very important role as facilitators of transactions in these offshore jurisdictions. So long as the role of these facilitators is confined to legitimate purposes, it is acceptable. However, on a percentage basis, large commissions or certain fixed charges, some of these facilitators also provide services to the criminals in order to legitimize their proceeds. The lawyer–client relationship comes in very useful in operating the financial entities in these offshore jurisdictions, as disclosure of information passed between lawyer and client is not permitted, being privileged information under the law. Likewise, nominee-operated financial entities, wherein a nominee can be an auditor, a company formation agent, or any local resident, may be useful in concealing both legitimate and illegitimate assets; in many instances there is a nominee of a nominee of a nominee *ad infinitum* and it becomes well-nigh impossible in such cases to determine who is the real beneficiary and the financial entities in control.

Location of offshore jurisdictions

The location of offshore jurisdictions plays a very important role regarding their usefulness. For instance, offshore centres in the Caribbean are preferred by persons in the North American and South American continents. Likewise, offshore centres in the Pacific are popular with the countries in South-East Asia.

Flags of convenience

Several offshore jurisdictions also offer flags of convenience, which are flags of that jurisdiction given to ships owned by persons in other countries. Ships flying these flags of convenience can be used by criminals in a variety of ways in their money laundering operations.

Financial havens

The various features of those entities in offshore jurisdictions described above, together with convenient geographic locations and the facility of providing a flag of convenience, make these offshore jurisdictions financial havens. In such a financial haven both legitimate and illegitimate transactions are conducted. The degree of legitimate and illegitimate transactions depends upon the availability and combination of various factors described above, as well as the capability and will to regulate the financial entities in these so-called financial havens.

Categories of financial havens

The first category of financial havens are those which serve as entry points for money into the international financial circuit, such as the small islands in the Caribbean, the Pacific and the Mediterranean. In general the financial havens which serve as entry points are minuscule economies with minimal or no regulations and are often politically unstable jurisdictions. The second category of financial havens are those which have developed financial markets and have a very high turnover, both of money and other related financial transactions; these can be termed intermediate points and are useful for camouflaging the flow of money in the international money laundering circuit. Another very important feature of intermediate financial havens is that they have comparatively stable political regimes – for example, Hong Kong and Singapore.

The third category of financial centres are those which have a thriving national economy, highly developed financial and banking sectors and stable political regimes that have evolved over a period of time; financial havens in this category have been used as such for the last two hundred years or so. Countries such as Switzerland and Austria fall into this category.

Countries and their tax havens

Another peculiar feature of the international financial and banking system is that most countries tend to have their own tax havens; for example, the French have Andorra, Germany has Liechtenstein, the US has islands in the Caribbean, India has Mauritius, countries in South-East Asia have Singapore and Hong Kong, Australia and New Zealand have islands in the Pacific. It is the vested business interests in each of these countries that dictate the existence of these proximate financial havens. A list of financial havens is given in Appendix 1 of this chapter.

Introduction of money into the international financial circuit

Criminals have devised several ways of moving money to 'entry point safe havens' in order to circulate it and eventually launder the same. The easiest and the crudest way is using cash: however, criminals are now also aware of more sophisticated ways of moving money. They now know that money can be exchanged for a valuable security that can be traded internationally and, being a piece of paper, can be easily taken out of the country.

Wire transfer of money

Once introduced into the international financial circuit, money can be moved around the world through wire transfers. Indeed, by wire transfer of money one can move it to several jurisdictions several times in a matter of 24 hours. Wire transfer of money is useful at disguising the origin of dirty money by inserting several layers, corresponding to particular jurisdictions in terms of each wire transfer. The electronic movement of money is accomplished through international protocols. Two of these protocols which exist in the United States are the 'CHIPS' system and the 'Fedwire' system. Internationally, the 'SWIFT' protocol is also used for financial transactions. Under the CHIPS and Fedwire systems, which in fact are a network of banks, the transfer of dollars is accomplished on a daily basis in the United States. Under the SWIFT system, the financial transactions are effected, but actual transfer of dollars is accomplished through 'correspondent accounts' in conjunction with CHIPS/Fedwire protocols.

In international financial transactions, the dollars generally do not move out of the US and the balancing of the accounts is done through correspondent banking relationships. Of course, the Euro-dollars which were referred to earlier and which will be discussed in greater detail later in this book are a totally different matter, and their movement in the international market is dictated by a different logic.

The money laundering circuit

The money laundering circuit at the international level makes use of all of the financial entities in the financial havens, plus the different types of financial havens offering distinct services and wire transfer of money. It can be briefly described as the removal or the placement of money in the international financial circuit, disguising and layering of the money in order to obliterate or blur its trail, and finally its emergence as legitimate money through certain processes which can also be described as integration of dirty money with legitimate money. There are various ways and means, techniques and categories that are devised to launder money through the international money laundering circuit. These techniques and categories of money laundering at the international level will be discussed at greater length in the next chapter.

Money movement through financial havens

Criminal money, or 'hot money' is generally moving towards a secure financial haven. In other words, from entry points such as the Cook Islands the money passes through the intermediate financial havens such as Hong Kong and Singapore and finally ends up in secure and stable financial havens like Switzerland and Austria.

Hot money and currency of choice

Hot money is generally seeking a secure and stable currency. Until recently the dollar was the currency preferred, because it was the most stable and widely traded. With the introduction of the euro in the European Economic Community, this is also likely to become a currency of choice.

Euro-dollars[1] and hot money

The emergence of Euro-dollars has already been referred to during the course of this chapter. Following the Middle East war of the 1970s, world oil prices were raised by the

---

[1]   Euro-dollars are discussed at length in a subsequent chapter.

oil-producing countries. The Arab oil kingdoms, which felt threatened in terms of their own banking systems and currencies, decided to put large sums of money, which were the sale proceeds of oil, into the Euro-dollar market. Narco-dollars, which again ran into hundreds of billions of dollars, also flooded the Euro-dollar market in the 1970s and 1980s.

The advantages/problems of several jurisdictions

In the international financial circuit, for a criminal who is laundering his proceeds of crime, there is an in-built advantage in his money having passed through several legal jurisdictions; anyone wanting to track down these criminal proceeds would have to master several legal jurisdictions through which the money has passed. It has been the experience that challenging a single legal jurisdiction takes several years; therefore to challenge a number of these jurisdictions would take a very long time.

Audit/paper trail in the international money laundering circuit

A silver lining concerning the money that is being laundered through the international money laundering circuit is that there is a paper trail or an audit trail that can be followed, though the chances of success in tracking down the laundered money are extremely bleak due to the manner in which the international money laundering circuit is structured.

SOME INTERESTING STATISTICS

In his address to the Financial Action Task Force in 1991, the Managing Director of the International Monetary Fund stated that money laundering comprised 2–5 per cent of world GDP. According to the World Bank, money laundering is a US$1,000 billion enterprise.

According to the United Nations booklet entitled *Financial Havens, Banking Secrecy and Money Laundering*, offshore banking centres have more than 1 million anonymous corporations. Moreover, the offshore centres have US$5,000 billion in assets, of which US$1,000 billion are in bank deposits and another US$4,000 billion are held in the form of stocks, bonds, real estate and commodities.

In 1997 the extent of laundered funds being moved every day through wire transfers was estimated at US$300 million, 0.5–1 per cent of more than US$2 trillion being moved via around 700,000 wire transfers. From this it becomes clear that special techniques are needed to track down funds moving through the wire transfer systems.[2]

---

[2]   See the booklet entitled *Information Technologies for the Control of Money Laundering* published by the Office of Technology Assessment, Congress of the United States.

Another interesting statistic is the inverse relationship between cash transactions, cheque transactions and electronic transactions in terms of money involved in each. In 1995, according to the US payment structure, cash transactions totalling 550 billion accounted for US$2,200 billion, cheque transactions numbering 62 billion accounted for US$73,000 billion, and electronic transactions totalling 19 billion accounted for US$544,000 billion.[3]

The total amount of US dollars in circulation in the world are in the region of US$500 billion, of which US$400 billion are in circulation outside the United States; these billions of US dollars outside the US are also useful in the process of money laundering through the international financial circuit.[4]

The above statistics have been provided to give readers an idea of the enormity of the problem and the difficulties that can be encountered in tracking down laundered money.

MONEY LAUNDERING VIS-A-VIS CAPITAL FLIGHT

In the chapter on the mechanics and typologies of money laundering, laundering will be viewed in its strictest sense by excluding all those cases which are listed by several authors as money laundering but actually fall into the category of simple spending sprees. Another distinction that has to be borne in mind while discussing the subject of money laundering techniques is that money laundering should not be confused with capital flight, which happens quite often. Capital flight is the movement of money out of jurisdictions due to unstable political or economic conditions; capital flight assures that the net worth of the capital is not eroded because flight capital is converted into a stable currency or a precious commodity such as gold.

LAWS ON MONEY LAUNDERING – UN REPORT

The United Nations special report on *Financial Havens, Banking Secrecy and Money Laundering* has also endeavoured to advance certain laws pertaining to money laundering; ten such laws are listed in this UN report, the essence of these laws being that money laundering operations, in order to be successful, try to approximate to normal business practices to the maximum possible extent.

GRAPHIC REPRESENTATION OF THE MONEY LAUNDERING CIRCUIT

In Appendix 2 of this chapter, the complete money laundering circuit is portrayed graphically; this graphic representation lists all the practices, trends, concepts and entities associated with money laundering at the international level discussed in this chapter.

---

[3] Figures are from the United Nations booklet entitled *Financial Havens, Banking Secrecy and Money Laundering*.
[4] Ibid.

APPENDIX 1

Major financial havens

Europe	Andorra
	Campione
	Cyprus
	Gibraltar
	Guernsey
	Ireland (Dublin)
	Isle of Man
	Jersey
	Liechtenstein
	Luxembourg
	Madeira
	Malta
	Monaco
	Sark
	Switzerland
The Caribbean	Anguilla
	Antigua
	Aruba
	Bahamas
	Barbados
	Belize
	Bermuda
	British Virgin Islands
	Cayman Islands
	Costa Rica
	Netherlands Antilles
	Panama
	Saint Kitts and Nevis
	Saint Lucia
	Saint Vincent and the Grenadines
	Turks and Caicos Islands
Africa–Indian Ocean	Liberia
	Mauritius
	Seychelles

Asia-Pacific/Middle East Bahrain
         Cook Islands
         Dubai
         Hong Kong SAR
         Labuan
         Lebanon
         Macao
         Marianas
         Marshall Islands
         Nauru
         Niue
         Singapore
         Vanuatu
         Samoa

APPENDIX 2

MONEY LAUNDERING CIRCUIT

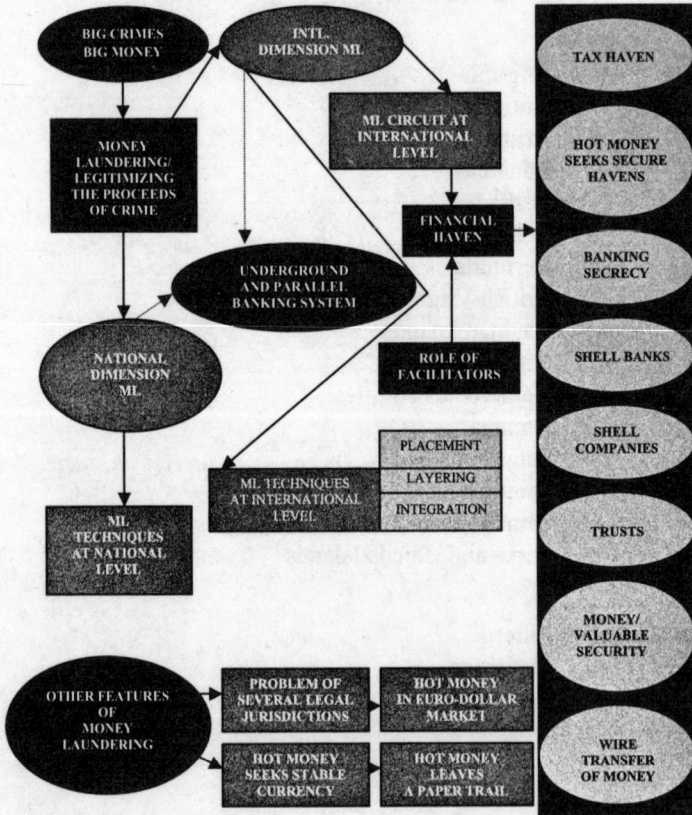

CHAPTER XI

MECHANICS AND TYPOLOGIES OF MONEY LAUNDERING

POINTS HAVING A VITAL BEARING ON MONEY LAUNDERING

In the previous chapter, while discussing the basics of money laundering, the following points were made, these also being relevant to the mechanics/classifications of money laundering:

(a) Money laundering has both a national and an international dimension; thus typologies of money laundering are observed at both levels.

(b) Money can be laundered exclusively in the national sphere.

(c) In any money laundering operation having an international dimension, a national dimension is a must.

(d) There is often an overlap between the national and international dimensions of money laundering.

(e) Driven by the free market economy, most countries are embracing economic liberalization; a corollary of economic liberalization is greater integration of the financial and banking system worldwide, which again is a key element for any successful money laundering operation.

On the issue of typologies, a point to be borne in mind is that money laundering is not something that can be taught or learned in a comprehensive course. It is a dynamic and continually evolving process and one has to keep abreast of the latest developments in the field, with regard to both techniques and the instruments through which it is effected. While discussing the various techniques of money laundering, it will be observed that some are foolproof methods, some are half-hearted attempts and some are downright amateurish attempts.

TECHNIQUES/TYPOLOGIES AT THE NATIONAL LEVEL

During the course of this chapter, money laundering techniques which have a strictly national orientation will be discussed first. These are:

Retail businesses

These businesses are merely fronts where most of the sales are fictitious; for instance, a general merchant could have a limited stock, but in its accounts books fictitious sales could be shown. The extent to which the sales are fictitious is the extent to which money can be laundered and ultimately projected as legitimate sales proceeds of business.

Retail businesses with a large turnover, such as fast food restaurants, are another convenient medium for laundering money. In these retail businesses with large turnovers, the illegal money can be commingled quite easily with legitimate sales without coming to anyone's notice because of the arduous mechanics of keeping accurate accounts. In this case the extent to which illegal money is commingled with the final sales proceeds is the extent to which money can be laundered.

Retail businesses that are exclusive and deal in very expensive items, e.g., high-end fashion designers' retail outlets, are also a very convenient vehicle to launder money. In these high-end fashion shops, sales of garments are shown at highly inflated prices, whereas the garments would actually be sold at much lower prices, or the sales could even be totally fictitious. In this instance, illegal money can be passed off as legitimate to the extent of the price inflation.

Simulation of a retail business can also be another way to launder money. For instance, one can set up a jewellery shop, having a limited stock of genuine jewellery items. All of the sales that would be effected in the shop would be of counterfeit jewellery, but sale transactions would be projected as sales of genuine jewellery. Illegal money can very easily be shown as the sale proceeds of counterfeit jewellery being sold off as genuine – in this instance, sales proceeds minus the price of counterfeit jewellery would be the laundered money.

Wholesale trade

As regards money laundering techniques, what is true of the retail trade (as indicated above) is also true of the wholesale trade, by and large. However, in both the retail and wholesale trade, a lot of explaining has sometimes to be done; in such instances, greasing the palms of inspectors is often resorted to, to make them turn a blind eye towards the nefarious business activities.

Manufacturing units

Another way to launder money is through a bogus manufacturing unit. Such a unit would have a building and a billboard indicating a factory. By projecting sales through this bogus manufacturing unit, money is laundered to the extent that bogus sales are effected.

Manufacturing units which are genuine can also be used to launder money. In such units, inflated invoices are issued for the product that is manufactured; the extent to which the price has been inflated is the extent to which money can be laundered.

Charity shows

Organizing charity/entertainment shows is another way to launder money. In this *modus operandi*, fraudulent sale of tickets can be resorted to, because a person buying a ticket is not under an obligation to attend the show. The extent to which fraudulent tickets have been sold is the extent to which money can be laundered. However, there is a price to be paid for this type of money laundering in the form of entertainment tax.

Lottery tickets

Lottery tickets is big business in several countries, especially India. Money launderers buy lottery tickets from genuine winners at a premium with their illegally acquired proceeds. Encashment of lottery tickets results in money being legitimized by these criminals.

Racecourses

Like the purchase of lottery tickets, the purchase of winning tickets at racecourses is another way to launder money. Money launderers use their proceeds to buy winning tickets at a premium from the actual winners. By encashing the winning tickets, the money launderers launder their money at a price, which in this instance is the premium paid on the winning tickets.

Casinos

Casinos, which are popular in most countries, is another convenient way to launder money. Money launderers take their proceeds to these casinos, buy a large number of chips and do little or practically no gambling. At the end of the day, the launderer encashes his chips by passing them off as genuine winnings. For the money laundering operation to be really effective in casinos, encashment of chips is done by money launderers in the form of cheques drawn on banks. Often there is complicity on the part of persons running the casinos in money laundering being effected through them.

Large numbers of bank accounts

A large number of accounts with small sums of money, in an individual's own name or in fictitious names, in bank branches scattered all over, is another way to avoid arousing suspicion as to the origins of illicit money. This is an unimaginative way to launder money, in which a façade of bank accounts is used to project the money as legitimate.

Property

In the property business, the sale of worthless houses at highly inflated prices is also resorted to in order to launder money; the extent to which the price has been inflated in these property deals is the extent to which criminal proceeds can be laundered. Of course, there is a price to be paid in this *modus operandi* in the form of higher registration fees for the sale of property.

Purchase of property with a high black money component is another way to disguise the money. In India, the black money component in property sales is approximately 50 per cent of the sale price. The extent to which the purchase price is in black money is the extent to which illegal money is disguised in the purchase of property. This disguised money can always be made liquid in the subsequent sale of property – but in that case this black money component would again need to be legitimized. Strictly speaking, this *modus operandi* cannot be termed as money laundering, but nevertheless it is a clever way to disguise illicit money.

Commissions from property deals could be highly inflated to launder money. Commissions from fictitious property deals amongst relatives could also be used to pass off illegal proceeds as legitimate.

By floating a property finance company and taking a loan from it, the criminal could launder the money to the extent that a loan has been taken. In such a *modus operandi* the property company could be a front and its assets the illicit proceeds of crimes.

Inheritance laws

In India the use of inheritance laws pertaining to jewellery is another way to launder money. According to inheritance law, any married women can have Rs. 500,000-worth of jewellery; to this extent illegal money can be laundered by each family. By systematic structuring of a group of families, which might even be members of criminal gangs, substantial amounts of illegal money could be laundered.

'Stree Dhan' is given to women in India at the time of the marriage. Illegal proceeds can also be passed off as legal, by projecting these as the Stree Dhan which the woman received at the time of her marriage.

Commodities market

Commodities markets, which deal in futures contracts in commodities, are also a very effective medium for laundering money. Illegal proceeds can easily be passed off as fabricated or inflated gains on futures trading in commodities.

Securities market

The capitalization of markets, in other words raising capital from the general public or financial institutions, is one of the principal ways to mobilize funds for economic growth. The markets so capitalized are also known as securities markets or stock exchanges. In the stock market, capital raised is in two forms; one is equity capital, which denotes ownership in the form of company shares; the other form of capital is interest-bearing bonds, which are debt instruments issued to the general public or financial institutions.

Another feature of the securities/stock markets is that so long as the price of shares or equities, indicated by the stock market index, is moving up or down, the participants in this market make money. When the stock market share price index is moving down, the 'Bears' make money, and when it is going up, the 'Bulls' make money. In the securities market, profits can easily be recorded on paper to launder the illegal proceeds. Losses on paper can also be recorded in the securities market to save on income tax. Although quite a few securities markets ask for identification from customers, money launderers are able to get around that by having aliases or false identities.

Insurance sector

Insurance companies are also frequently used by money launderers to legitimize their proceeds. Insurance companies generally offer life insurance and other forms of general insurance, including health and property insurance. Money launderers generally take out very expensive insurance policies and after paying a few premiums, apply for premature encashment of policies at a discounted rate. The cheques paid out by the insurance companies for premature surrender of policies is generally passed of as legitimate money. In this *modus operandi*, aliases and false identities come in very handy and a certain complicity of insurance officials is sometimes also observed when the premium paid in cash is a large sum of money.

Agricultural sector in India

In some countries certain sectors of the economy are exempt from income tax. For instance, in India the agricultural sector is exempt from it in order to give a boost to agriculture and relief to farmers who are engaged in an occupation that is otherwise not very remunerative. Money launderers buy up land in such a situation and show highly inflated gains from agriculture, purportedly through the use of advanced and sophisticated agricultural techniques. Inflated gains in an agricultural scenario can very easily account for illicit proceeds. Another advantage of laundering money through the agricultural sector is that one also saves on income tax.

Extension services in the agriculture sector, such as dairy farming and poultry, which are also exempt from income tax, are also utilized to launder money. The *modus operandi* in these extension services is the same – inflated gains account for illegal proceeds and therefore make them appear legitimate.

Amnesty schemes

Often when the black money component in the national economy is high, due to the negative effects which black money exerts on the national economy, governments want to mobilize this black money by bringing it into the open so that it might be utilized in a more productive manner. To bring black money into the open, governments often introduce amnesty schemes, whereby people can declare their illegally acquired proceeds or black money to government on payment of a certain amount of tax; in these amnesty schemes, no questions are asked about the source of the money and after payment of tax it becomes legitimate money which can be used openly in the economy. These amnesty schemes have often been criticized as government-sponsored money laundering schemes which reward the criminal elements at the expense of honest taxpayers.

Indira Vikas Patras: bearer certificates with no identification requirement

In India, where the black money component in the economy is as high as 50 per cent, the government felt at one point that a substantial portion of this money should be used in a more productive way. This could only be done by channelling it through government institutions. In order to give legitimacy to the black money, the government introduced bearer certificates, also known as 'Indira Vikas Patras'; anyone could buy any number of bearer certificates of high denomination issued by the post offices without any questions being asked. With these bearer certificates, offering a good rate of interest, one could double one's money in six years. Moreover these bearer certificates, having no identification, could easily be traded and the holder could encash the same on maturity. A number of criminals and tax evaders invested their money in the Indira Vikas Patras and doubled it in six years. On encashment of these Indira Vikas Patras, if the money came from a black money source, it would go back to that source or be reinvested in more Indira Vikas Patras. These had become very popular with criminals and tax evaders as an anonymous way of holding money with the added incentive of a handsome return.

There was an ingenious way in which criminals holding Indira Vikas Patras could launder their money by floating a finance company. In this *modus operandi* the criminals would take deposits, offering handsome interest to the depositors; moreover, they would give Indira Vikas Patras, which had a high credibility, as collateral to the person making the deposit. In this case, all deposits in the finance company would become legitimate, having been received in the form of cheques. The criminals could then reinvest the deposits in the finance company in other business enterprises. Ultimately, on maturity, the criminal would pay back the deposit with interest from the resources of the finance company. The legitimate business enterprises in this case would become a money laundering vehicle for the criminals. In such an arrangement, even if the finance company was fraudulently declared bankrupt, no one would suffer because Indira Vikas Patras given as collateral could always be encashed by the depositors and the fraudulent nature of bankruptcy enabled the criminals to siphon off laundered money in the form of bad loans to the business enterprises floated by them.

Realizing that a very large portion of illicit finance was being channelled through the Indira Vikas Patras, the government finally discontinued this scheme three years ago. The scheme had been in operation for 15 years or so. Considering that the GDP of India was INR 15,981 billion in 1998–99, the black economy component, computed at 50 per cent, works out at INR 7,990.5 billion, and even if half of this black economy component was invested in the Indira Vikas Patras, then substantial illegal proceeds to the extent of INR 3,995.25 billion were being processed through them.[1]

The Indira Vikas Patras were remarkable in many respects:

(i) They enabled black money to be channelled through post offices for more productive utilization.
(ii) They offered a convenient way for criminals to earn handsome returns on their illicit gains.
(iii) The criminals could also use them to launder their money through various ingenious schemes.

The merits and demerits of Indira Vikas Patras in an economy where the black money component is high can be debated at considerable length.

Use of gold/diamonds/precious gems

Criminals can also buy gold, diamonds and precious gems and use them to launder money. For instance, in India there is a great demand for gold; India is also the largest centre in the world for the cutting and polishing of diamonds. Before the Gold Control Order was abolished, the amount of gold smuggled into the country was estimated to be in the region of 500–700 tons, worth roughly US$5–7 billion. The diamond trade today runs to US$8 billion. Considerable smuggling of gold into India is still going on; large numbers of diamonds are also diverted from exports, ultimately to be sold in the retail black market. With their illicit proceeds, the criminals buy gold and diamonds. By choosing gold and diamonds as a convenient store for holding money, using the same *modus operandi* as that of the finance company and Indira Vikas Patras described above, the criminals could launder their proceeds.

Use of false identities to launder money

False or stolen identities are also useful for money launderers, who could utilize false and stolen identities in the various operations in the national sphere described above; in such cases the investigation would generally come to a dead end. False or stolen identities are also very useful for introducing money into the international money laundering circuit and its subsequent legitimization.

Role of facilitators

In the money laundering exercise in the national sphere, financial experts, accountants and auditors play a very important role in advising the criminals. There is also complicity of various financial institutions such as banks, insurance companies and brokerage

---

[1] The Indira Vikas Patras scheme was discontinued three years ago; hence, the GDP and related figure for the year 1998–99 have been indicated.

houses in the securities and commodities markets in laundering the money. However, money laundering carried out at the national level is highly vulnerable to investigation and even the most perfect of schemes can be prised open once adequate intelligence is available and the political and bureaucratic will is there to see these money laundering investigations through to their logical conclusion.

It should be mentioned that in a country such as India where the black money component is very high, the need, incentive or desire to launder money is rather limited. In economies with a large component of black money, money laundering is generally directed towards maximizing wealth and, to a limited extent, providing a façade of legitimate money.

TECHNIQUES/TYPOLOGIES AT THE INTERNATIONAL LEVEL

Having discussed money laundering at the national level in its various facets, let us now examine the international dimension. Once the international dimension of money laundering comes into play, money is laundered more effectively and it becomes extremely difficult, if not impossible, to unravel the complex web of transactions in order to expose the origin of money that is the proceeds of crime.

At the outset, one may also ask where the money that has been laundered through the international circuit goes. One answer is that the money that moves from the national jurisdiction to the international circuit returns to the national jurisdiction. Another trend is that money which has gone from the national jurisdiction to the international circuit need never return to the original national jurisdiction.

In Chapter X the concepts, practices, trends and structures related to money laundering in its international dimension have already been discussed. The international money laundering circuit, comprising the three stages of money laundering, i.e., placement, layering and integration, whereby illegal money is transformed to legitimate money, has also been mentioned briefly.

The international money laundering circuit can be structured in various ways, so that each corresponds to a particular technique or classification of money laundering. The structuring of the money laundering circuit is one of several permutations and combinations of concepts, practices, trends and structures. In a particular money laundering circuit/technique/typology, some features might be preferred to others, depending upon services rendered by the particular financial haven being used. These structured variations, permutations and combinations in the international money laundering circuit will become clear when discussing placement, layering of money and its integration in greater detail later in this chapter.

INTRODUCTION/PLACEMENT OF MONEY

Physical placement

The introduction or placement of illegal money in the international money laundering circuit is not only an essential step in the money laundering exercise, but also the most vulnerable operation. Money is generally introduced into the international money laundering circuit through those financial havens classified as 'entry point safe havens' in the previous chapter. There are various ways in which money can be placed in these financial havens. The crudest way is through movement of cash: cash, however, means bulk, because crime money generally comprises small bills. In order to reduce this bulk, the criminals convert these small bills into high-denomination currency notes. Cash movement is effected through couriers who carry a certain amount of cash on their person and in accompanying baggage on a particular trip. Money in the form of cash is also sent via speedboats and aeroplanes to entry point financial havens; cash is also moved to entry point financial havens concealed in cargoes being transported by ships or aeroplanes. However, because of its sheer bulk, physical movement of large sums of cash can sometimes create insurmountable problems for the money launderer. On one occasion Pablo Escobar, one of the heads of the Colombian cocaine drug cartels, lost up to US$500 million lying in cash in a warehouse in California due to its rotting, because of his inability to move it in time.

Conversion to valuable securities

Criminals have now become smart and they know that cash can be exchanged for a valuable security such as a banker's cheque (also known as a cashier's cheque), bank drafts, equity shares and company bonds. Cash so converted into any of these valuable securities can easily be smuggled out of the country in a convenient manner because the 'bulk' has been done away with. Most countries that have money laundering legislation have also introduced cash reporting requirements pertaining to monetary instruments and cash.

'Smurfing'

Transactions exceeding a certain amount have to be reported – in the US this reporting requirement applies to all transactions exceeding US$10,000. To overcome this reporting requirement, criminals resort to a technique which is known as 'smurfing'; in smurfing, cash is converted into a valuable security of an amount which is less than the reporting requirement. Thus, through smurfing, a large number of cashier's cheques, drafts, equity shares and bonds which are the proceeds of crime are available for moving out of the country in several ways, of which smuggling is one, in order to be placed on the international money laundering circuit.

Money orders

Money orders issued by post offices, which in the US can be a maximum of US$3,000, are also used by criminals to move their money out of the country.

Brokerage houses

Brokerage houses dealing in securities, commodities futures and foreign exchange, by the very nature of the functions they perform, are also very convenient channels for moving illegal money out of the country to be placed in the international money laundering circuit. By using brokerage houses, one may introduce illegal money not only through entry-level financial havens, but also through intermediate financial havens such as Hong Kong and Singapore.

Expensive art objects

Antiques and precious items of art are also purchased by the criminals from their illicit funds in order to introduce money into the international money laundering circuit. Antiques and precious items of art purchased by the criminals can easily be smuggled out of the country and sold abroad. The sale proceeds can then be introduced through a convenient safe haven in order to pass through the complete money laundering cycle before reappearing as legitimate money.

Correspondent banking channels

Correspondent banking is another very convenient way to move illegal money out of the country and to bring laundered money back into it. In order to understand this, an understanding of correspondent banking is necessary. Banks in the world normally do not maintain branches in every country, as that would be a very expensive exercise with numerous overheads. The bankers generally enter into a correspondent relationship with other banks having branches in each other's countries. In this correspondent relationship, deposits are maintained in the other country's currency by the banks concerned: thus, by advising the correspondent bank, the money can be moved from one correspondent account to another as and when required. Of course, the account books have to be balanced at the end of the day in this correspondent relationship.

Underground systems

Another way to place money in the international money laundering circuit is through underground and parallel banking systems, which eliminate the physical movement of money. This aspect of moving money will be discussed in greater detail in the next chapter, which is devoted entirely to underground and parallel banking systems.

Exempt financial entities

In any country that has enacted money laundering legislation, there are also financial entities which are exempt from financial transaction reporting requirements because of overriding business considerations. Through these entities in the exempt list money is introduced or placed on the international money laundering circuit by the criminals by way of wire transfers to a convenient haven.

DISGUISING/LAYERING OF MONEY

For disguising the trail of money, or what is also known as layering, entities such as shell companies, shell corporations, shell banks and offshore trusts are used in conjunction with offshore jurisdictions offering their brand of services. Money is passed through shell companies, shell banks, shell corporations, offshore trusts and offshore jurisdictions through various permutations and combinations which are only limited by the laws/regulations of those offshore jurisdictions. While disguising the money trail, money could also be made to move through legitimate businesses and genuine banks in the world of international finance. In the layering process, electronic transfer of money is very useful because it enables movement of money through various entities and several jurisdictions in a matter of hours. In layering dirty money, another trend that has been noted is that the money moves from unstable/not so stable financial havens to intermediate havens to secure financial havens.

LEGITIMIZATION/INTEGRATION OF MONEY

The ultimate aim of the international money laundering circuit is to make the illicit money appear as legitimate; this legitimization process is also known as integration of money. The legitimization process to some extent utilizes the same *modus operandi* as that used in disguising the trail of money, in order to further reinforce the steps before money becomes legitimized. At the integration stage in the international financial circuit illegal money, by way of investments in legitimate commercial enterprises, is made to appear legitimate. From these legitimate commercial enterprises operating in other countries, the money can be repatriated to the home country as legitimate earnings. Money from these legitimate business enterprises operating abroad can also be shown as a loan to the money launderer in the home country; of course, the money launderer can always default on the loan, and even if he repays it a cycle has been established to launder money. In the integration process, money from the legitimate enterprises or bank accounts abroad need never came back to the home country, as already stated, and can be further utilized abroad for legal or illegal activities.

Illegal money, introduced in the international financial circuit through a process of layering, is also often secreted away in the form of gold in Swiss bank vaults. The veil of secrecy which these Swiss vaults guarantees ensures that criminals can always draw upon this source of money and surreptitiously pass it off as legitimate.

While going around the international money laundering circuit during the integration stage, the illegal money can eventually also end up in the Euro-dollar market (discussed in the previous chapter), where the money not only earns a decent interest rate, but becomes very difficult to track down because the Euro-dollar market itself is very large and runs into trillions of dollars.

INTERNATIONAL TRADE AND MONEY LAUNDERING

The business of imports and exports is one of the most important gateways for laundering money through the international financial circuit. However, before proceeding to discuss how money is laundered through imports and exports, a brief idea of how this international trade is conducted is necessary. In the import and export business, since one is dealing between two countries often separated by considerable distances, the shipment of and payment for goods between the buyer and seller is facilitated by two basic instruments: the letter of credit and bill of lading. By depositing money with a bank, the buyer obtains a letter of credit issued from his bank to the seller's bank. Through this letter of credit the seller's bank can release the payment to the seller after the goods have been shipped by him. As proof of shipment of goods, bills of lading are made out and sent to the buyer's bank. On receipt of the bills of lading, the buyer's bank gives the seller's bank the go-ahead to release the payment, already guaranteed by letter of credit to the seller. In the import–export trade there are several forms of letters of credit and bills of lading, in which conditions are stipulated concerning the release of payment and the receipt of goods.

Invoice manipulation: opportunities to launder money

By manipulating the price of goods, whether for import or export or through bogus imports and exports, money is laundered; pricing of goods in international trade is more commonly known as 'invoicing'. By under-invoicing of imports, the importer has to pay the sellers abroad more than the stated price of the imports; illegal proceeds are useful to pay the differential between the actual price and the stated price of imports. In over-invoicing of exports, the seller receives more money than the stated price of the exports; in this case illegal money can be shown as legitimate to the extent that the stated price of the exports exceeds the actual price of the exports paid by the buyer.

By simulating a bogus trade in import and export, illicit proceeds can be brought into the country on the strength of purported exports and can also be taken out of the country on the strength of purported imports; in the case of bogus imports and exports, another layer of financial entities would be needed to make the money laundering process more credible and not subject to suspicion.

By over-invoicing of imports, excess foreign exchange released can be retained abroad in a legal form; likewise, by under-invoicing of exports, once again the differential between the actual price of the exports and the stated price of the exports is retained abroad in a legal manner. Thus, as a result of over-invoicing of imports and under-invoicing of exports, with the foreign exchange retained abroad, a criminal could set up a legitimate enterprise through which he can route the illegal proceeds, either to disguise their trail or to make them reappear as legitimate.

In fact, several variations on the invoice manipulation theme are possible in order to launder money. The only limitation is human ingenuity. In countries with foreign exchange control regulations, the role of invoice manipulation increases significantly to facilitate money laundering.

SOME OTHER FEATURES OF MONEY LAUNDERING AT INTERNATIONAL LEVEL

Country development bonds and money laundering

At some point in time developing countries are confronted with a crippling foreign exchange crisis, in which they do not have enough foreign exchange reserves to pay for even a fortnight's worth of imports. India was confronted with such a situation in both 1991 and 1999 due to economic sanctions following its test explosion of nuclear devices. Since a very large section of the Indian population is settled in various countries of the world, there is a base from which funds can be tapped in these times of crisis. To tap funds from non-resident Indians, also characterized as the Indian diaspora, the government of India floated development bonds at interest rates slightly higher than those prevailing in the international market to mobilize foreign exchange. In this process of floating Indian Development Bonds, no questions were asked about the source of the money. In 1991 US$5 billion were mobilized through the Indian Development Bonds; in 1999 another US$4.2 billion were mobilized through the India Resurgent Bonds. It is conceivable that some of the money mobilized through development bonds could be the proceeds of crime. In the case of some developing countries, illegal proceeds constitute a major chunk of the corpus of the development bonds floated.

Gifts of foreign currency and money laundering

Countries which have a trade deficit in their international trade and a precarious balance of payments position with regard to foreign exchange reserves, have also devised a number of other ways to attract foreign exchange. In the case of India, gifts in foreign exchange from non-resident Indians could be given to anyone in India; not only are these gifts exempt from income tax, but there is also no limit as to the amount of the gift that could be received. Quite a few criminals receive such gifts in foreign exchange from non-resident Indians in order to pass off their proceeds of crime as legitimate; in this *modus operandi*, it is ensured that the proceeds of crime reach the non-resident Indian in the form of foreign exchange (often through underground banking channels) to enable him to send the same as a gift.

Underground banking

The underground and parallel banking systems also play a very important role in facilitating money laundering in countries which have foreign exchange controls; the techniques and classifications of money laundering in the Indian context where foreign exchange controls operate will be discussed in the next chapter.

Gold and diamonds

Gold and diamonds also play a very important role in money laundering, especially in the context of and in conjunction with the underground and parallel banking systems; hence, this aspect has also been dealt with in greater detail in the following chapter.

New technologies

How the new developments in information technology such as e-commerce, electronic banking, electronic cash, smart cards and e-gambling are utilized to launder money is discussed in Chapter XVIII.

SOME INTERESTING CASES OF MONEY LAUNDERING

Operation Casablanca

Operation Casablanca is the largest undercover operation pertaining to money laundering so far carried out. This operation was carried out by the US Customs Service in 1998. The fact that US$100 million in currency were seized, 167 individuals were arrested, 26 Mexican bank officials were implicated and three Mexican banks indicted is indicative of the magnitude of this operation. Moreover, this operation spanned several continents and involved some 200 undercover agents; in terms of sheer logistics, to keep the operation under wraps was a tremendous achievement in itself.

In this case, the US Customs officials penetrated the Cali and Juarez drugs cartels; they were trusted sufficiently to be given the drugs proceeds realized as a result of dealing the drugs in major US cities. The customs officials would then deposit these proceeds in undercover accounts of US Customs in Los Angeles. The proceeds were wire transferred from the undercover accounts to banks in Mexico. The Mexican banks in turn issued bank drafts – drawn on the US accounts of Mexican banks – and couriered these to the customs undercover agents. Ultimately the funds were disbursed to the money launderers. This case came to be known as Casablanca because the sting operation was carried out in a casino by the name of *Casablanca* which is located on the outskirts of Las Vegas.

BCCI case

The Bank of Credit and Commerce International (BCCI) was floated by a Pakistani national, Agha Hasan Abedi. It was intended to cater to the needs of the developing world, having its headquarters in Luxembourg, with branches all over the world. It may come as a surprise to readers to know that it is perhaps the only bank in the world that was set up on the basis of a back-to-back loan with no equity. Over a period of time, because of the nature of its activities, this bank came to be known as the 'Bank of Crooks and Criminals International'. BCCI was used with impunity by drug traffickers, dictators, terrorists, fraudsters, intelligence agencies, arms dealers and several other unscrupulous elements to carry out their activities, which included the laundering of money. BCCI was able to do this because of lack of controls or lax controls relating to banking and other financial entities in offshore jurisdictions. BCCI operated through several entities which included banks within banks, shell companies, shell corporations, trusts and nominee-operated accounts; in fact, it was able to build multiple layers of secrecy by structuring financial entities. Because of its global operations, BCCI was not accountable or subject to any particular jurisdiction. In July 1991, when enforcement authorities in the United States and United Kingdom cracked down on BCCI, they seized US$12 billion-worth of assets.

Following the BCCI episode, the Basle Committee on Banking Supervision proposed a set of core principles to regulate international banking; the role of the Basle Committee on Banking Supervision is discussed in a subsequent chapter. The BCCI case in its totality is the biggest money laundering case in the world.

The case of a Tamil Nadu minister

During my visit to Tamil Nadu in the course of the present study, the Director General, Vigilance – the agency charged with tackling corruption – stated that he was unable to indict a minister in Tamil Nadu who was corrupt, because the minister was showing all of his illegally acquired money as gifts from non-resident Indians (NRIs) (he had openly declared INR 30 million as gifts from NRIs). Obviously the money in the present instance was sent to the NRIs through underground banking channels, and once again due to the sketchy evidence that one gets in the investigation of underground banking cases, it was not possible to register a case against him.

ULFA terrorists in Assam

ULFA is a terrorist organization in Assam which has been able to mobilize massive funds through ransom from kidnapping and other illegal activities over the years – these funds are estimated to be in the region of INR 6–10 billion. ULFA has invested these funds abroad to run legitimate businesses, with restaurants constituting the majority of such businesses. Obviously the money to run a legitimate business and thereby launder it was sent out of the country through underground banking channels.

LTTE case

One of the functionaries of the LTTE is a man named Padmanabhan, based in Singapore. According to intelligence reports, Padmanabhan is alleged to have mobilized money to the extent of US$100–800 million by running a shipping company in Singapore, a large part of which may be laundered money.

117

CHAPTER XII

UNDERGROUND AND PARALLEL BANKING SYSTEMS

WHY USE OF THE TERM 'UNDERGROUND' IN ADDRESSING THESE SYSTEMS?

Underground and parallel banking systems are another way of moving money around the world. The reason these systems are called underground and parallel banking is because they have evolved as a result of traditional banking practices followed by communities in some countries over several centuries. Moreover, the parallel that has generally been drawn between these underground systems and correspondent banking has also contributed to their being termed as 'underground' banking systems.[1]

THE RECENT TREND OF STYLING THESE AS INFORMAL MONEY TRANSMISSION SERVICES

The latest trend is to refer to these underground banking systems as informal money transmission services. The reason for their activities being referred to as such is because, according to some, their activities do not strictly fall within the definition of commercial banking according to the Banking Acts of several countries. At this point, an explanation about commercial banking is in order, because it entails maintaining some cash reserves as per the directions of the central bank, taking deposits, giving out loans, which leads to multiple expansion of money, a concept which is at the heart of commercial banking.

TYPES OF SYSTEMS AND THEIR EVOLUTION

There are three principal underground banking systems, namely, 'hundi/hawala', 'chop shop/chitti banking' and 'black market peso exchange'. The hundi/hawala system has its origin in the Indian subcontinent and in trade related to the Arabs, the chop shop/chitti banking system has its origin in the traditional Chinese banking practices, and the black market peso exchange system prevalent in Latin America is of recent origin.

---

[1]   The concept of correspondent banking has already been explained in Chapter XI.

Hundi/hawala system

The hundi/hawala system was used by Indians like a form of modern-day banking, in order to facilitate trade. 'Hundi' which means 'trust' and 'hawala' which means 'transfer related to money' can actually be likened to modern-day letters of credit. In former times if a trader was going from one city to another, he would take a hundi as a letter of credit from a hundi banker in his own city to the hundi banker located in the city with which trade was to be transacted. The hundi bankers, by honouring these so-called letters of credit, facilitated trade between two regions in those ancient times. Of course, at the end of the day, the hawala bankers had to balance their books, which was quite easily accomplished due to trade and commerce in either direction. It is this traditional hundi/hawala banking system which has survived to the present day as an underground banking system.

Chop shop/chitti banking

Chop shop/chitti banking is basically the Chinese underground banking system and has been covered by William L. Cassidy in his article 'Fei-Chien or Flying Money'.[2] This article is perhaps the most authentic study in the context of Chinese underground banking.

'Chops' are basically seals that facilitate money transactions. Several varieties of chops exist, such as general purpose chops indicating ownership, goods delivery chops and debt acknowledgement chops. The word 'chitti', which means 'a pass' in Hindi – one of the languages used in India – was generally given to servants as a means of payment by the British during the colonial rule of India. It was through the British that the word chitti crept into use in the context of Chinese underground banking.

Very briefly, the traditional Chinese banking practices can be described as comprising the primitive credit institutions/Chinese banks; an instance of such primitive banks were the Shansi banks, which sold money through drafts for a fee, and these could again be likened to the modern-day travellers cheques. Promissory notes and bills of exchange in the context of traditional Chinese banking practices were also very common. Another trend of the traditional Chinese banking system was that of gold shops and silver shops branching out into banking activities. Other terms quite common in the Chinese banking system are 'shroffs' and 'chops'. 'Shroffs' was in fact a means to verify the authenticity of a currency; 'chops' have already been referred to in a different context; they were also used as seals indicating not only ownership, but also other off-the-record currency transactions. Such an elaborate network of traditional Chinese banking has survived to the present day as the Chinese underground banking system.

---

[2] The article entitled 'Fei-Chien or Flying Money' by William L. Cassidy can be accessed on the Internet at: http://users.deltant.com/~wcassidy/wlrc/Flyingmoney.html, 1994.

Black market peso exchange

As already mentioned, this underground banking system is of recent origin and operates in the context of North America, Latin America and some countries in Europe; it is linked to drug traffickers and other criminal syndicates. Under this system peso-brokers based in Colombia buy dollars at a discount from the drug traffickers, giving them pesos in return, with which the drug traffickers service their needs in Colombia. The dollars now available with the peso-brokers are again sold at a premium to persons engaged in the import and export trade. Through invoice manipulation, these importers and exporters further avoid customs duties which in turn causes a lot of damage to the already fragile Latin American economies. These dollars are also sold by peso-brokers to smugglers who again wreak havoc on the economies of Latin America. The only reason this system can be classified as an underground banking system is because it eliminates the physical movement of money and also incorporates certain principles of correspondent banking.

THE FRONTS THROUGH WHICH THESE SYSTEMS OPERATE

The underground banks operate through fronts such as money transmission services, in places like Hong Kong, Singapore, Dubai, London and New York. In the context of the Chinese underground banking system, the underground bankers also operate through gold shops and silver shops as fronts: anyone who has been to Bangkok can see a series of gold shops in a certain street which are in essence underground banks. Foreign exchange dealers/moneychangers are also very popular fronts for underground banking, especially amongst the ethnic communities such as Indians, Chinese and the Hispanics. Then, of course, there are legitimate businesses all over the world which provide an effective umbrella for these underground bankers to carry out their activities under a highly effective camouflage.

THEIR *MODUS OPERANDI*

For these underground and parallel banking systems to operate, communication of data from one underground banker to another has to take place. The methods adopted by underground bankers are generally quite unconventional, and they do not leave a paper trail or try to obscure them. As an example, one piece of a playing card or a currency note torn into two pieces when matched with the other piece facilitates payment. In another instance, a man might go to a Chinese gold shop with a sugar cube having an elephant drawn on it; such a sugar cube might denote a payment of £1 million-worth of gold. On seeing the sugar cube the gold shop owner transfers the gold from one shelf to another to facilitate the transaction in the favour of the holder of the sugar cube: after this, the sugar cube can just be swallowed, having done its job.

WHAT MAKES THEM TICK?

These underground systems exist in the Indian and Chinese context because both those communities feel comfortable with them, having used them over several centuries. Moreover, they find these systems cheaper, speedier and more reliable than conventional banking systems. Trust engendered over several countries is the central pillar around which these systems revolve. In contrast, in the Latin American context, the underground system operates mainly because of expediency; as already mentioned, fear is the key to these Latin American underground systems and greed is a critical element which fuels them.

GEOGRAPHICAL SPREAD

The geographical spread of these underground banking systems is wide, amongst both the Indian and Chinese communities. The main reason for this is the Indian diaspora, spread all over the world, due to population pressure, plus the urge to seek opportunities abroad; as a result one finds that Indians are settled in practically every continent of the world, especially in Europe, America and the Middle East. The existence of the Chinese diaspora, which in fact is more widespread, can be gauged from the fact that in most of the big cities of the world there is what is known as Chinatown. More or less the same reasons as those indicated for the Indian diaspora are responsible for the Chinese diaspora; however, one major factor which led the Chinese to move out of mainland China in large numbers was the persecution, insecurity and lack of freedom which they had to face when communism was on the rise in China.

Regarding the spread of the Latin American underground banking system, it is again linked to the distribution of the Hispanic population in North America. Detailed demographic studies to measure the extent and spread of these communities all over the world might yield some interesting information with regard to the underground banking practices being followed by them. It is also necessary to mention here that ethnic and family ties have further reinforced the Indian/Chinese/Hispanic diaspora worldwide.

The Indian and Chinese communities in their countries of adoption have also spawned local variants of the underground and parallel banking systems, e.g., 'Poey-Kuan' in Thailand and 'Che-Whe' in Trinidad and Tobago.

OPERATION IN RELATION TO ECONOMIC SYSTEMS AND CURRENCIES

These underground and parallel banking systems operate in both developed and developing economies. They also operate in relation to fully convertible currencies and currencies subject to exchange controls. A deliberate misconception that has been generated is that the systems operate because of beneficial exchange rates in the context of developing countries. This misconception becomes amply clear or falls by the wayside because even in developed countries with no exchange control regulations, people and criminals do stay underground for reasons other than beneficial exchange rates. In the context of this misconception, the linking of the passage of the Foreign Exchange

Maintenance Act (FEMA) which has now replaced the Foreign Exchange Regulation Act (FERA) with the passage of the Money Laundering Bill in India was one of the most unfortunate developments for quite some time. It was only when the simple basic point was brought out in informal discussions that beneficial exchange rates were not the main driving force behind the underground and parallel banking system that the passage of FEMA independently of the Money Laundering Bill took place in the Indian Parliament.

AVAILABILITY OF FUNDS IN ORDER TO OPERATE

It is quite obvious that underground bankers must have funds/money to make this system operate. The major source of funds for these underground bankers are the legitimate earnings of the Indian and Chinese communities. Invoice manipulation in the context of imports and exports from developing countries constitutes a major portion of funds that become available to the underground bankers. Money from crimes such as organized crimes/drug trafficking/bribery and corruption, especially in defence deals, is another major source of funds for the underground banks. These funds are mopped up by underground bankers through agents operating in a tier system.

Advertising in the local press is another method used by underground bankers to mobilize these funds: through these advertisement generally the Indian and Chinese communities are targeted for mobilization of funds. Underground bankers also manage to obtain large portions of their funds by seeking hot money in financial havens.

AS A MEANS OF LAUNDERING MONEY

The underground banking systems are useful for laundering money in countries with exchange controls. They are also used fairly extensively to launder money in countries where there are no exchange controls. The underground and parallel banking systems offer two great advantages for laundering money; the first is that they eliminate the physical movement of money; the second is that they obliterate or obscure the paper trail. Moreover, these systems used in conjunction with conventional money laundering make the task of tracking down money well-nigh impossible, because in a certain batch of transactions, the paper trail is missing and even the silver lining of a paper trail in the conventional money laundering circuit is of no use, because it would lead to a dead end.

SOME EXAMPLES OF LAUNDERING THROUGH UNDERGROUND BANKING SYSTEMS

A straightforward case of money laundering through the underground system[3]

The simplest example that can be given is that of simulating a fake export of, say, highly sophisticated machinery, while the thing being exported is actually junk; the value of

---

[3] See Figure XII.1 for a depiction of this type of operation.

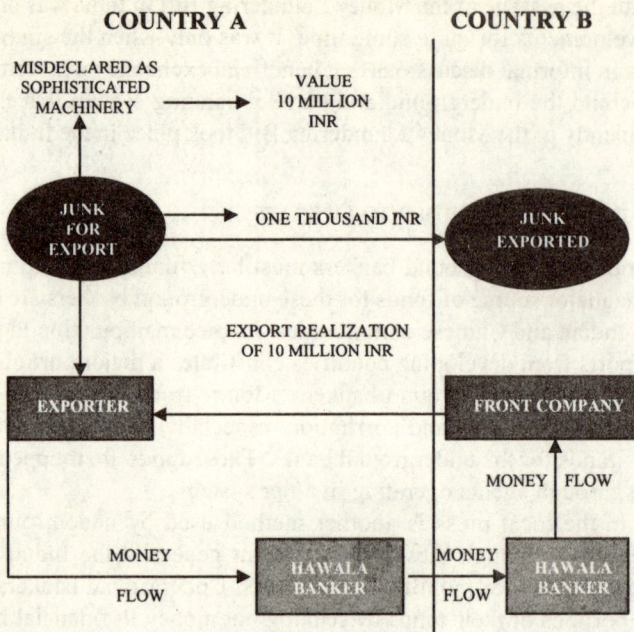

COUNTRY A   COUNTRY B

MISDECLARED AS
SOPHISTICATED   VALUE
MACHINERY   10 MILLION
                                          INR

JUNK
FOR   ONE THOUSAND INR   JUNK
EXPORT   EXPORTED

                    EXPORT REALIZATION
                    OF 10 MILLION INR

EXPORTER   FRONT COMPANY

                                                MONEY   FLOW

MONEY   HAWALA   MONEY   HAWALA
               BANKER   BANKER
FLOW   FLOW

Figure XII.1. A simple case of money laundering through hawala.

junk in this case is nominal, say INR 1,000/-, whereas the stated value of the export runs into a few million INR; in this *modus operandi*, the hawala route is used to send the stated value of exports (which could be criminal money) outside the country, to be repatriated as laundered export proceeds, in the form of foreign exchange through fronts/fictitious companies or business associates based abroad.

*A case of laundering through the underground banking system,
with the element of fraud*[4]

Another illustration is that of the export of garments, which involves both money laundering and fraud; in this case some rags worth 50 million INR were exported to the Middle East, although the stated value of these rags was in the region of 1 billion INR as they were mis-declared as garments; the fraud aspect here is that money amounting to 200 million INR, in the form of duty drawbacks, which is a form of incentive given to exporters, was received

---

[4] See Figure XII.2 for a depiction of this type of operation.

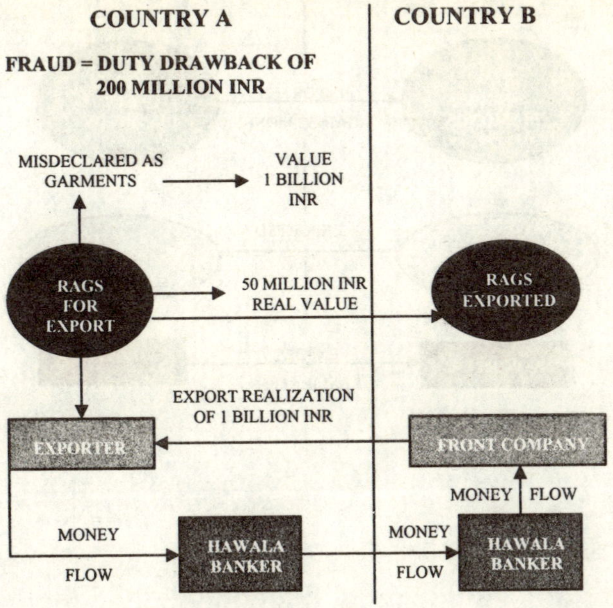

COUNTRY A | COUNTRY B

FRAUD = DUTY DRAWBACK OF
200 MILLION INR

MISDECLARED AS
GARMENTS ⟶ VALUE
1 BILLION
INR

RAGS
FOR
EXPORT

50 MILLION INR
REAL VALUE

RAGS
EXPORTED

EXPORT REALIZATION
OF 1 BILLION INR

EXPORTER ← FRONT COMPANY

MONEY FLOW

MONEY

FLOW

HAWALA
BANKER

MONEY

FLOW

HAWALA
BANKER

Figure XII.2 A case of money laundering plus fraud through hawala.

from the government on the fraudulent value of exports, in this case stated to be 1 billion INR. Coming to the money laundering aspect of the case, 1 billion INR of criminal money is sent out through the hawala route to the Middle East, and then realized as laundered export earnings in the form of foreign exchange through a front company.

The diamond trade, underground banking systems and money laundering[5]

Perhaps the most interesting example of underground banking in the context of money laundering is that of the diamond trade in India, which runs into 400 billion INR, or US$9 billion. Prior to the last budget there was no duty on either uncut raw diamonds or cut and polished diamonds – although it was a controlled activity and continues to be so. The diamond trade is dominated by a very close-knit group of Gujaratis; it also utilizes a section of a community hailing from the south of India which specializes in smuggling of diamonds and uses the hawala route to launder money.

[5] See Figures XII.3, (a), (b) and (c) for a depiction of the *modus operandi* of the diamond trade, underground banking systems and money laundering.

(a)

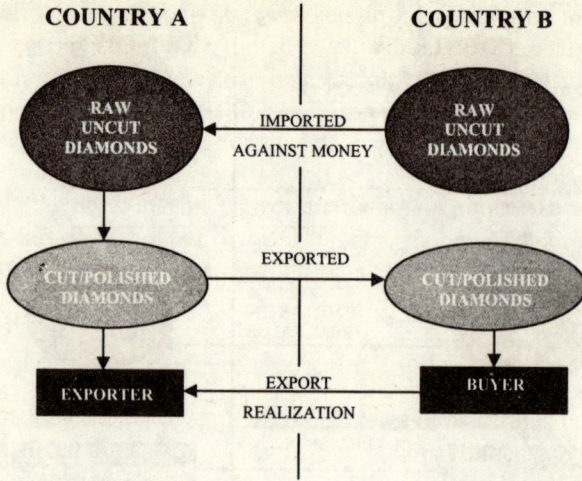

(b)

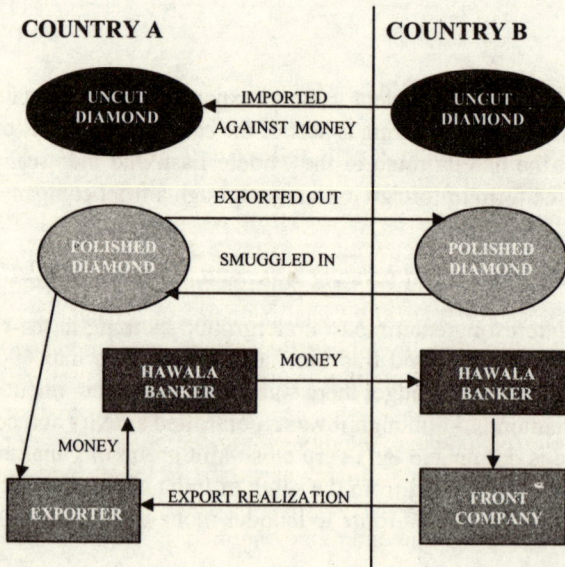

(c)

COUNTRY A   **COUNTRY B**

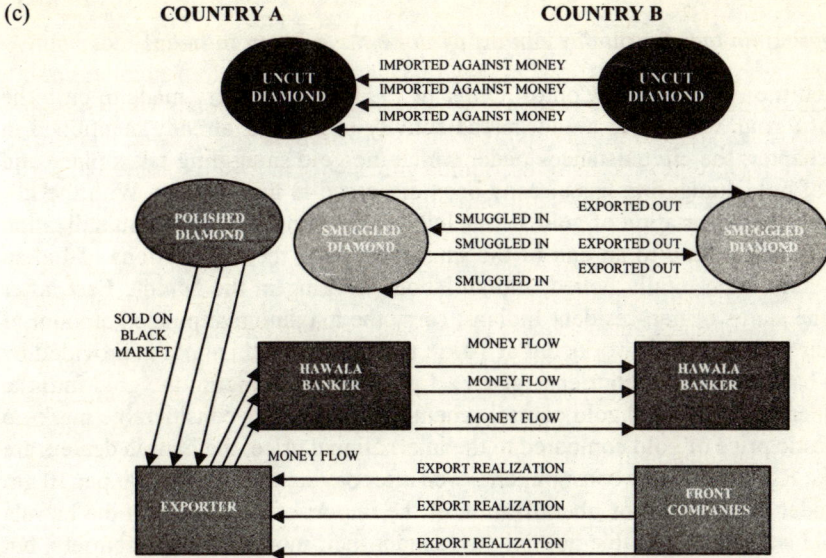

Figure XII.3. (a), (b), (c) The diamond trade and smuggling: money laundering through hawala.

The mechanics of this trade are that first raw diamonds are imported into the country; one consignment of these diamonds is polished, and then exported to a centre in Europe, say Brussels; then this same consignment of diamonds which was exported is smuggled in and out of the country on a number of occasions, to show an export on paper against raw diamonds, which are being continually imported, cut and polished to be sold on the black market in the national economy at a premium, instead of being exported. For each import of raw diamonds and for each consignment of smuggled diamonds that has been re-exported, an export realization has to be extant, for which money is sent out through the hawala route; it is by way of this export realization in foreign exchange through the hawala route that the premium earned in the black market sale of diamonds is laundered.

In all the cases referred to above, the money launderers are killing two birds with one stone: they are laundering criminal money as export proceeds, and they are saving on income tax, because only 20 per cent of export proceeds are taxable at present.

The illustration relating to fraud and money laundering becomes all the more relevant in the context of the widespread complicity of Indian customs in such crimes, as is evident in the arrest of top custom boss B.P. Verma on bribery charges by the Central Bureau of Investigation in 2000.

Gold smuggling (in the present day context of money laundering in India)

With the abolition of the Gold Control Order in 1993 attempts were made to curb the smuggling of gold, which was a widespread activity in India as already mentioned in an earlier chapter; the circumstances under which the gold smuggling takes place and the extent of gold smuggling has already been discussed in that chapter. With the liberalization of the importation of gold, it was felt that the approach of decriminalization of an activity might lead to an end of the same. However, the expectations of Indian authorities have been totally belied; Indian labour working in the Middle East, after achieving the status of non-resident Indians, carry the maximum stipulated amount of gold on their person, which works out at 10 kg; the money for this gold is provided by the hawala bankers and the courier is given a free ticket for bringing the gold into the country under the liberalized gold control scheme. Since there is considerable mark-up in the domestic price of gold compared to the international price, the hawala dealers are able to make Rs. 400,000 per consignment, even after paying duty of Rs. 400 per 10 gm of gold. Under this scheme of liberalization of the import of gold through the hawala dealers, gold smugglers are able not only to launder their money through couriers, but also to earn substantial profits; this whole process can also be termed 'disguised smuggling'.

Funding of terrorism in Jammu and Kashmir[6]

As already mentioned, terrorists use the underground banking system very extensively to send funds to their areas of operation. For example, terrorism in Jammu and Kashmir is being funded extensively through the hawala route. Money which ends up with hawala operators in big cities like Delhi finds its way to terrorists in Jammu and Kashmir through the network of wholesale and retail dealers. Movement of funds through underground banking systems to finance the terrorist incidents of 11 September 2001 have also been noted.

Underground banking in the context of national economy

Another sinister development regarding countries with a very high level of black economy is the use of underground banking to move the money in the local economy. For instance, in India where the black money component is as high as 50 per cent of GDP, most black marketeers do not carry money on their person while travelling from one place to another; these black marketeers have coded numbers which are honoured by a domestic network of underground bankers to facilitate transactions in black money. Obviously, such a development has implications as regards money laundering, because it makes the task of tracking down black money more difficult still.

---

[6] See Figure XII.4 for a depiction of this type operation.

MIDDLE EAST | INDIA

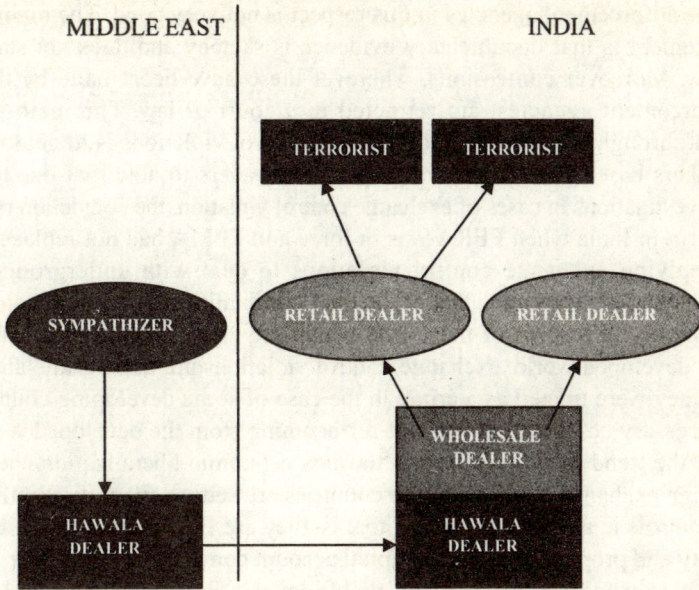

Figure XII.4. Funding of terrorism in Jammu and Kashmir.

LINKAGE BETWEEN DRUG TRAFFICKING, GOLD SMUGGLING AND HAWALA

There has been a lot of theorizing on the possibility that proceeds of drugs go to pay for smuggling (gold and other luxury goods) and that these transactions are conducted through underground bankers (hawala) in the context of the Indian subcontinent. There seems to be some truth in barter arrangements in the context of the Middle East.

ESTIMATES OF AMOUNTS INVOLVED

In 1991, the Indian Working Group on underground banking, on the basis of certain parameters, had made some projections of the amount of money transactions through hawala bankers; it was estimated that this system processed $10–20 billion per year; this figure must obviously be much higher today.

HOW TO COUNTER THESE UNDERGROUND AND PARALLEL BANKING SYSTEMS

Exchange control regulations

In most of the developing countries attempts have been made to tackle these systems through detection of the violation of exchange control regulations; however, the track record of the enforcement agencies in this respect is not very good. The main reason for poor enforcement is that documentary evidence is sketchy and does not stand up in a court of law. Moreover confessions, wherever these have been made by the accused before enforcement agencies, are retracted in a court of law. The main problem in enforcement through the approach of exchange control violations is to get to the underground bankers based abroad. It is of interest for readers to note that due to the tardy nature of investigations in cases of exchange control violation, the conviction rate was less than 1 per cent in India when FERA was in force and FEMA had not replaced it.

While applying exchange control violations to deal with underground bankers, another problem that crops up is that of the dual criminality requirement; countries offer co-operation only in respect of those acts which are also crimes in their countries. In most of the developed world, exchange control violations are not a crime and therefore even when they were treated as a crime in the case of some developing countries in the past, the necessary co-operation was not forthcoming from the developed world.

However, the trend worldwide now is towards economic liberalization and the abolition of foreign exchange controls. Some countries are setting about dismantling foreign exchange controls in a phased manner – that is, they are first shifting to current account convertibility and propose to go on to capital account convertibility at a later stage when their foreign exchange reserves reach viable levels. Even now the trend is to treat exchange control violations in a lenient manner because several countries have enacted laws treating them as civil offences. The above trends with regard to exchange control violations are also operating in India.

However, the leniency with regard to exchange control violations needs to be circumscribed, particularly when these violations are used to pursue acts of a serious criminal nature. This criminalization of exchange control violations can be done by including them in the schedule of offences of laws/proposed laws to deal with transnational crimes. In the law on money laundering in the Indian context, to place FEMA in the schedule of offences of the Indian Money Laundering Act – which is not the case now – would go a long way in ensuring that underground banking systems are not used to launder money.

By licensing their activities

Some countries have devised a system of licences to deal with underground bankers. Under this system, the underground bankers are required to obtain licences from the appropriate authorities and to operate under certain regulations. Informal money transmission services/houses in free ports such as Hong Kong and Singapore have generally been brought under such an ambit of licensing. The principal deterrence in this system of licensing the activities of underground bankers is the threat of the revocation of a licence in the case of misuse of the same. However, licensing by its very nature also brings certain attendant problems, the main problem being with regard to supervision when there are a very large number of licencees, and the other being corruption in such a system of attendant controls.

By use of fiscal laws

Some countries have also sought to tackle the underground and parallel banking systems through use of their fiscal laws. In the UK, such an approach was tried whereby the entire proceeds of the underground bankers were taxed if they were unable to explain the source of the funds.

Moreover, countries also need to be aware of the implications of avoidance of double taxation treaties regarding exchange of information between countries with regard to underground banking systems. Often very useful information can be exchanged under these treaties, which is admissible evidence in a court of law. These treaties are also another way to circumvent the problem of dual criminality which generally crops up with regard to extending co-operation in exchange control violation cases.

By criminalizing the underground banking systems

Perhaps the most effective way to deal with underground banking systems is to criminalize them. Once criminalization of the systems takes place, co-ordination of several agencies charged with enforcement would need to be ensured at the national level; a central enforcement agency could perform such a function.

Another problem with which the criminalization of the underground and parallel banking systems would have to deal is the amorphous nature of proof that is generally available in these cases. This problem could be overcome by making undercover operations and electronic surveillance admissible evidence; these provisions of law would also ensure that successful prosecution of underground bankers takes place in the long run.

Since underground bankers are operating across several countries, provision for search and seizure of documentary evidence in other countries and admissibility of the same would also need to be incorporated in treaties and conventions on the subject.

Another requirement of the criminal law relating to the recording of oral evidence of witnesses based in other countries which is a hindrance in the successful prosecution of cases, is the prohibitive costs involved in witnesses travelling to record their evidence in the country where the trial is to take place and also enabling their necessary cross-examination. With rapid advances in technology these prohibitive costs with regard to recording of oral evidence of witnesses could be made considerably cheaper, for example, through video conferencing.

Development of data banks

To deal effectively with underground bankers, databanks at the national level/regional levels are a must. They are non-existent at the national level, even in countries where underground banking is fairly prevalent, e.g., India. Of course, the inputs into these databanks have to be meaningful and would need to cover not only all the relevant information about the underground bankers, but also information pertaining to their associates;

the *modi operandi* of these underground bankers would also be a very useful input. With the help of these databanks, strategic intelligence could be developed, which by giving an overall picture of their activities would enable enforcement agencies to come up with well-co-ordinated enforcement actions to deal with underground bankers in an effective manner.

Databanks are also very useful tools for developing tactical intelligence for investigation of cases. Intelligence analysts perform a very useful role in developing tactical intelligence to work on certain important cases having a wide network, and they must be an integral part of every databank. While on the issue of information and databanks, the role of hard intelligence in countering the activities of underground bankers can never be discounted. Hard intelligence goes a long way towards hitting the underground bankers where it hurts them most; for instance, a large haul of gold linked to underground banking can knock the bottom out of several underground banks and put an end to their thriving activities.

Role of regional/international organizations

The role of regional/international organizations would become much more important in areas of strategic/tactical intelligence once databanks are in place. Moreover regional/international organizations could play a very critical role in co-ordination of investigations against underground bankers spread across several countries. These regional/international organizations could also provide a useful forum for symposiums/seminars/working group meetings to chalk out effective strategies and better co-ordination in the investigation of cases.

By making regular banking channels more attractive

Making regular banking channels more attractive is another way of dealing with underground and parallel banking systems, in the context of developing countries. The endeavour should be to make the banking channels speedier, cheaper and more reliable; computerization and technology would obviously play a very important role in this process. Moreover, the regular banking channels would have to become more competitive in terms of exchange rates, to put the underground bankers out of business.

By floating development bonds offering attractive rates of interest

There was a time in the early 1990s when the foreign exchange reserves of India were so low that only 15 days' imports could be catered for. At that point in time the Central Bank of the Government of India (Reserve Bank of India) had to lift gold and take it out of the country to raise the much-needed foreign exchange reserves. Of course, this withdrawal of gold to raise foreign exchange reserves is not a process that could go on indefinitely. Ultimately, the Indian government came up with a scheme for India Development Bonds offering an attractive rate of interest, which was higher than that prevailing in the international market. These India Development Bonds were basically targeted at the very large NRI population. Apart from handsome returns being offered by the bonds, another factor that prompted the NRIs to invest in them was patriotic fervour and a sort of craving to uphold the dignity of the country; ultimately US$5 billion were mopped up through these India Development Bonds. Similarly, following the testing of nuclear devices in 1999, many countries imposed embargoes on development aid to India; these embargoes were also overcome by floating the Resurgent India Bonds along the same lines as the India Development Bonds; through the Resurgent India Bonds another US$4.2 billion were mobilized by the Government of India. In fact, this system of floating bonds gave a tremendous boost to India's foreign exchange reserves; despite being a trade deficit country vis-à-vis exports versus imports, India's foreign exchange reserves today stand at a staggering $72 billion; of course, a substantial portion of that sum is in the form of NRI remittances.

Thus, it can be seen that floating development bonds can also effectively starve the underground bankers of much-needed funds to operate the underground systems.

By attacking links between the underground banking systems

Mention has already been made of how these systems are linked to various activities, some of which are not only undesirable but downright criminal. Attacking these links between the underground banking systems is another important way of indirectly tackling them. Some of the important links that need to be tackled on a war footing in order to deal effectively with underground bankers are those relating to invoice manipulation and proceeds of crime as a source of funds for these systems. In a more positive sense, another very important link that needs to be tackled is to make existing banking channels more attractive by making them more reliable, speedier and cheaper.

One could list several such links and they might vary from country to country; perhaps each country/region has to devise effective strategies to counter those links which fuel the underground banking systems.

PART III

HOW CRIME AND MONEY LAUNDERING IMPINGE ON NATIONAL SECURITY AND ECONOMIC LIBERALIZATION

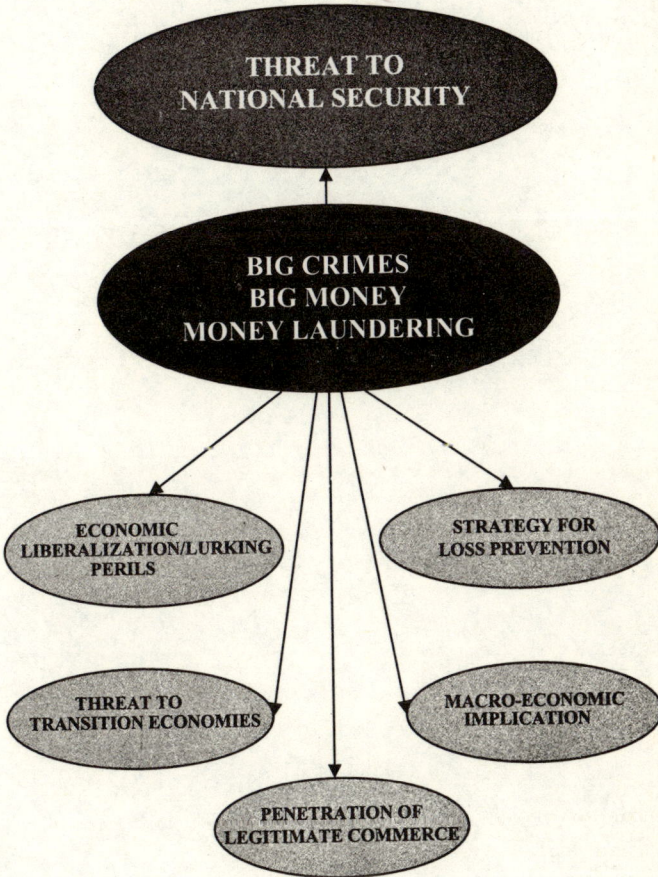

CHAPTER XIII

MONEY LAUNDERING: IMPLICATIONS FOR NATIONAL SECURITY

NATIONAL SECURITY

Importance in affairs of state

National security is certainly a matter of utmost concern demanding the highest attention. To illustrate this point, I would like to take the readers many years back in time when I was working for Interpol in France; the year was 1989 and the Berlin Wall was coming down. During those momentous days an article appeared in *The Times* written by a mysterious person called only 'Z'. This article dealt with the collapse of communism in the Soviet Union and the erstwhile totalitarian states of Eastern Europe and what the Western response to it should be in political and economic terms. This was one article that highlighted the national security concerns on a global scale in a very dramatic manner in a scenario which could hardly be visualized at the time the article was written. Considering the important issues raised in this article by 'Z', it was ascribed to the highest of quarters by the persons who are supposed to be 'in the know' in the intelligence world. Subsequently, in a sequel to the article (which was a bit of a damp squib) it was revealed that 'Z' was a university professor in the United States.

Attempts to define it

One of the objectives of this book is to analyse the national security dimension and to project how the proceeds of crime and money laundering impinge upon national security. In order to analyse the national security dimension one has first to define national security. Moreover, in the context of this study, the economic element of national security needs to be highlighted.

I have read many books and articles on national security in order to educate myself on the subject; with the same objective in view, I have also interacted with experts in the field. Most of the articles and books dwell on the concept of national security with 'defence' as the main theme; of course, the nuclear dimension is also thrown in when one is talking about defence.

There is not much literature on national security as an all-embracing concept. As regards the economic aspect of national security, it has periodically engaged the attention of thinkers, and some have written at length on this concept. To be frank, I have not come across a really suitable and comprehensive definition of national security.

137

Some thinkers (Merton Berkowitz and P.G. Bock) have attempted to define national security in terms of ensuring the value system for which a nation stands: this value system could be secularism and democracy in the context of a particular nation. Though from a philosophical standpoint this definition might be eminently suitable, for a more pragmatic approach by a practitioner in the field it might not be adequate in terms of all of the parameters that have to be tackled.

Most articles on national security, whether they have a defence, economic or other orientation, are generally based on a situational context, for example, a cold war or post-cold war scenario, and touch upon some aspects of national security in terms of models of various sorts, e.g. a mercantilist model, laissez-faire or liberal model, geo-economic model or political economy of national security model. At this stage, these 'economic models' – selected deliberately in the context of this study – should briefly be explained.

In the mercantilist model – whose greatest proponent was Gustav Schmoller – the aim is to enhance the power of the state through economic means. This model ultimately found a logical corollary in the laissez-faire model of Adam Smith; laissez-faire means 'let act', and this model, while advocating free trade, also recommends certain restrictions in areas which touch upon national security. According to the geo-economic model – which had as its main proponent Edward Luttwak – since economic power is the major source of all power, economic domination is the ultimate agenda in a world where the likelihood of military conflict is becoming increasingly remote. The political economy of national security model – propounded by Aswin Ray – sets forth the argument as to how this model led to the emergence of power blocks in the world which were not in the interest of many of the countries concerned.

Even the cabinet secretariat resolution no. 281/29.6.98/TS of 16 April 1999 setting up the National Security Council for India fails to give a satisfactory definition of national security. To appreciate this point the resolution is quoted in full:

> *'The Central Government recognizes that national security management requires integrated thinking and coordinated application of the political, military, diplomatic, scientific and technological resources of the state to protect and promote national security goals and objectives. National security in the context of the nation, needs to be viewed not only in military terms but also in terms of internal security, economic security, technological strength and foreign policy. The role of the council is to advise the Central Government on the said matters.'*

Another feature of the articles written on national security in the context of India is that they are more concerned with setting up an institutional framework for national security, because it has been the perception of most 'experts' that lack of such an institutional framework was responsible for India not being able to safeguard its national security adequately the 1948 war with Pakistan, the 1962 war with China, the 1965 war with Pakistan and the Kargil fiasco in 1999. India's success in the 1971 war, which led to the creation of Bangladesh, has been attributed to charismatic leadership that enabled a 'makeshift inter-disciplinary working group' to co-ordinate the war effort in a very successful manner. Most of the articles concerned with the institutional framework do not make any attempt to define national security, or even if they do so, it is in a very cursory manner. Perhaps they assume that everyone knows what national security is: to cite an example, at the most the article might quote someone like McNamara, who described national security as follows: 'security means development into a modernizing society; security is not just military hardware though it may involve it – security is not a traditional activity though it may encompass it'. Such a definition coming from a former Defence Secretary of the US would be in order, but it is certainly not an appropriate definition to be quoted by a person claiming to be an authority on this subject.

HISTORICAL PERSPECTIVE

At this stage a historical perspective, particularly from an economic angle, is also worth examining before arriving at a comprehensive definition of national security. Lord Macaulay once made the statement that seeds of power lie in army and religion. When he made this statement perhaps he was slightly off the mark, because he totally discounted the enormous economic power which Great Britain wielded as a result of its vast territorial empire: perhaps His Lordship took the economic prowess for granted. Although the nineteenth century belonged to Great Britain, the twentieth century in its first half also witnessed two world wars which resulted from the conflicting economic and imperial interests of the European powers. In the context of world wars, the importance of the economic factor needs to be emphasized, because most countries also had a ministry for economic warfare to undermine the economic strength of the enemy. Coming on the heels of the two world wars, the process of decolonization was supposed to usher in an era of 'freedom' in the world. Quite a few have argued, however, that though decolonization led to the demise of one form of imperialism, i.e. political imperialism, it led in turn to growth of another form of imperialism, economic imperialism. The great powers of yore realized that perhaps it was more profitable and less cumbersome to practise economic imperialism, which was not easily discernible.

The post-Second World War world also became divided into two blocs; one advocating planned economy and socialism, the other advocating free market economy. This struggle between socialism and free market economy has finally been resolved in favour of the free market economy and the whole world, since the demise of communism in the 1990s, has embraced the liberal economic model. Today economic liberalization and greater integration are the two phrases by which most nations love to swear, but several, lacking the necessary courage or wherewithal, are hesitant to take the final plunge, pondering over the famous words of Lloyd George that 'there can be no greater mistake in life than to try and cross an abyss in two leaps'.

Economic liberalization and greater integration of the world economy can also be considered a mixed blessing in the context of the economic security of nations; if, on the one hand, it affords opportunities for growth, on the other hand it makes one vulnerable on the same count. As stated earlier, several nations, realizing that 'military wars are passé', are swearing by the doctrine of economic domination as their overriding goal because, in their perception, this domination would enable them to wield enormous power in all domains affecting nations.

It would also be pertinent to examine – in the context of historical perspective – how the concept of national security has been treated by kings, queens, states/nations over the ages. A cursory survey of history reveals that there have been sagacious statesmen who were well aware of this concept of national security, in a subconscious sense, and who took decisions in their own peculiar way which were wise and proved to be profitable not only to their own kingdoms/states but also to other actors in the drama. On the other hand, there have also been the 'great blunderers' of history who had no grasp of this concept of national security and in utter disregard of the interest of nations, including their own, plunged the world into devastating wars.

Prior to the two world wars in the twentieth century, one could say that nations/states had only a hazy idea about the concept of national security as it is understood today. In fact, it was the haziness associated with this concept that made the United States prevaricate to an extent before taking the decision to enter the two world wars on the side of the Allies. It was the dilemma 'to be or not to be' confronting the United States in both world wars that led many people subsequently to think about the concept of national security and to evolve and clarify the issues related thereto. Initially, of course, the thrust of national security definitely had a defence-oriented bias which became further accentuated due to the nuclear dimension in the cold war era. Subsequently, of course, several other aspects of national security were explored. Not only was the United States content with theorizing on the concept of national security, but it also put into place a National Security Council as long ago as 1947.

ANOTHER ATTEMPT AT DEFINITION

What exactly is national security? Simply put, it means securing the nation. The nation has to be made secure both externally and internally; thus, it has both an external and an internal dimension. In its most restrictive sense, national security is confined to the defence of 'a state' from external and internal enemies. Taken in a broader perspective, it would embrace all those sectors which make a nation strong and also those which sap its strength. Defence-preparedness and economic strength are perhaps the bedrock on which national security rests. In India, a Group of Ministers in 2001, while finalizing the recommendations of the Sub-Committees on National Security following the Kargil fiasco, indirectly attempted to define national security by stating that 'military might alone does not guarantee either sovereignty or security. The more realistic approach also includes economic strength, internal cohesion and technologies. A strong sense of nationalism and good governance also form an integral part of national security.' It would not be wrong to state here that such indirect definitions of national security, though strong on rhetoric, are lacking in substance.

NATIONAL SECURITY: IN TERMS OF COMPONENTS OF THE STATE

Perhaps a definition of national security in the conventional sense is not possible. The definitional aspect of national security can best be tackled by elaborating the various components of a state and by explaining how these components are or become related to national security. Vis-à-vis national security, the components of a state which need to be considered in all their ramifications are polity, population, economic well-being, the socio-cultural milieu, strategic interests, diplomacy, intelligence and good governance.

Polity

In the context of national security, 'polity' would encompass whether the state is a republic or a monarchy, whether it is a democracy or a totalitarian state, whether it is a federation, confederation or otherwise, whether it is secular or based on religion, whether the form of government is based on division of functions between the executive, judiciary and legislature, or otherwise. The extent to which these features of a nation's polity are considered as 'ensuring the value system of the nation', as stated earlier, is the extent to which they become vital in the context of the national security of a given state.

Population

It is obvious that the age range of the population is linked to their productive levels, the rate of growth of population over a period of time and not only their literacy levels, but also the content and quality of education they receive, have a strong bearing on national security.

Economic well-being

When one considers the economic well-being of a nation, the spheres of economic activity which assume importance are agriculture, industry, services, national resources and technology levels; capacity for resource mobilization in the most effective manner is an important concomitant of economic well-being, and the ultimate yardstick to judge it is, of course, the standard of living. From the above, it is evident that economic well-being is an important indicator of the economic strength of the state, which in turn is a vital component of national security.

Socio-cultural milieu

When one refers to socio-cultural milieu, the matters that one would be referring to are those relating to religion, language, ethnicity, social ferment, fine arts and thought processes – all of which, depending upon the orientation that they assume, could be cementing factors or disturbing elements for a national security matrix.

Strategic interests

Strategic interests for any state would be determined in the first instance by its geopolitical situation, which means both the physical geography and the political environment: a landlocked country is at a disadvantage, as is a country surrounded by hostile neighbours. The geographical spread of the population of a state in other regions of the world could also be a factor in determining its strategic interest. For some states the security of supply of certain vital commodities, for example oil, might be the overriding strategic interest, because these states might be lacking this natural resource. Strategic interests which obviously have a very vital bearing on national security would differ from state to state and would have to be determined by every state in a comprehensive manner in order to be able to safeguard them.

Military prowess

To ensure its national security, military prowess is the ultimate weapon in the armoury of the state. States need the back-up of military prowess to defend themselves or to push through their strategic interests in the international arena. Military prowess is again of two types: one comprises the conventional forces and the other the nuclear arsenal. Most states endeavour to optimize their conventional forces, a nuclear arsenal being possessed by a select few; moreover, there is a worldwide effort at the containment of the nuclear ability, considering its destructive potential. It should be pointed out here that the nuclear dimension plays a very critical role in the national security environment; several doctrines such as the 'nuclear umbrella', 'deterrence' (in its various manifestations) and 'disarmament' have been developed with regard to these weapons.

Foreign policy

Foreign policy is another important component of the state which has a bearing on its national security. It is the lament of not a few diplomats the world over that the full potential of diplomacy, which is a lower-cost option than defence, has not been exploited in the realm of national security.

Intelligence

Intelligence can be described as a form of foreknowledge which eases the pain of decision-making in matters affecting the security of the state; many legends exist as to the role played by intelligence in safeguarding the same. Intelligence comes into play in internal matters of the state and also in the external sphere. As an instrument of state policy, intelligence needs to be fully exploited because it is the lowest-cost option, compared to both defence and diplomacy, in ensuring the security of the state.

Good governance

Good governance, especially in the present-day set-up, is another essential prerequisite for safeguarding the state; in fact, good governance would go a long way in strengthening all the components of the state discussed so far in relation to national security.

INSTITUTIONAL FRAMEWORK FOR NATIONAL SECURITY

Although with most states national security is a prime concern the primacy accorded to it and the National Security Council in the United States is perhaps unique. Following much debate as to how best to deal with national security, India, which has recently acquired nuclear capability, has also set up an institutional framework of sorts – also known as the National Security Council, and the National Security Advisory Board. However, one should caution that too much obsession with national security, which has recently been witnessed in India, is also not desirable, because then it tends to become an end in itself. The main objective that needs to be always borne in mind, so far as national security is concerned, is whether it ensures peace, which in turn, would create conditions for a better life.

NATIONAL SECURITY: IN THE CONTEXT OF GLOBALIZATION

To be relevant, any discussion of national security must also be viewed in the international context. One is living today in a fast-changing world. Trade and commerce propelled by the World Trade Organization are likely to increase still further. The world is also heading towards a greater integration of its financial and banking systems. Several demographic changes due to shifts of population driven by greater opportunities are also taking place. The way tourism is spreading, the world is almost like a global village. Most of the recent advances are due to the ease of communication which is technology driven. The advances in computer science have led to the growth of a new environment, known as cyberspace, which is posing a serious challenge to established national boundaries. Here one is also tempted to refer to the economic boundaries of nations about which the German philosopher Fichte talked in the nineteenth century and which are becoming real in the context of regional economic groupings like the European Economic Community and ASEAN. Revolutionary advances in biotechnology are likely to further alter the quality of life in the world. Increasing globalization seems to be the trend now and the national security matrix of any given state has to take account of this new world order.

MANIFESTATION OF CRIME IN THE CONTEXT OF COMPONENTS OF THE STATE

Having discussed and defined national security at length, let us now examine two other points impinging upon national security in the context of this book. The first relates to major crimes and their proceeds, the second relates to the money laundering dimension of these proceeds of crime. Before one considers the interplay between national security, crime and

NATIONAL SECURITY	**Polity**	a.	Republic/monarchy
		b.	Democracy/totalitarian
		c.	Federation/confederation/otherwise
		d.	Secular/based on religion
		e.	Government based on division of functions between the executive, judiciary and legislature or otherwise.
	Population	a.	Health
		b.	Age group and productivity levels
		c.	Rate of growth
		d.	Literacy level – content and quality of education.
	Economic well-being	a.	Agriculture
		b.	Industry
		c.	Services
		d.	Natural resources
		e.	Technology levels
		f.	Capacity for resource mobilization in the most effective manner.
	Socio-cultural milieu	a.	Religion
		b.	Language
		c.	Ethnicity
		d.	Social ferment
		e.	Fine arts
		f.	Thought processes.
	Strategic interests	a.	Geo-political situation
		b.	Geographical spread
		c.	Security of supply of vital commodities
		d.	Individual interests of states.
	Military prowess	a.	Conventional forces
		b.	Nuclear arsenal.
	Foreign policy/ diplomacy		Low-cost option.
	Intelligence		Lowest-cost option.
	Good governance		Essential in itself and for all the other components.

Figure XIII.1. Components/sub-components of the state.

money laundering, it would be of interest to look at Figure XIII.1, in which national security has been broken down into various components and sub-components of the state.

From a cursory glance, it is quite obvious that crime would have to be categorized as a negative socio-economic ferment of its socio-cultural milieu; it could also be considered as a negative element of the economic well-being, because of large-scale economic scams/economic crimes that are surfacing due to the activities of white-collar criminals. Crime could also be categorized under the heading of military prowess, in the context of large-scale bribes and commissions that take place in defence deals and which have been referred to earlier. In the highly materialistic culture which is prevalent in the world today, treason or selling of state secrets is another serious crime that has to be contended with.

One could continue to discuss the crime aspects of all the state-related components of national security listed in the chart at great length, but such a detailed discussion is beyond the scope of this book. Suffice it to say that crime has an impact on practically all aspects of the components of the state, which in turn affect national security. The polity of a nation can be compromised if criminals come to power. The morals of the population and its health can be corrupted by large-scale crimes. Through economic crimes of the types discussed in earlier chapters, tremendous economic damage can be caused to the nation for the sake of personal gain. The socio-cultural milieu can be totally distorted due to widespread crime: even religion, language and ethnicity can be exploited by criminal groups (on their own and at the behest of certain inimical nations) along communal lines in order to further their criminal designs or weaken the nation. Compromising of strategic interests, amounting to treason, has already been referred to, as has military prowess and its connection to crime. Foreign policy and diplomacy are at a discount in the world today because diplomats have failed to become true professionals in addressing the various needs of the nation. Moreover, diplomats can also be influenced by criminals and there have been instances where they have fraternized with them. Intelligence can also be a double-edged sword and has to be utilized with great care by professionals in the field of national security. Good governance is the crying need of large segments of society today in order to enjoy the basic elements of security and certain civic amenities. Thus, it can be seen that crime can impact on practically every facet of national security; only the extent to which it does so may vary.

THREATS TO NATIONAL SECURITY AS A RESULT OF MONEY LAUNDERING

Coming to the money laundering dimension and national security, it is quite obvious that crime money that has been legitimized and washed poses a still greater danger to all the components of national security under discussion. The insidious nature of laundered crime money renders it difficult or even impossible to discover how the vital components of the nation are being sapped by unscrupulous elements. It is obvious that there are certain areas of national security where laundered money would operate in a highly camouflaged way – for instance, the economic well-being of a nation. The socio-cultural milieu and population are other areas where legitimized crime money poses great danger. Dangers posed by proceeds of crime to various components of state impinging upon national security have been mentioned briefly: suffice it to say that with laundered money, there would be a manifold increase in the threat to these components because of their greater vulnerability.

Long ago, following the French Revolution, de Tocqueville remarked that 'eternal vigilance is the price of liberty'. Here one may add a rider that 'eternal vigilance is the price of national security – which in turn can guarantee the liberty of individuals'.

CHAPTER XIV

ECONOMIC LIBERALIZATION: PERILS FACED BY A GROWING ECONOMY

RATIONALE FOR ECONOMIC LIBERALIZATION

The economic well-being of people has always been a matter of prime concern. With this end in view, several economic models have been experimented with, namely, the free market economy, the state-controlled economy (in other words, communism) and the mixed economy (which provides for co-existence of both state and private enterprises). However, it finally dawned on economic thinkers and government policy-makers that excessive government interference in the economy has not been conducive to economic growth: on the contrary, as has often been witnessed, it is detrimental to or has stunted it. Thus, starting in the late 1980s and early 1990s, most governments of the world decided to adopt economic liberalization, with the free market economy as the ultimate goal.

The phenomenon of economic liberalization has been more evident in the developing world. The economic rationale behind economic liberalization has been to achieve higher economic growth, which would ultimately lead to the eradication of poverty through universal prosperity and more equitable distribution of wealth. Other broad objectives of the economic liberalization process have been diversification of the economy and a boost for external trade. The specifics have obviously differed from country to country depending upon the level of state control.

HOW IT TOOK OFF IN INDIA

In India the process of economic liberalization was precipitated by an acute balance of payment crisis in 1991, when its foreign exchange reserves had fallen to such a level that it could barely afford to pay for 15 days of imports. On the foreign exchange front, India's credibility was so low that it had to withdraw gold and pledge it to a bank in London before the much-needed foreign exchange could be released to tide over the crisis. At that time, all of the macro-economic indicators in the economy could aptly be described as 'sick'. Low economic growth rate, widespread poverty, high fiscal deficit as a percentage of gross domestic product (GDP), inflation in double figures, a high interest rate regime and weak external trade were all macro-economic factors mirroring the sickness of the Indian economy. At that critical juncture, a new regime had also taken over in India with a renowned economist as the Finance Minister to put the Indian economy back on the rails.

To set the macro-economic parameters right, a series of reforms were needed immediately in the Indian economy. This series of reforms which were undertaken in the first instance by Dr Manmohan Singh – the then Finance Minister – have also been described as the process of economic liberalization; in economic terms these reforms are known as reforms at the micro-economic level and they basically meant structural reforms in several sectors of the economy.

ECONOMIC LIBERALIZATION IN THE INDIAN CONTEXT AND THE PERILS LURKING

Industrial sector

In the Indian context, economic liberalization in its initial phases meant opening up of the industrial sector (areas reserved for government) to private participation (both from India and abroad) – mostly heavy and medium industries were covered under this; of course, certain critical sectors of the economy relating to defence and impinging upon national security were not deregulated. This process of opening up of Indian industry has been further carried forward in the areas of minerals and mining and oil exploration and refining. At the inception of the opening up of the industrial sector, a certain element of screening was inevitable to ensure that only serious players entered the field and undesirable elements and non-serious participants were excluded.

Infrastructure

For all-round economic development to take place in India, infrastructure development, which had lagged behind considerably and was unable to cope with the demands of a rapidly growing economy, also had to be undertaken as an integral part of economic liberalization. The critical areas of infrastructure development in the Indian context are electricity, roads, ports and irrigation facilities in the form of mega-hydro-electric projects. Since infrastructure development calls for massive investments, which are generally not available to the governments of developing economies, private sector participation and foreign investment become necessary inputs. In the Indian context industrial development in the form of roads – the great quadrilateral (linking the four metro cities, Delhi, Mumbai, Chennai and Kolkata) and the north–south and east–west corridor – are presently under construction, financed through a nominal tax on fuel and other ingenious schemes.

Likewise, ports are being corporatized and their capacity increased to meet the growing demand of external trade. Some of the irrigation projects which had run into rough weather because of environmental issues should, on balance, proceed along the right lines. Electricity generation continues to be a matter of concern because of massive debts under which this sector is groaning; private investment is shying away from it, and power generation is one sector which needs a major overhaul, especially in the context of doing away with 'freebies' and theft of electricity which is generally sought to be passed off as transmission losses.

Agricultural sector

The agricultural sector, which constituted INR 3056.43 billion, or 14.7 per cent of GDP (in 2000–01), is of course critical in any scheme of economic liberalization. The prime requirement of Indian agriculture is greater investment as a percentage of GDP; the rate of investment has declined from 1.6 per cent of GDP in 1993–94 to 1.3 per cent in 1998–99. To ensure an adequate growth rate in the agricultural sector, which should be much above the present level (0.2 per cent in 1999–2000, 5 per cent in 2000–01), greater diversification in cash crops, horticulture, animal husbandry and agriculture-based industries is also needed; such a diversification would also, of course, affect the earning and consumption patterns of the economy as a whole in a positive sense. However, one major problem facing the Indian agricultural sector is being caused by the massive buffer stocks of wheat and paddy which are running as high as 60 million tons at present. These buffer stocks were basically intended to ensure adequate supply of food grains in case of drought; according to experts, 18–20 million tons of buffer stock is sufficient for the country. Excess buffer stock of 40 million tons has created its own peculiar problems in terms of storage/loss and massive food subsidies which are given in the form of minimum support prices to the farmers. The problems of excessive buffer stock are being tackled through exports, food-for-work programmes, greater uptake through the public distribution system, removal of restrictions on free movement of food grains for trade within the country, construction by the private sector of highly sophisticated silos for storage of food grains, etc. However, the problem of excessive subsidy on the food grains, which has also been termed the 'food economy', coupled with unsustainable levels of buffer stock, has to be tackled as a major aspect of economic reforms within the country. The food economy is also highly vulnerable to corruption. The Food Corporation of India, the procurement agency of the government, is notorious for corruption; for instance, when millions of tons of food grains are procured, fudging of the price of a gunny bag of one quintal capacity by INR 1 can lead to misappropriation of millions of INR.

Subsidies

Another area in the context of economic reforms/economic liberalization that needs to be addressed is the question of subsidies. Some forms of subsidies in the Indian context, such as those on food, electricity and fertilizer, are totally undesirable, have contributed significantly to the fiscal deficit and should be done away with in a phased manner, in order to minimize the adverse impact on the farmers. Some other subsidies on exports, in the form of duty drawbacks and tax breaks, are desirable, especially when a country like India is experiencing a trade deficit in terms of imports versus exports. While on the issue of subsidies, it is pertinent to point out that quite a few of these are liable to misuse through fraudulent practices which are further aggravated by the problem of corruption.

Capitalization of markets

Capital is one of the essential requirements of economic development. Thus, increasing capitalization of markets in order to raise equity and debt are an essential requirement of any programme of economic reforms. Equity can be raised directly by companies in the form of primary issues or it could be mobilized through secondary issues which are traded openly in the securities market. Loans can be raised through bonds and several forms of debentures.

The reform process in India, in its initial phases, also gave a tremendous boost to the capitalization of markets. By permitting foreign institutional investors to participate in the Indian equity market a further boost was sought to be given to the same. However, two stock market scams, one in 1992 (the Harshad Mehta scam), the other in 2000 (the Ketan Parikh scam) have dented the credibility of the securities market to a considerable extent. Rather than mete out salutary punishments to the wrongdoers, to describe some of these scams as 'sysmetic failures' did not reflect very well on the government and was certainly not a measure which would help in restoring a positive attitude in the capital market. It has been the experience that even the foreign institutional investors have not brought in the necessary capital and have generally proved to be fairweather friends, withdrawing from the markets at critical junctures. However, further easing of restrictions on foreign institutional investment and those by non-resident Indians have been introduced to give a much-needed boost to the capital markets. In view of the 11 September 2001 terrorist attacks in the US, confidence in the capital markets worldwide is low and has affected the Indian stock exchanges. Capitalization of markets is one of the most vulnerable areas in any reform or liberalization process and calls for utmost vigilance because a market crash has a contagious effect on the economy as a whole.

Foreign direct investment

Foreign direct investment (FDI) is an integral part of any reform process in an economy embarking on economic liberalization. The investment to a very large extent depends on the 'feel-good factor' which in turn depends to a very large extent on the success of reforms undertaken. In the case of India, FDI since 1991 has been US$31.4 billion as against approvals of US$76 billion[1] granted by the government. A comparison is often made between India and China and other East-Asian economies (tiger economies) with regard to their ability to attract foreign investment. Low FDI in India has been ascribed to bottlenecks and slowdown of the reforms process. China attracts more FDI in one year than India has attracted since the reform process began more than ten years ago; it should be added that China embarked on the process of economic liberalization in the 1970s and has a highly developed infrastructure to support that process. The East-Asian economies on the other hand have opted for short-term debt which has had disastrous consequences for those economies, as evidenced below.

---

[1]   *Indian Express*, 7 February 2003.

A further point as regards foreign direct investment is that countries embarking on the path of economic liberalization have first of all to ensure that in the initial stages it is channelled into priority sectors. Of course, at a later stage, the FDI regime could be further liberalized. Foreign direct investment can also imply the takeover of certain industries and, while welcoming such investment, one has to be very wary of unscrupulous corporate raiders.

Boost to exports

Increase in external trade is another integral part of the reform process. This implies a boost to exports and adequate imports linked to economic growth. The desirable position in terms of external trade is obviously to have a favourable balance of trade – that is, exports should exceed imports. Moreover, exports should be fairly diversified so that the economy is not vulnerable due to its lack of variety in any liberalization process. Incentives to exporters by way of tax breaks and special economic zones are a must. Special economic zones incorporating the features of financial havens have also been created by a number of countries to give a boost to their exports.

On the import side, while certain sectors of the economy such as the agricultural sector in India need to be protected through compensatory duties, the quantitative restrictions on imports ultimately need to be abolished and custom duties brought into line with normal customs tariffs levied by other countries in order to make local industry more competitive. An extremely vigilant eye would need to be kept on external trade, because the scope for international economic crimes and other forms of commercial crimes is vast; threats to this area of economic activity have already been discussed in Chapter VII.

The balance of payments position: foreign exchange reserves

To strive for comfortable foreign exchange reserves is also one of the goals of any economic reform process. According to accepted international norms, the foreign exchange reserves of a country should be able to cater for nine months of imports; this, of course, implies a favourable balance of payments position. In the case of India, ever since it has embarked on the economic liberalization process its foreign exchange reserves have shown a marked improvement. Today foreign exchange reserves are in the region of US$72 billion which can cater for almost one year of import requirements. Although India is a trade deficit country (imports were US$50.536 billion and exports were US$44.56 billion per annum in 2000–01) in terms of import/export trade the balance of payments position has improved because of NRI remittances, bonds such as the India Millenium Bond and Resurgent India Bonds targeting NRIs floated by the Indian government, increasing FII and FDI investments as a result of economic reforms, a certain quantum of concessional aid and other invisible repatriations of foreign exchange. With such comfortable foreign exchange reserves, India has opted for full current account convertibility, but there was still a negative balance of 0.5 per cent on this account in 2000–01. India has not yet embraced full capital account convertibility because of the cautious approach adopted by it, dictated as it is by the consideration that it should first become a trade surplus country. In the context of foreign exchange markets, the rupee has managed to remain stable compared to the dollar and other hard currencies based on market considerations and with minimal interference by the Reserves Bank of India.

While discussing the foreign exchange sector, it must always be borne in mind in the context of India that there is a thriving underground and parallel banking system operating in the form of hawala. This underground and parallel banking system facilitates not only money laundering, but also capital flight to a very large extent. Of course, other avenues for money laundering and capital flight are also being exploited by criminals and anti-social elements.

Management of external debts[2]

Prudent management of external debt is another feature of economic reforms. In the case of developing countries, the servicing of the past debt itself often forms a major portion of the external debt – in other words, the countries fall into a debt trap from which they find it very difficult to escape. External debt of a country generally comprises government borrowings and external commercial borrowings apart from debt-servicing charges that have been referred to. Moreover, the external debt can be long-term or a short-term debt. The critical factor to be borne in mind is that short-term external debt as a percentage of the total debt should never be in excess of 10 per cent. In the case of India, short-term debt is US$4.657 billion, i.e., 4.74 per cent of the total external debt of US$99.005 billion. Of the total external debt, 11.4 per cent constitutes debt-servicing charges. Short-term external debt has also been referred to earlier in the context of the tiger economies of South-East Asia that collapsed a few years ago. The economic crisis in most of these economies was attributed to a very high level of short-term external debt, which in some instances amounted to almost 80–90 per cent of the total external debt. Although this short-term external debt led to rapid economic growth, following a series of defaults, coupled with frauds and malpractices, it also led to a crisis of confidence and ultimately a complete check of short-term debt and its rollover by foreign banks. The net result was that the tiger economies were unable to keep their ongoing projects functioning and their currencies plummeted by substantial amounts due to the crisis in the economy. Moreover, several of these South-East Asian tiger economies also tried to hide their true financial/economic position by transferring or disguising their losses through offshore financial havens, in order to escape the scrutiny of the IMF, World Bank and other creditors/financial institutions. Thus, opacity and lack of transparency, coupled with a very high level of short-term debt and some unethical

---

2 Figures in this paragraph are for the year 1999; See *India's external debt*, a status report issued by the Ministry of Finance.

practices, were responsible for the South-East Asian economic crisis. A massive infusion of concessional aid and restructuring of loans had ultimately to be undertaken to put these economies back on the rails.

India and China remained insulated from these crises, because of prudent management of their external debt. Today India is in the category of lesser-indebted nations, according to the World Bank index of debtor nations. An extremely vigilant eye needs to be kept on external commercial borrowings to ensure that short-term external debt never exceeds a certain ratio which might jeopardize the economic position or economic security of the country in the long run.

Reigning in the fiscal deficit

Governments the world over are guilty of profligacy, including those committed to the reform process. The principal reason for this profligacy on the part of governments is that they refuse to take certain hard decisions – more so with regard to taxation – which, though perceived as a hard measure by the general population and therefore undesirable according to their reckoning, is also treated by the governments as an extreme step which might erode their popular base and re-election prospects. The net result of this financial profligacy is that the budget does not balance and total expenditure far exceeds the total tax revenue. In the case of India, for instance, the expenditure is divided under two headings – planned expenditure and non-planned expenditure. Planned expenditure relates to developmental plans; non-planned expenditure is generally of an administrative nature. In the budget for the year 2001–02, planned expenditure was 4.4 per cent of GDP whereas non-planned expenditure was 12 per cent; the fiscal deficit was INR 1163.17 billion, or 5.1 per cent of GDP, which the government of India bridged by borrowing from the market or from the Central Bank. The implications of a high fiscal deficit is that debt-servicing charges are continuously rising and there is very little government money to finance economic development. The only option for the governments that have embarked on the process of economic reforms is to cut down on non-planned/ administrative expenditure by downsizing the government, increasing tax revenues through better compliance and extending the tax base.

In the context of India, even the states have taken to financial profligacy and likewise their fiscal deficit is also running at 5 per cent of GDP. In all, with 10 per cent of the total GDP as fiscal deficit at the central and state level, it is very difficult to sustain an economic reforms programme which would yield a growth rate of 7–8 per cent, which is an essential condition for economic well-being and eradication of poverty. In order to introduce fiscal discipline within the government, it has introduced the Fiscal Responsibility Bill to ensure that the fiscal deficit eventually decreases to 2 per cent of GDP, which is considered an acceptable level.

While on the issue of profligacy of governments and fiscal deficit, evasion of taxes and the black economy need to be curbed. Another focus area in the context of economic reforms is ensuring that allocation of resources due to corruption and other extraneous/ political considerations does not come about.

Reforms in taxation

Tax reforms are also a vital area of the liberalization process, and are relevant to direct taxes and indirect taxes. As far as direct taxes are concerned, tax reforms in the Indian context have meant rationalization, i.e., bringing down the tax rate to an acceptable level of a maximum 30 per cent tax on income. Enlarging the tax base is also a very important component of tax reforms. in the year 1997–98, 40 per cent of manufacturing units did not file any income tax return and only 1.2 per cent of the population paid taxes. Two other areas which would need to be taxed are the farm sector and the export sector, to mop up more resources; in order to increase the number of taxpayers, it must also be ensured that people are not able to evade taxes. Coming to indirect taxes, the process of rationalization of central excise and customs duties has also been an integral part of the reform process. In the budget for 2001–02, Central Excise has already been rationalized to a single tariff of 16 per cent. Customs duties have been brought down to two levels – 30 per cent and 20 per cent – the objective being to further reduce them to a single level of 20 per cent. To increase revenue from taxes, better compliance is the key, and to ensure the same, the complicity of tax officials with taxpayers in order to evade taxes needs to be dramatically curbed. Tax dodging, tax manipulation, tax evasion and non-payment of taxes are crimes to which so-called white-collar criminals, economic offenders and other notorious criminals indulging in dangerous crime resort, in any liberalization process. Tax laws and tax machinery would need to be considerably strengthened to ensure that mischief-makers do not have a field day during the process of economic liberalization.

Credit and monetary policy

Credit and monetary policy is another very important tool of economic liberalization. Lowering of the interest-rate regime to give a fillip to industry and consumer demand is one of the primary goals of economic liberalization. At the same time, the central banks have to exercise control over the money supply to contain inflation within reasonable limits; the Central Bank controls the growth of money supply through open-market operations in government securities or by adjusting the statutory liquidity ratio of the commercial banks to ensure that an objective and judicious amount of broad money (m3) is available. The autonomy of the central banks must also be ensured by the federal government so that they function in an objective manner. Credit and monetary policies can also be the subject of machinations by industrialists and other business groups, through intensive lobbying by professional bodies constituted to represent the interests of these groups. Governments must be very vigilant to ensure that the liberalization/reform process does not lose its primary focus and become too subservient to the vested interests of some industries.

Banking sector

The banking sector is another critical area wherein major reforms are necessary to ensure the success of the liberalization process. These reforms would need to cut down flab in inefficient public-sector banks, to give a fillip to private banking and to make the banking sector as a whole more competitive by greater opening up of the sector to foreign banks and through Indian banks developing more extensive correspondent relationships with foreign banks. Due to increased economic activity within the country and in terms of external trade and other resulting money flows in the foreign exchange markets, the banking sector could become vulnerable to unscrupulous elements. To keep a strict watch over the activities of these criminal elements, due diligence/better compliance procedures in opening of accounts and large-scale transactions would have to be ensured. Banks would have to be very vigilant about suspicious money transactions, which would mostly relate to large money flows. In the case of suspicious transactions, the banks would have to resort to 'whistle-blowing' to ensure timely enforcement action. The tax haven route, with all the attendant features of these tax havens, would also need to be closely monitored by the banking sector.

In the process of economic liberalization, the banking sector would also become a part of international protocols on wire transfer and electronic transfer of money, another area where the banks would have to be vigilant to keep a check on criminal money. The biggest scam in the banking sector today is that loans are mostly taken by large enterprises in order to default on the payments for one reason or the other, thereby leading to the banks having massive non-performing assets. Through the law on securitization of loans, banks, in concert with the government, are trying to go into overdrive to recover these massive non-performing assets and make themselves viable financial institutions not vulnerable to depredations of unscrupulous elements.

Services sector

The growth of the services sector offers the maximum potential in the growth process initiated by economic liberalization. In the Indian context, the information technology sector (especially export of software), the telecommunication sector (which includes a tremendous boost to cellular services) and rapid advances in e-commerce are some of the main features of the growth of the service sector. To deal with several interrelated issues listed above, a convergence bill has been introduced in the Parliament. The services sector is again vulnerable to misuse – for instance, cellular services are very useful for the terrorists and need to be monitored; in the field of e-commerce there is a tremendous scope for fraud, and the same would also need to be curbed.

International trading in securities

When an economy is opening up, it also wants to access the international capital market to raise finance. India sought to do this through ADRs and GDRs (American Depositary Receipts and Global Depositary Receipts). Initially the domestic equity and ADRs and GDRs were treated as separate entities. With the increased pace of economic reforms, fungibility of ADRs and GDRs has been ensured, which means that these can be converted into local equity and vice versa. Manipulation of domestic capital markets through such fungibility is a distinct possibility and a vigilant eye would have to be kept in this area of economic activity.

One of the ultimate goals of the liberalization process is a highly developed capital market wherein international security or debt instruments are freely traded. A vibrant Indian economy would also command the same treatment with regard to the securities and debt instruments of Indian origin in the principal capital markets of the world. Such an enlargement of trade in the capital markets would obviously need to be regulated to make sure that unscrupulous elements do not indulge in insider trading or other malpractices.

Insurance sector

The insurance sector, which has been a highly protected sector in India and which has failed to deliver the maximum benefit to the common man, also needs to be opened up to financial competition as a part of the liberalization process. Foreign companies have made an entry into the insurance sector and already competition is beginning to pay dividends in the form of better returns for the consumers. The insurance sector is perhaps one of the larger money-spinners in the Indian economy. This is a sector which is particularly prone to fraudulent claims and investment scams, especially by public-sector insurance companies. A vigilant eye needs to be kept on the insurance sector to provide safeguards from crime.

Financial entities other than banks

The non-banking financial institutions, the chit funds and other collective investment schemes are another area of the financial sector that needs to be constantly monitored, considering the massive frauds that are taking place in them. These financial sectors should be made to play a constructive role in the process of economic reforms. Indeed the management of this financial sector needs to be cleansed of all the criminal elements.

Public-sector reforms

Public-sector enterprises, which occupy the commanding heights of the Indian economy and were regarded as temples of progress in the initial stages of economic expansion within the framework of the mixed economy, are now considered an encumbrance; the public sector is one area in which government participation is not considered desirable by some. The rationale for this line of thinking is that public-sector units are not being run along competitive lines, they are not providing adequate returns on investment and a number of them have become ailing and are a massive drain on the state's financial resources. On the other hand, there is another school of thought which holds the view that the public sector performed a stellar role in the formative years of the Indian economy because it was possible for the government alone to make such massive investments in certain sectors to ensure development; moreover, according to this school of thought, it is this very large public sector which fostered and encouraged the growth of the private sector in India in a benign economic atmosphere.

As already indicated above, going by the logic of one school of thought, the public sector needs to be privatized and government has no business to become involved in commercial matters. However, there are quite a few people who feel that public-sector units are like the family jewels and should not be given away to private enterprises at throwaway prices; they feel that these public-sector units should be turned into viable economic units. At present there is a great debate raging on this subject in the country. Of course, the whole process of disinvestment by government in the public sector needs to be reviewed and well thought out – even though government is preparing to mobilize substantial amounts of money through disinvestment. In some areas disinvestment is not desirable, and efforts should be made to turn loss-making public-sector units into profit-making enterprises. In other areas privatization would be the desired goal, because government should not be dabbling in certain areas of economic activity. Moreover, extreme caution would need to be exercised so that those public-sector units are not privatized at throwaway prices or for less than the value that they could fetch – it would certainly make the government look ridiculous, if it sold a hotel for INR 800 million and after three months the private party acquiring it sold the very same hotel at a profit of INR 300 million; this has happened in India, in the case of the Centaur Hotel in Mumbai. Moreover, it must be ensured that proceeds of disinvestment do not go to pay for the profligacy of the government by adjusting it against the high fiscal deficit. In fact the proceeds of disinvestment in public sector enterprises should go exclusively for the reduction of the national debt so that debt-servicing charges of the economy as a whole decrease over a period of time. Moreover, because of the huge sums of money involved in any disinvestment exercise by the government, there is always scope for massive corruption, which would need to be curbed, by ensuring transparency in the disinvestment process.

FIRST-GENERATION AND SECOND-GENERATION REFORMS

Another debate that has raged in the context of economic liberalization in India has been with regard to first-generation and second-generation reforms. A moot point here is whether any such distinction can be made in a reform process which is a continuous exercise. Perhaps it would be more appropriate to say that having initiated the reform process (which can be categorized as first-generation reforms), this needs to be further extended to other areas of economic activity. Moreover, the structural reforms already undertaken would need to be further deepened and widened to ensure that the economic momentum is maintained.

Thus, the discussion between first- and second-generation reforms is essentially polemical in nature. The basic idea is to ensure that the reforms serve the objective for which they have been initiated and that the process of economic reforms is not hijacked by criminal, anti-social and subversive elements.

SUMMING UP: THE REFORM PROCESS AND IMPLICATIONS FOR MONEY LAUNDERING

To sum up, one can say that much still needs to be done in the sphere of economic reforms and economic liberalization. To illustrate this point, an analysis of India's external trade is revealing: out of total exports of US$44.36 billion in 2000–01, textiles, gems and jewellery constituted 33 per cent of exports; as regards imports, diamonds, gold and oil constituted 56 per cent of the total imports of US$50.53 billion. If one were to take commercial frauds and international economic crimes into consideration, India's export trade presents a fairly dismal picture. Thus, much requires to be done in terms of diversification and increasing competitiveness and volumes with regard to India's external trade. The trade deficit, which is a matter of prime concern for the Indian economy, would also have to be turned into a surplus over a period of time, by sustained efforts.

All of the perils indicated so for in the economic liberalization/reform process would lead to generation of larger proceeds of crimes and also laundering of the same on a more extensive scale.

Note: If not otherwise indicated, figures in this chapter have been taken from the *Economic Survey 2001–02*, published by the Ministry of Finance, Government of India.

CHAPTER XV

FEATURES OF TRANSITION ECONOMIES AND SCOPE FOR MONEY LAUNDERING

WHAT ARE TRANSITION ECONOMIES?

When discussing economies in transition, one is basically looking at the former Communist economies. It was with the fall of the Berlin Wall in 1989 that the whole process of the demise of communism began. In the context of East Germany, the unification of the two Germanies was a logical corollary to the demise of communism in the eastern part. This unification could be managed in a comparatively orderly manner due to the vast resources of West Germany and its experience with the market economy. The other East-European countries which also shed communism were helped to a very large extent by Germany, other EEC (European Economic Community) member countries and the United States.

After the demise of communism in Eastern Europe, it was only a matter of time before the same process occurred in the former Soviet Union. The Baltic republics were the first to break free from the Soviet Union and they were helped to a considerable extent by the Scandinavian countries. The final crunch in the demise of communism came with the break-up of the Soviet Union into separate countries. This process was fairly cathartic and even entailed a counter-coup and widespread public unrest.

PAINS OF TRANSITION

Thus, when communism came to an end virtually worldwide, its legacy was a number of transition economies trying to cope with a totally new and unfamiliar situation. At this point, it would be worth recounting some of the immediate and future problems with which these transition economies had to contend. Transition economies meant a shift of trade and industry from state control to private hands. Since even the basic expertise of the market economy was lacking, this process was a particularly painful one. With no infrastructure available to facilitate the transition from state control to market economy, the problem was further compounded because of a mismatch that occurred due to disruption of production lines and consumer demands in the market. The scenario in these transition economies was one of complete confusion – there was runaway inflation which was further compounded by rapid currency devaluation. In conditions of scarcity the black-marketeers had a field day. Income disparities were surfacing between the criminal class and honest citizens. For the general run of the people, whatever government jobs were available were vastly underpaid; with their savings more or less eroded, honest citizens had to undergo tremendous hardships. In this dismal picture of the transition economies, two things were obvious – one was the new class, which was thoroughly unscrupulous in its pursuit of wealth, and the other was organized-crime groups who had a field day in terms of proceeds of crime in general and black marke-teering in particular. While discussing the problems faced by transition economies, it is also necessary to keep in mind that in the former Communist economies there was always a thriving underground economy which further excaberated the problems that the transition economies encountered.

IMMEDIATE PROBLEMS

The newly democratic regimes that emerged to occupy the position of power in the former Communist countries had to cope up with a number of problems. First and foremost was resistance by the Old Guard. To put the new regime on a sound legal footing, constitutions and other laws had to be enacted; a massive restructuring of banking and financial sectors of the economy had to be undertaken to gear them to the needs of the market economy. The new government had to cope with a massive infusion of aid and to ensure that pilfering was curbed and misappropriation of funds did not take place. Transition economies were also laying a lot of store by private enterprises and hoping that, impelled by the force of self-interest, all problems would be resolved; these hopes were belied to a large extent and ultimately they realized that even private enterprises would need some form of regulation. These transition economies had massive state-owned assets; unscrupulous politicians, in league with businessmen and organized-crime groups, indulged in a massive rip-off/ skimming of the state-owned enterprises. For instance, in Russia when Boris Yeltsin, the then President of Russia, went to the Duma (the Russian Parliament) for money to run the government, his request was refused. As a result, Yeltsin pledged state enterprises to raise loans from the market to run the government. In effect, most of these state enterprises had been pledged to unscrupulous politicians, businessmen and organized-crime groups, who were generally in collusion. In the absence of any finance forthcoming in the future, the Russian government defaulted on loans, and massive state enterprises passed into crim-inal hands at throwaway prices, initiating the rip-off and the skimming.

   Due to unstable economic conditions in the transition economies, the money from state enterprises took the form of capital flight and the money coming from crime came to be laundered. Former intelligence (KGB) officers also joined in this process and, with their expertise, made the task easier. In fact, today it is estimated that there are 30,000 offshore Russian corporations operating out of Cyprus and remote islands in the Pacific, such as the Cook Islands and Naoru. It is through these offshore corporations that capital flight and money laundering is taking place to Western Europe and North America. Even in the existing laws in Russia and other transition economies there are enough loopholes, which have been exploited to take the wealth out of the country. The magnitude of the problem of money laundering hit the world in 2000 when the Bank of New York was implicated in a case of money laundering from Russia running to US$4–7 billion; of course later, on realizing the complexities of transition economies, it emerged that the money laundering case involving the Bank of New York might be more in the nature of capital flight from Russia, the amount of which has been estimated at US$100–400 billion over the past decade.

PREMISES TO KEEP IN TIME TO COME

The transition economies had ultimately to strive for stabilization for their sheer survival. This meant holding out certain premises for the future in terms of living standards, basic amenities and the other benefits of a consumerist society. These transition economies ultimately also had to contend with the question of their integration into the world economy. Learning from each other's experience has been a big contributory factor for these transition economies in coming to grips with their problems; they have drawn on experiments undertaken by economies on the liberalization track, inputs from developed countries and international agencies such as the IMF/World Bank and other multilateral aid organizations. The main tasks ahead of these transition economies is to increase the growth rate of the economy which in turn would raise the standard of living of the people and also lead to more equitable distribution of wealth due to all-round economic prosperity in the new market set-up.

Managing some of the vast state enterprises as profitable and viable units is another challenge that these economies have to contend with. Conversion of some of the state-owned enterprises into private enterprises, once again in order to make them profitable and viable, is another challenge. By creating stable economic conditions and thereby managing the problem of capital flight and reversing the outflow of capital back into the country is another area which would have to be attended to as a priority by these transition economies if they are to emerge as competitive entities on the world scene. Those transition economies which have fledgling democracies would also have to build up democratic institutions and put them on a firm footing, a process which in turn would foster private enterprise. Organized-crime groups that have emerged in several of these economies would also have to be curbed; hence, a sustained campaign would have to be launched against the corruption which has afflicted these economies to a very large extent. Those transition economies which are new to the free market set-up would also have to introduce a set of laws to deal with economic offences; although it might seem quite strange, several economic offences are not perceived and treated as such in these economies. Above all, these transition economies would have to manage all the other areas which a free market economy entails – mobilization of resources, balancing the budget, keeping the fiscal deficit low, having an appropriate credit and monetary policy in place, among other things.

Although each country would also have to deal with its own peculiar economic problems, the need for international co-operation to tackle the majority of these problems cannot be over-emphasized. In the context of the new World Trade Organization (WTO) regime, too, these transition economies would need to set their sights higher and increase their share in world trade in consonance with their inherent economic strength and resources.

CHAPTER XVI

ANOTHER LOOK AT THREATS FACED BY ECONOMIES

Proceeds of crime obviously pose a great threat to economies that are undergoing the liberalization process and also the former Communist economies that are in a state of transition, but as already mentioned, the threat posed by laundered money because of its disguised nature is more serious because it is difficult to perceive in operation.

PENETRATION OF LEGITIMATE COMMERCE

The major threat posed by proceeds of crime/laundered money is to legitimate commercial activity. It is now well documented that criminals worldwide have penetrated or branched out into legitimate commerce in order to camouflage their criminal activities, in order to further maximize their profits and also to gain respectability. With their criminal mindsets, these elements pose a very serious threat to legitimate commerce. The magnitude of this threat operates both on a large scale and at micro-levels. In today's world one should not be too surprised to know that a mega-multinational corporation is in fact controlled by a mafia group or a criminal syndicate. Likewise, retail-level outlets and even medium-level enterprises are known to be controlled by some crime syndicates. For instance, in India the Mumbai underworld has entered into the construction business and film industry in a big way; similarly, in New York the mafia gangs are known to dominate the construction industry, and most of their money comes from all sorts of rackets associated with it. The casinos in Las Vegas are again notorious fronts for the crime syndicates operating in the United States.

Another general threat which these commercial enterprises pose to liberalizing economies/economies in transition is that of unfair competition. Whether they are in commercial activity or legitimate commerce these unscrupulous elements do not follow the rules of the market and are not averse to indulging in extortion, kidnapping, murders, engineered accidents, etc. When criminals are playing with the rules of the marketplace in such a manner, it has a tendency to force/persuade the honest and legitimate businessman to retaliate by similar criminal means in order simply to survive as a viable business entity. Thus, there is the danger of the whole market being tainted by an atmosphere of crime. The tendency of legitimate commercial businesses to resort to unfair means in the face of hostile competition from criminal elements has also been characterized as the contamination effect of crime and its proceeds, laundered or unlaundered.

TEMPTATION TO USE PROCEEDS OF CRIME FOR ECONOMIC DEVELOPMENT

Sometimes there is a great temptation for politicians and even some economists and development experts to harness the proceeds of crime for much-needed economic development, especially in the case of developing economies. Economies undergoing liberalization and in transition are generally in need of funds and sometimes this overriding concern blinds them to their source. However, in the long run the consequences of development achieved with laundered money can only lead to dangerous consequences – one of the possibilities being that the whole polity of the nation passes into criminal hands. All economies, whether developing, in the process of liberalization, in transition or developed, should make a distinction between bad money and good money; it must always be borne in mind by people in a position of responsibility that bad money ultimately leads to undesirable results.

CRIME MONEY: IMPLICATIONS FOR ECONOMIC POLICY FORMULATION

Proceeds of crime whether, laundered or unlaundered, which run into large sums, can also have very serious macro-economic implications for economies undergoing liberalization and in a state of transition. These large proceeds of crime, because of their disguised and underground nature, can give a highly distorted view of the economy to policy planners if they tend to ignore them. Thus, based on published and openly available data, policy-makers often make the mistake of ignoring the vast amount of black money in circulation, with the result that policy projections devised by them at the macro-economic level are seriously skewed. For instance, the money supply in the economy could be totally unrelated to the projections and because of a different volume of money in operation, all projected calculations relating to incomes, prices and employment could go wrong. The credit policy formulations, especially with regard to interest rates, might also go totally awry and not lead to the desired results of economic growth because of the same fallacious assumptions. The inflationary pressures that could be generated because of large-scale proceeds of crime might be totally out of the control of the macro-economic policy-makers. Moreover, if 50 per cent of the national economy is a black economy, wrong projection of fiscal deficit as a percentage of GDP can make a mockery of all projections relating to economic growth.

Quite unsuspectingly the policy planners can also be manipulated into misallocation of resources on extraneous and other political considerations as a result of the machinations of criminals with their vast proceeds of illegal wealth. Such misallocations can be of stupendous financial magnitude if one considers that these might involve the relocation of massive hydro-electric projects/thermal electricity generation plants, for example.

ROLE OF POWER BROKERS

Power brokers play a pivotal role in undermining most of the economic systems undergoing liberalization; it would not be an exaggeration to say that the role of power brokers is all-pervasive in practically every scam that occurs in these economies. Therefore, they need to be identified, isolated and cut off from the mainstream of economic activity.

CHAPTER XVII

STRATEGIES FOR LOSS PREVENTION

In the context of damage that can be caused to economies undergoing liberalization or in transition, the main endeavour is to contend with the mischief done by unscrupulous elements. The best way to minimize this mischief is by devising an effective strategy for loss prevention.

PROACTIVE INTELLIGENCE-ORIENTED APPROACH

Any strategy for loss prevention has to have a proactive approach. Only an intelligence-oriented approach can be proactive, because intelligence is something that implies fore-knowledge and that forewarns of possible damage, so that effective steps can be taken in time to plug the losses. Of course, in a highly diversified field of economic activity, such an intelligence-oriented approach would call for a great deal of expertise in several areas of economic activity. Such expertise is not always easily available and sometimes the basic knowledge has to be honed to the requirements of intelligence gathering.

For any intelligence-oriented approach, a narrow focus on just the economic crime in question would not suffice; an intelligence-oriented approach would have to explore all avenues relating to commerce, industry, agriculture, banking and the financial services sector, and so on. It is from these various channels that intelligence would flow and it is through these same channels that losses would have to be prevented.

A proactive intelligence approach aimed at loss prevention, in order to be really effective, would obviously in the first instance have to identify the vulnerable areas of economic activity that are to be targeted. These areas would relate to stock markets, banks and financial institutions having large money flows wherein suspicious movement of money takes place on a large scale. Corporate raiders are another entity that would have to be kept in check. In fact, one can produce a comprehensive list of vulnerable areas based on the previous discussion on threats faced by liberalized economies and economies in transition.

TRADITIONAL LAW ENFORCEMENT AS A TOOL TO PREVENT LOSSES

In contrast to the proactive intelligence approach for loss prevention, there is also the traditional law enforcement approach. Such a traditional approach also works; by being basically passive in nature it only comes into play when considerable damage has been done. The correct perspective to view such a traditional law enforcement approach would be to consider it as a means of meting out retributive justice to the criminals. The traditional approach of dealing with white-collar criminals with kid gloves would not suffice;

to provide adequate protection to economies undergoing liberalization or in transition, all economic criminals must be dealt with very severely so that they know that crime does not pay and so that others are not encouraged to venture into criminal activities.

THE ROLE OF DIFFERENT ENTITIES IN LOSS PREVENTION

Regulatory bodies

The role of some entities, such as the Securities and Exchange Board of India, the Telecommunication Regulatory Authority of India and the Insurance Regulatory Authority, in the context of India, is critical in the areas of loss prevention because, being at the cutting edge of their areas of operation, they are in a very good position to ascertain malpractices and frauds. These regulatory bodies also need to be given adequate powers to monitor their areas of activity in an effective manner and also to hand out salutary punishments whenever wrongdoing is detected.

Professionals

The role of professionals in economies undergoing liberalization or in transition is another area that needs to be scrutinized in a proper manner. Professionals such as chartered accountants and lawyers tend to be the facilitators of most of the crimes committed in these transition economies. A very tight control and vigilant eye needs to be kept on these facilitators both by the relevant government vigilance organizations, as well as their self-regulatory bodies, to ensure that they do not make the process of crime easy and rewarding.

Banks and other financial entities

Another area demanding special focus in these economies on the path of liberalization is the role of banks and other financial institutions. The banks must report all suspicious transactions to the appropriate enforcement authority; 'whistle-blowing' or alerting the enforcement authorities should be made an obligatory duty of all banks and financial institutions. Of course, in order to detect suspicious transactions, the bank and other financial institution staff would have to be properly trained and learn to draw a distinction between information, intelligence and evidence.

Intelligence agencies

In any set-up in the area of loss prevention, the role of intelligence agencies can hardly be minimized. In the Indian context, the Economic Intelligence Bureau, Directorate of Revenue Intelligence, Central Bureau of Investigation, Directorate of Enforcement, Directorate of Inspections, Economic Offences wings of various states and other internal vigilance systems within the organizations could play a stellar role in gathering intelligence in order to prevent losses. Of course, a good deal of co-ordination would have to go into the overall intelligence effort, so that it becomes meaningful and focused and leads to effective action, instead of dissipation of their energies in a diffused manner. To ensure such co-ordination in the sphere of intelligence, a central supervisory agency would obviously have to be set up. Perhaps the Économic Intelligence Bureau can perform such a role in the Indian context. Co-ordination would be necessary not only amongst the various economic intelligence wings, but also between the intelligence as well as the law enforcement wings, so that effective follow-up action could be taken against the criminals.

THE SCOPE FOR PREVENTING LOSSES

In any strategy aimed at loss prevention, one may ask the logical questions: what is possible and what should be endeavoured? The endeavours in any such strategy can be categorized in the following order. The first possibility is that the loss can be totally prevented by putting preventive steps and systems in place. The second possibility is that the loss can be minimized, again because of adequate preventive steps or early detection. The third possibility is that losses can be recovered in an unencumbered manner and without much legal fuss, again because of timely detection. In fact, the key to any successful strategy aimed at loss prevention is that criminals must be made to understand that crime does not pay. When is it that crimes does not pay? Only when the proceeds of crime which are the losses of economic and other enterprises are either prevented, or, having taken place, are restored to the losers who have been the target of unscrupulous elements.

Some of the international/regional organizations dealing with matters of law enforcement could also have a unit to target frauds/crimes in areas/countries/continents in their respective sphere of activity, with a view to chalking out effective strategies and also taking necessary steps to ensure loss prevention.

PART IV

RECENT ADVANCES AND OTHER ASPECTS

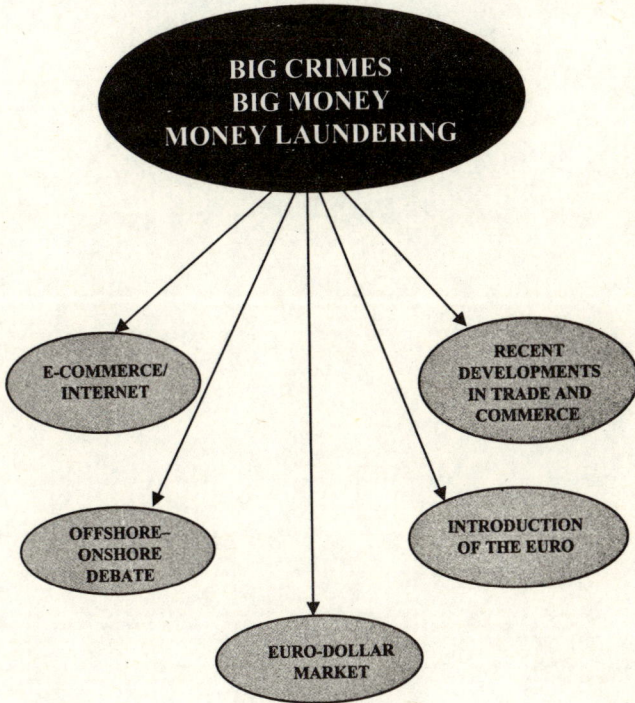

CHAPTER XVIII

E-COMMERCE, THE INTERNET AND MONEY LAUNDERING

SPREAD OF INFORMATION TECHNOLOGY

The world has experienced an information boom in the past two decades. The Internet has been largely responsible for this information explosion. Through this medium, which has been networked to various servers, it has become possible for people in the comfort of their own homes to access information about practically anything in the world, from the various websites, through their personal computers – of which there were estimated to be one billion in 2002:[1] To give some idea of the spread and reach of this information boom, the population of Internet users worldwide has been estimated at half a billion in 2002.

Starting out with the information boom, e-commerce has also opened up several opportunities for trade and commerce. It is now possible to draw up contracts, letters of credits and other instruments of trade and to communicate the same on the Internet; prior to communication, all of these documents can also be certified by digital signatures. Even hard copies can be scanned and contracts and other papers sent to trading partners via the Internet. To make these commercial transactions secure and also to ensure the privacy of individuals, cryptography is being utilized.

E-COMMERCE: GAINING IN STRENGTH

Today the whole of a commercial transaction could be paperless; relevant data is stored in computers at either end after it has been communicated through electronic impulses. Of course, it is always possible to reduce the whole transaction to hard copy by taking a printout of the data. In fact, e-commerce has witnessed a tremendous increase over the years. In 2002, e-commerce transactions are estimated to be worth hundreds of billions of dollars. By all accounts, e-commerce will witness an exponential increase in the future.

E-BANKING, E-MONEY, SECURITIES TRADING ONLINE AND INTERNET GAMBLING

The spread of this new electronic medium has also extended to other areas which have facilitated the process of e-commerce. E-banking, or banking on the Internet, is increasingly being used by individuals all over the world; it would be no exaggeration to say

---

[1]   Alvin Toffler, 'Tomorrow's Economy', *India Today*, 17 March 2003.

that most banking transactions in times to come will probably be through this medium. Electronic money, in other words digital cash, also known as smart/cash cards, is very much in vogue; like e-banking, the use of e-money is also bound to increase over the next few years. Both e-banking and e-money aid e-commerce by ensuring that the speed of payments keeps pace with the speed of commercial transactions.

Another area in which the Internet has become increasingly popular and where is being used extensively is that relating to trading in securities on the capital markets; the computerization of stock exchanges and their link through the Internet was one of the early developments which led to this new medium being heavily used for securities trading. Internet gambling is another activity that has caught on like wildfire. Both trading in securities on the Internet and online gambling offer huge scope to criminals to launder their proceeds.

REASONS FOR PREFERRING THIS NEW ELECTRONIC MEDIUM

At this stage it would be worth examining the reasons for the increasing use of e-commerce, e-banking, e-money, securities trading on the Internet and online gambling. With this new electronic medium of the Internet, the world seems to have become a much smaller place where one can reach out to areas which were once considered inaccessible; this in turn has led to the greater use of this medium in the field of e-commerce and related activities. E-commerce and other related activities have received a further boost through this new medium because there are no national frontiers to contend with. The speed of transactions is perhaps one of the key factors which has influenced the increasing use of e-commerce. The security of the medium has also been a big contributory factor in the growth of e-commerce and other related activities. Amongst the other features that have led to its growth are that one-to-one contact or detailed time-consuming correspondence are no longer necessary for conducting business.

VULNERABILITIES OF THE INTERNET

Like anything else in this world, the new electronic medium of the Internet is also vulnerable both as a medium and in terms of the uses to which it is put. Jurisdiction and the borderless environment are the most problematic areas of this new medium. Anonymity, by which one does not know with whom one is dealing, is another great weakness of the Internet. The security offered by this system is also not foolproof; scope for breaches of security is inherent in the interconnectivity through which the system operates: there have been numerous instances of hackers breaching security and viruses corrupting and destroying data on a very large scale. In this medium of electronic impulses, one is dealing with virtual data which has been digitalized on the computers; virtual data in itself is a concept that most people have yet to come to grips with in terms of its admissibility as evidence in the context of laws currently in force. Other problems relating to data relate to corruption and loss of it due to the impermanent nature of data, i.e., it need not be kept beyond a certain period of time. This medium is also a totally unsupervised one; thus, lack of supervision is another vulnerable area; even if one has a modicum of built-in software for supervision, this has its limitations. In any given situation human intervention is always a useful input; in this medium there is no human intervention and hence no alarms and no suspects. It is also vulnerable because of the opportunities it offers to create virtual jurisdictions in cyberspace; to establish contact and to exercise control over these virtual jurisdictions would be one of the great challenges with which this medium would have to contend.

THE EMERGENCE OF CYBERCRIME

Apart from the vulnerabilities of the Internet that have been described, it is also a new medium that is prone to crime. Since it is new, what types of crime might be occurring in this medium is still a grey area, as many of the crimes have not yet been identified or detected. It must also be recognized that as the medium evolves and grows, the potential for the occurrence of computer crimes will also increase.

Cybercrime is another name given to computer-related crime. Computer crimes can be categorized under three headings. The first type of computer crimes are those where the Internet and the computer are the target: hacking, stealing of data, destruction and corruption of data are some of the crimes which would fall into this category. The second type of computer crimes are those where the computer becomes a tool for committing crimes; computer-related frauds, computer-related forgeries, pornography and cybersquatting, amongst many others, are crimes that would fall into this second category. The third type of computer-related crime is that in which the computer is incidental to the crime; instances of such crime occur where data/evidence relating to the crime is stored in the computer – for instance, in cases of frauds/white-collar crimes.

A draft European Convention on Cyber Crimes has been the first international initiative by the Council of Europe to categorize types of cybercrime. This Convention has categorized cybercrimes under four headings. The first pertains to offences against the confidentiality, integrity and availability of computer data and systems; types of crime under this heading are illegal access, illegal interception, data interference, system interference and misuse of devices; these types of crime are those in which the computer/Internet are the target. The second heading pertains to computer-related offences: computer-related forgery and computer-related frauds fall into this catagory; these types of crime are those in which the computer is the tool with which to commit the crime. Heading three of this Convention relates to contract-related offences; child pornography is covered under this heading. Under heading four of the Convention, offences related to infringement of copyright and related rights are dealt with.

There is also an interesting study by the Australian Institute of Criminology which has categorized computer crimes as theft of telecommunications services, communications in furtherance of criminal conspiracies, telecommunications piracy, dissemination of offensive materials, electronic money laundering and tax evasion, electronic vandalism, terrorism and extortion, sales and investment frauds, illegal interception of telecommunications and electronic funds transfer frauds.

MONEY LAUNDERING AND E-COMMERCE: SOME DISTINCT ADVANTAGES

Another outcome of the increasing use of e-commerce will be that the money laundering process will become much easier. Anonymity, security, speed, ease of communication, borderless trading and lack of supervision are all facets of the Internet that would facilitate the process of money laundering. This new medium would also make the placement of money much easier through Internet banking and through digital cash (smart cards/cash cards) where no banks are involved. The process of layering of money and integrating the same as laundered money would also become easier through the medium of the Internet, because money can pass through a greater number of jurisdictions with relative ease and speed, with all the other attendant advantages that this medium offers.

Intermediaries located in financial havens, also known as facilitators, generally play a very important role in money laundering. These intermediaries are generally chartered accountants, lawyers, company formation agents and other professionals in the field of finance. This medium would do away with the need for these intermediaries and therefore make not only e-commerce but also money laundering more cost-effective and cheaper.

The newness of the medium is another feature that will aid the process of money laundering. In this new electronic medium, since the rules of the game have yet to be fully laid out, especially with regard to regulations and enforcement, the process of money laundering could be greatly facilitated.

Internet trading in securities is now known to be a *modus operandi* widely used by the money launderers to explain their proceeds of crime. In the layering and integration process, the securities markets, especially those where international trading of securities takes place, are very useful for passing off criminal proceeds as legitimate earnings from stock exchanges.

Likewise, Internet gambling is increasingly being used to launder money. A number of financial havens have private Internet casinos in place. These Internet casinos are a very convenient tool for laundering money. The potential for Internet gambling being used to launder money can be gauged from the fact that in-house gambling was estimated at a staggering US$49 billion worldwide in 1998.[2] The way in which Internet gambling is spreading, coupled with the intense competition amongst financial havens to extend this facility further, will result in more money being laundered using this method. Most of the servers of these Internet casinos, including the casinos themselves, are located in the financial havens; sometimes the server is in one financial haven and the casino in another. The customers of these Internet casinos can be from principal onshore centres, other financial havens, or anywhere in the world. Some of the 'captive Internet casinos' are sometimes simply fronts for passing off illegal proceeds as earnings from gambling and thereby launder the same. Sometimes these casinos may be in collusion with the criminals and book their bets in a doctored manner to pass them off as casino winnings, once again with the intention of laundering the money.

---

[2] Website source: http://www.ascusc.org/jcmc/vol2/issue2/janower.html.

Reporting of suspicious transactions in which a large turnover of money takes place, such as in banks, brokerage houses, money changers, money transmission agents and the securities market, is nowadays considered to be one of the principal tools for countering money laundering; in such a fast-moving medium as the Internet, suspicious transactions tend to go unreported, especially when norms for reporting such transactions are not clearly laid out. Moreover, intelligent reporting of suspicious transactions would always remain a remote possibility on the Internet because of lack of the physical presence of human intelligence; perhaps refining of software might help to some extent in expeditious analysis. Even due diligence processes such as 'know your customer', which again are an integral part of the fight against money laundering, tend to be ignored in this new medium.

PROBLEMS WITH REGARD TO ENFORCEMENT

Several problematic areas peculiar to law enforcement also have to be tackled in the context of this new medium of the Internet. The first problem is that of jurisdiction; in the event of an offence being committed on the Internet, which country has the jurisdiction to take cognizance? Since the Internet is a borderless world, the consensus is now veering toward the view that the country where the server is located is the one which should exercise jurisdiction to investigate and take further follow-up action in relation to a crime. Law enforcement is also greatly hampered due to the fact that in most countries there are no laws to deal with computer crimes, or even to regulate this new and fast-moving medium. Moreover, as has already been discussed, cybercrimes have not yet been comprehensively identified; to codify a criminal code for effective policing of the Internet is therefore still a long way off. 'Criminal intention' or '*mens rea*', which is one of the essential requirements to treat an act as a crime, is very difficult to prove in this electronic medium. Since one is dealing with virtual data, the question of its admissibility as evidence is yet to be resolved; the virtual nature of data also poses other problems with regard to effective law enforcement. Even the assets in this new medium, which are of an intangible nature, tend to confound law enforcement when it comes to search and seizure of such assets. Since the computerized networked environment is a totally new and unfamiliar medium, ways for conducting searches and seizures within it have yet to be fully devised by law enforcement.

Admissibility of new forms of evidence that could emerge in this new medium must also be evaluated; the question of new forms of evidence becomes all the more important because they will tend to conflict with the existing laws to a large extent. Several other problem areas relating to law enforcement in this new medium could be listed. Many other new areas that law enforcement has never dealt with before are also likely to emerge in the future.

SOME OTHER IMPORTANT DIMENSIONS

Right to privacy and use of cryptography

The right of privacy in this electronic medium is another issue around which a great debate is raging. Some argue that the right of privacy is absolute, which of course is a totally untenable position. If there is wrongdoing or some crime that has been committed in this new medium, it must be investigated and to that extent the right of privacy needs to be curtailed. The rules of the game with regard to privacy and access to regulatory authorities have to be defined and put into place. Cryptography, which is integral to privacy in this new medium, would have to be considerably regulated; several countries are even talking about keeping cryptographic keys with third-party mediators to resolve all issues relating to rights of privacy as opposed to access to information.

Need for an effective audit trail

In order to monitor this electronic medium effectively and ensure that it is not abused, an effective audit trail would need to be built up with respect to all communications and data that passes through it. Digital signatures would of course be a very important element in this audit trail. Adequate software could also be devised indicating the source, the destination and the intermediate points for communication of data. Digital cash, which may result in the elimination of banks, would also need to be closely monitored because it could be misused for laundering money and committing a host of other crimes and irregular acts. The monitoring of digital cash at the time of loading could, of course, be ensured, but once this cash enters the electronic medium and moves around the world, monitoring it could be highly problematic; effective ways and means would have to be devised to do the same.

The concept of cyberspace

Under this new electronic medium one can not only operate through regular jurisdictions, but also create virtual jurisdiction in cyberspace and operate out of the same. These virtual jurisdictions would offer limitless opportunities for all kinds of clandestine operations, as they might be very difficult to detect. How to detect and police these virtual jurisdictions in cyberspace will be a great challenge for enforcement.

Enactment of suitable laws to counter cybercrime

Substantive laws, procedural laws and evidentiary laws to deal with cybercrime would also have to be framed by all countries to police this new medium effectively; these laws must take into account all the peculiar problems of the medium that have been referred to earlier with regard to law enforcement.

Technology and the changing role of the judiciary

The judiciary would also have to lend itself to change in this fast-moving new electronic medium of the Internet. Once new crimes are detected, new laws come into force to deal with them and a regulatory framework is put into place to deal with several other issues, the courts would have to move into a different gear altogether. The concept of 'E-courts' would have to be put into place to deal with the problems thrown up by this new medium. Such E-courts are already functioning in Singapore, and in them virtual data stored on computers is admissible evidence; so also are the depositions of witnesses through video conferencing, under certain circumstances. It has been the Singapore experience that these E-courts are able to administer justice in a very speedy manner. Deposition of evidence through video conferencing in this fast-moving borderless world, where witnesses could be located at long distances, would be a practical and cost-effective method of trials by E-courts while administering justice. Likewise, many other cost-effective and new methods for administering justice through E-courts will emerge in the future.

Further need to discipline offshore jurisdictions

Amongst some of the other issues pertaining to this new medium are the recalcitrant offshore jurisdictions which are providing opportunities for its abuse; these would have to be effectively disciplined and brought into line with accepted norms of good conduct. The potential for increasing the mischief, once underground banking systems are used in conjunction with this new medium, would also have to be taken into account and countered effectively. The need for bilateral, regional and international co-operation cannot be over-emphasized, and suitable treaties and conventions would have to be drawn up to ensure this.

CONVERGENCE OF TECHNOLOGIES TO BE RECOGNIZED

Another factor that needs to be recognized in the context of information technology/ the Internet is the convergence of other fast-evolving technologies such as telecommunications and broadcasting with the Internet. Considering the level of convergence that is likely to emerge, it would be appropriate to introduce a convergence law to regulate these interrelated technologies and deal with the problems that they might pose collectively or individually in terms of crime or otherwise. India is planning to introduce such a convergence law, and a convergence bill in this respect is pending with the Indian legislature for enactment into law.

SOME ESTIMATES OF THE EXTENT OF COMPUTER-RELATED CRIME

According to a study carried out in 2000 by Price Waterhouse Coopers,[3] computer fraud is costing Australian organizations almost $4 billion per annum; the worldwide extent of these computer frauds is estimated to be around $250 billion. The 'I love you' computer virus originating from the Philippines (in 2000) affected almost 10 million people

---

[3] Adam Gosling, 'Cyber cops for hire', *IT News*, 22 June 2000.

worldwide, causing an estimated loss of US$10 billion. It is conjectured that the 'I love you' computer virus could have been a failed attempt at bank robbery or identity theft; this virus, while infecting computers, was also reading and copying passwords from files in every computer it infiltrated, to a website in the Philippines. The dilemma facing law enforcement agencies as to how to deal with computer crime is clearly brought out by the response of the Philippines enforcement authorities to the 'I love you' virus; for several days they could not take action because they were searching for an appropriate law to apply in this case.

According to the US Federal Bureau of Investigation (FBI), recent statistics indicate that computer crime rose by 600 per cent in 1998; of course, today the rate of growth, as also the extent of crime, must be much higher and much larger. The FBI is one federal agency that is targeting computer crimes at a national level in the United States through a network of agents. Up to 1999 it had dealt with almost 18,000 complaints from within the United States and outside; the average loss per victim was estimated at US$800. While the Price Waterhouse Coopers study appears to have overstated the extent of computer frauds, the law enforcement response as evidenced by the FBI indicates that it is still trying to come to grips with a crime in a totally new medium.

Perhaps the weakest link in the chain in the fight against computer crimes are the law enforcement agencies. Law enforcement officers worldwide are known to be averse to the use of computers and do not like to work in unfamiliar mediums. In this world of fast-moving convergent technologies, law enforcement officers would have to become computer-literate in order to deal with this type of crime, for which they would also need relevant training.

CHAPTER XIX

THE OFFSHORE–ONSHORE DEBATE

In the context of money laundering, one of the greatest debates is centred round the offshore and onshore jurisdictions. In order to understand this debate and its implications it will be helpful to clarify what exactly is meant by offshore and onshore jurisdictions.

THE MEANING OF 'OFFSHORE'

In common parlance, offshore jurisdictions mainly refer to islands offering financial services in a manner which strictly speaking is not desirable for the international financial world. In a similar vein, going offshore means operating an account in another jurisdiction in a currency other than that of the jurisdiction.

Technically speaking, the offshore concept is primarily related to banks opening accounts in other jurisdictions to avail themselves of tax breaks and to circumvent currency reserve requirements and a host of other banking regulations in the home country. As already mentioned, the offshore accounts are denominated in a currency other than that of the jurisdiction concerned – offshore accounts are generally maintained in dollars. It is possible for both offshore and onshore accounts to exist in the same jurisdiction, i.e., for a country to be offshore and onshore at the same time. For example, in the UK a multinational bank can have an onshore branch in London to carry on regular banking activity: at the same time the same bank can also have an offshore bank branch licensed in the UK, say, in London, to operate an account which is in dollars.

Whereas onshore accounts deal primarily with retail banking, offshore accounts are basically meant to service banks – in other words, they are primarily meant for inter-bank transactions. If, say, a multinational bank as described above has an offshore and onshore account in London, a kind of firewall is supposed to exist between the two accounts/branches so that both confine themselves to their respective areas of activity; however, some unethical banks tend to breach this firewall, even in major financial centres having a clean track record in terms of banking integrity.

ORIGINS OF 'OFFSHORE BANKING'

The origin of offshore banking can be traced to the City of London where the offshore banks were first incorporated. Several banks worldwide opened offshore branches in London in the late 1940s and early 1950s to bypass the exchange control laws of the UK and enjoy the benefits of the worldwide financial network that the City of London offered.

However, it was from 1960 onwards that offshore banks really took off. There were three principal reasons for this expansion of offshore banking. First, a series of bank failures leading to a banking crisis in the United States in the 1960s led to the imposition of several controls there; in order to avoid these domestic controls a number of banks went offshore. Second, the banks wanted to enter the more profitable business of long-term lending, instead of the short-term lending in which they were generally engaged. The banks were able to enter the business of long-term lending because of the very large number of petro-dollars that had flooded the world markets in the 1970s, following the Middle East war crisis; the subsequent narco-dollars in the 1980s further swelled the funds waiting to be tapped by these offshore banks. The third reason for banks going offshore was to enter the profitable arena of sovereign debt – an area that was formerly a preserve of governments. The booming South-Asian tiger economies also gave a fillip to offshore banking. It is now anticipated that with most of the governments in the world opting for economic liberalization, the need for offshore banking will be considerably reduced. However, offshore banking as a 'mega-reality' is very much in existence today.

Another feature of offshore banking is its existence in conjunction with banking secrecy. Such secrecy in some of the offshore centres has been primarily responsible for earning offshore banking a bad name; for instance, banking secrecy in the UK is not an impediment to an investigation in a criminal case, but in some other jurisdictions it can be a big stumbling block to such an investigation.

OFFSHORE CENTRES: SERVICES OFFERED AND THEIR ABUSE

Offshore banks exist in the major financial centres as well as the small islands dotting the world. Moreover, these offshore centres are designed to service the genuine needs of the financial industry, through banking secrecy and incorporation of banks, trusts, companies, corporations and other financial and legal entities. According to some, banking secrecy is one of the foremost features intended to service the genuine needs of the people; and it is argued that it is a necessary condition for business competition, to guard against confiscation of assets by discriminatory regimes, to hide wealth from greedy and avaricious relatives – several other examples are cited as to why banking secrecy is a genuine service. Incorporation of banks offshore is resorted to by some multinational banks in order to circumvent currency reserve requirements in the home country. Individuals and companies may also prefer to form offshore trusts to make provisions for needy relatives if the inheritance laws in their own country do not permit the same: for example, in Islamic countries Muslim women do not have any inheritance rights and trusts are useful to provide them with the same. Offshore corporations and companies, discussed in detail in an earlier chapter, are also intended to service the genuine needs of the financial world; for instance a multinational company might wish to have a holding company or a corporation in an offshore jurisdiction in order to take advantage of the tax breaks offered.

Most of these very features of offshore centres which are meant to service genuine needs are just a step away if one chooses to go the unscrupulous way. Banking secrecy, offshore trusts, shell banks, shell corporations and shell companies can be and are being utilized to launder money. False documentation coupled with unscrupulous facilitators such as chartered accountants, lawyers, company formation agents and other financial experts further aid the process of money laundering and other illegal activities through these offshore centres. Indeed, it is the experience that offshore centres which are also free trade zones have become the centre of activity for all kinds of illegal activity apart from money laundering, such as arms trafficking, gold smuggling and invoice manipulation.

ABUSE OF OFFSHORE CENTRES

By corporations

Offshore centres have been subject to abuse by corporate entities, a prime example of such a misuse being that of the Long Term Capital Management company, which was licensed offshore in the Grand Cayman Islands. Operating from the Caymans, with all the opacity and lack of transparency that these offshore jurisdictions offer, the Long Term Capital Management company was able to speculate in the US stock market and thereby exercise excessive leverage in the form of notional control of US$1.25 trillion (1,000 times the capital held by the firm). Since such a speculative act on its part had put at risk a number of financial institutions in the US stock market, the Federal Reserve had to intervene to ensure an arrangement to prevent massive defaults. In the case of the Long Term Capital Management company, the Head of US Commodities Future Trading was constrained to remark that 'lack of basic information about the positions held by hedge funds, about the nature and extent of their exposures, potentially allows them to take positions that may threaten our regulated markets, or indeed, our economy, without the knowledge of any federal regulatory authority'. Alan Greenspan, Chairman of the Federal Reserve, in his testimony before the US Congress, felt that the problem was one inherent in the new technologies that have accompanied financial globalization. Most hedge funds, he testified, are only a short step from cyberspace. Try to regulate them, he warned, and they flee to less-regulated jurisdictions. At best, according to Greenspan, countries like the US can only regulate global market entrepreneurs like Long Term Capital by regulating the domestic sources of their funds.

By governments

Offshore centres have also been misused by the governments of countries to hide the true state of their economy. Due to opacity and lack of transparency, these offshore centres played a cataclysmic role in the South-Asian and Latin American financial crises which overtook the world in the late 1990s. According to an IMF study, in Argentina some US$3–4 billion were lost or hidden offshore in 1995; in Venezuela, billions of dollars in problem loans were moved offshore in 1994; in Korea, offshore deals circumvented bank lending from 1993 to 1996; in Thailand, poor lending decisions were rolled over offshore from 1993 to 1996; and in Malaysia, some US$10 billion in losses were hidden offshore in 1997. In Russia its Central Bank, through the use of a commercial bank, FIMACO, had managed to put government liabilities offshore and thereby artificially boost the balance-sheet of the Russian government to mislead the IMF into believing that the Russian currency reserves were stabilizing.

By criminals

The gravity of the problems posed by offshore centres with regard to crimes is also very serious and is vividly illustrated in two other cases. In 2000 it came to light that through an obscure trading company called Benex, US$4 billion had been laundered or moved as capital flight from Russia through the Bank of New York. Following the collapse of the corrupt military regime of General Abuja in Nigeria, the Nigerian government requested the United States, the United Kingdom and the IMF to help them to recover US$55 billion stolen by the military regime which was supposedly hidden in offshore jurisdictions.

OTHER FEATURES OF OFFSHORE BANKING

Why some countries resort to offshore banking

At this stage, it is worth asking why a number of countries have resorted to offshore banking along with tight banking secrecy laws. The most obvious answer is to make money; but such an approach to making money raises the question of the 'morality' of the act. For a number of the small island republics which are unable to subsist in the absence of any other economic activity, offshore banking has provided them with the much-needed capital to run their economies and administration.

Geography as a factor in their location

Another feature that is noteworthy with regard to these offshore centres or financial havens is that geography plays an important part. For instance, the islands of the Caribbean constitute the offshore centres for North America and Latin America; islands in the Pacific service Australia and other countries in the southern hemisphere; Hong Kong and Singapore serve as major offshore centres for South-East Asia. In fact, it can be stated that a number of countries tend to have their exclusive offshore centres – Switzerland has Liechtenstein, France has Andorra, the Netherlands has Netherlands Antilles, the UK has the Channel Islands. A list of offshore centres/financial havens was provided as Appendix 1 in Chapter X.

Tendency to blame each other

There is quite rightly a tendency on the part of onshore centres to blame the offshore banking centres for most of the ills afflicting the international financial world. However, in most forums it will be seen that the spokesmen of the offshore centres, who are generally very highly paid former central bankers from the major financial centres (often those who have worked for the Bank of England) put up a very spirited defence for the offshore centres by citing the benefits they provide. They go to great lengths to explain measures that they have taken to prevent the misuse of these centres. In defence of them, these spokesmen sometimes even go to the extreme of stating that we are 'all offshore to each other'. Despite their eloquent presentations, whatever these spokesmen say is strong on rhetoric but lacking in substance.

Regulatory and other related issues

Today it is more appropriate to state that most of the offshore centres can be termed financial havens. The regulatory issues that these offshore centres need to address relate to trusts, corporations, companies, incorporation of banks and banking secrecy. They also need to have due diligence procedures in place and in this context 'know your customer' should be an integral part of their routine financial transactions. Reporting of suspicious transactions and facilitating investigations of crimes also need to be a part of the regulatory regime. There should also be a code of conduct which the facilitators should follow to prevent the misuse of the offshore centres. Another point that needs to be highlighted is that some of these offshore centres, especially small islands such as the Cook Islands with a minuscule population, lack the capabilities to put in place a basic infrastructure for any sort of regulatory regime. Intense competition amongst the offshore centres, which results in each offering greater facilities and opportunities than the other, also militates against regulation.

SOME INTERESTING OFFSHORE CENTRES

It is worthwhile looking at some of the interesting offshore centres. The Cayman Islands is one of the most important offshore jurisdictions and is generally judged as the fifth-largest financial centre in the world, after London, New York, Tokyo and Hong Kong. There are more than 570 banks licensed in the Cayman Islands with deposits of over US$500 billion; Bermuda has 40 per cent of the world's captive insurance companies; Panama has 100 banks from 30 countries and its banking sector accounts for 11 per cent of its GDP. It wants to rival London and New York as a financial centre – the dollar being the official currency of Panama makes it an attractive offshore centre. Luxembourg, with 22 banks in the city, is seventh in the world in terms of assets in foreign currencies. Liechtenstein could be called the world's best tax haven because even the Swiss go there to do their banking, its bank secrecy being tighter than that afforded by their own system.

EXTRACTING CO-OPERATION FROM THE OFFSHORE CENTRES

A number of country-specific, regional and international initiatives have been launched to regulate these offshore centres/financial havens, which are dealt with in greater detail in a subsequent chapter.

With regard to co-operation in money laundering or other criminal cases, one feature which is much touted by offshore centres are the so-called 'mutual legal assistance treaties'. In fact, it is these treaties that are the most pernicious element militating against effective bilateral, regional or international cooperation. First, they are very difficult to conclude by most countries, due to protracted negotiations and their limited resources. Most of the offshore centres/financial havens (e.g., Switzerland and Singapore) will refuse to extend co-operation in cases of banking secrecy and money laundering on the pretext that they do not have a mutual legal assistance treaty with the country concerned. If a country is a signatory to any international convention enabling co-operation in cases of transnational crimes and money laundering, or if it is a member of any such grouping whose objective is the countering of transnational crime and money laundering, that should be the back-up necessary to extend co-operation on a bilateral basis.

The latest initiative to discipline offshore jurisdictions was a threat (in 1999) by Jonathan Winer, then US Deputy Assistant Secretary of State, to:

'create financial cordon sanitaires that would prohibit financial transactions with non-cooperative jurisdictions partially or entirely, until they come into compliance with international norms to protect against financial crime.'

Continuing in the same vein the initiative stated:

'Such an approach might have been unthinkable in a period when the principal goal of western economists was to ensure the free flow of capital throughout the world's economies. By contrast, the risks posed by illicit flows have indeed engendered a counter-current, one which may yet become something of a new tidal wave.'

CHAPTER XX

IMPORTANT FACTORS IMPINGING ON THE PROCEEDS OF CRIME AND MONEY LAUNDERING

THE EURO-DOLLAR MARKET AND MONEY LAUNDERING

The emergence of the Euro-dollar market

The Euro-dollar market is just another name for offshore banking. However, it has some peculiar features which merit its examination as a distinct entity in the context of money laundering.

The Euro-dollar market came into being as a result of the Hungarian crisis of 1956, precipitated by Russian intervention in Hungary. As a result of the Hungarian crisis, the assets of the Dnerdoni Bank in the United States were frozen. Following this, Russia wanted to open a dollar-denominated account outside the US to service its financial needs. In order to do so, the Dnerdoni Bank approached a British correspondent bank, and following its request, the British correspondent bank opened a dollar-denominated account for the Russian bank. This is the genesis of the Euro-dollar market: a few even argue that the Hungarian crisis is also the genesis of offshore banking. However as indicated earlier in the discussion on offshore/onshore banking, offshore banking preceded the Hungarian crisis.

Its expansion

Following the Iran–Contra affair and the Falklands War, many other countries had their accounts in the US frozen. As a result, European banks began accepting deposits in dollar-denominated accounts from other countries to enable them to service their countries' financial needs and also to manipulate the balance deposits. The acts of these European banks in opening dollar-denominated accounts led to the further extension of the Euro-dollar market.

Other factors that fuelled the Euro-dollar market from 1960 onwards were the same as those that fuelled offshore banking in the same period; in brief, these can be recounted as the banking crisis in the United States in the 1960s which led to banks moving offshore to avoid cumbersome domestic requirements, the availability of petro-dollars in the 1970s, followed by narco-dollars in the 1980s, and the desire of the commercial banks to enter into the arena of long-term capital lending and sovereign debt in order to earn handsome returns from the surplus dollars available.

What are Euro-dollars?

Euro-dollars can be defined as US dollars held by non-residents of the United States, including banks, in a dollar-denominated account outside the United States. The two sources of Euro-dollars are generally large companies (petro-companies in the Middle East) who are bank customers, or other banks with surplus dollars. Euro-dollars are generally held as transfers between accounts amongst the banks or as certificates of the deposits with the banks. The advantage of holding a certificate of deposit in Euro-dollars is that it can be sold or discounted by the holder prior to maturity like any other bill of exchange.

The nature of the market

The Euro-dollar market is basically an inter-bank market wherein dollar deposits are loaned to other banks to facilitate their loan-making abilities. Euro-dollar loans are generally granted by banks as long-term loans. For every Euro-dollar loan given by a bank, it has to cover it by backing it up with a Euro-dollar deposit. These deposits, which are generally for short periods, are rolled over or re-deposited amongst the banks to enable the continuation of the long-term loans. In order to raise this Euro-dollar deposit to support a loan, the bank has to pay a fee to the other bank; this fee is known as the London Inter-Bank Offer Rate, or LIBOR. The cost of the Euro-dollar loan to the borrower totals the rate of interest charged by the bank plus LIBOR, which is the cost to the bank of raising the certificate of the deposit for the loan.

This inter-bank market in Euro-dollars, in which short-term certificates of deposit are being rolled over and re-deposited, is facilitated to a large extent by the CHIPS and Fedwire systems for electronic transfer of US dollars. Through the CHIPS and Fedwire systems, rapid settlement of all inter-bank transactions is carried out on a daily basis. Expeditious settlement amongst banks of loans on a daily basis and certificates of deposit for the short term has its obvious advantages.

The Euro-dollar market, though relatively stable, has also been vulnerable to defaults. If one looks into the failure of the Herstatt Bank (one of the Euro-dollar banks) in Germany in 1974, one realizes the dangers of such an inter-bank market of bank loans backed up by short-term certificates of deposit; when the Herstatt Bank became insolvent, it could not repay Euro-dollar deposits to other banks, which finally had to use their own funds to repay the Euro-dollar deposits that they owed. Considering that 500 million Euro-dollars were involved in the collapse of Herstatt Bank, its repercussions were felt throughout the international banking community.

A boon for criminals and money launderers

The Euro-dollar market by its very nature offers tremendous advantages to drug traffickers and transnational criminals. First, the offshore nature of the market enables and facilitates the money laundering process, particularly by providing a convenient channel for moving the money through other financial havens located around the world before money can eventually be deposited in the Euro-dollar market. The size of the market, which runs into trillions of dollars, and the nature of the market, which comprises mostly inter-bank transactions, lends further anonymity to the dollars: once they are deposited in the Euro-dollar market by the criminals, the funds are practically impossible to track down. Moreover, Euro-dollars held by criminals outside their countries' jurisdictions (especially the US) are safe, because they are not easily liable to seizure. The Euro-dollar market also enables the criminals to hold their money in a stable currency, thereby ensuring that it is not eroded by devaluation. In addition, money in the Euro-dollar market carries a decent interest rate for the criminals. Above all, the ease with which the money can be moved around the world through the Euro-dollar market has its obvious advantages to the criminal to meet his business and other commitments.

INTRODUCTION OF THE EURO AND MONEY LAUNDERING

At the beginning of 2002, 12 of the member countries of the European Union switched over to the euro, a common currency which is now the legal tender in these 12 countries, instead of their original national currencies. The introduction of the euro is a landmark in the world of international finance because it has become the currency of one of the biggest economic blocs in the world, rivalling the United States in economic might.

The introduction of the euro in some of the EU member countries was a massive operation involving the printing of 14.5 billion bank notes and their storage and transportation prior to circulation. As regards euro coins, 50 billion were minted. The mechanics involved in the introduction and circulation of the euro involved advance storage, security during storage and provision for dual circulation of currency in the interim, i.e., prior to the withdrawal and destruction of the national currencies by the stipulated date. A point worth mentioning is that in some countries 80–90 per cent of the euro banknotes were introduced through ATMs.

As a currency, the euro has enormous circulation potential, both within the European Community and elsewhere. Moreover, because of the economic might of the EU, the euro has become a transaction and reserve currency worldwide. It may very soon rival the dollar as an internationally accepted and traded currency. Such an international currency would obviously be very attractive for the criminals to hold the proceeds of crime and to launder the same. In coming years, the euro will perform the same role for the criminals as the US dollar.

During the changeover period from national currency to the euro, it was widely apprehended that criminals would be able to launder their proceeds and pass off euro money as legitimate; however, in the ultimate analysis, the source of money would still need to be explained and therefore such an apprehension was not entirely valid. Still, in such a gigantic operation involving changeover of currencies, the scope for money laundering could not be ruled out, because there are limitations to the extent that transactions can be monitored. Since the euro as a currency also has very large-denomination notes of €500, these large-denomination notes would certainly facilitate the process of money laundering by making placement of money in the money laundering circuit so much easier.

Over a period of time the euro and the dollar are going to be the most widely traded currencies internationally; because of mobility offered by these currencies they will be passed extensively through the financial havens for layering of dirty money and integration as laundered money. Moreover, most criminals would like to hold on to their money in euros and dollars because of the stability of these currencies, which in turn would ensure that the value of the money is not eroded. In all likelihood, as with the Euro-dollar market, a market in euro will also emerge on the world scene; thus criminals would have the added benefit of earning interest on their Euro-dollars and their counterpart, the euro.

Once a new currency such as the euro has been introduced on such a large scale in such a powerful economic bloc, its integrity has to be ensured against counterfeiting. Keeping in view the technological advances which are available to criminals to counterfeit the currency, the disparate laws to deal with counterfeit currency in the member countries of the EU, and also their capabilities to detect the same, very elaborate mechanisms have also been put into place to prevent the counterfeiting of the euro and to take effective action should it take place. Ultimately, the integrity of the currency and people's faith in it has to be ensured to make it widely accepted.

MERGER OF STOCK EXCHANGES

On 3 May 2000 a dramatic announcement was made to the world that the London Stock Exchange and Deutsche Bourse would be merging at the end of 2000; the merged stock exchange to be known as the iX exchange. On the same day, NASDAQ announced a joint venture with the company that was proposed to run the merged Anglo-German exchange, i.e., the iX. The idea behind such a merger was to provide 24-hour seamless trading in international securities.

The speed and suddenness of the above communications surprised many in the world of international finance. Though these mergers did not finally come about as proposed, they are bound to take place in the future, once agreements regarding the rules and regulations pertaining to merged exchanges have been settled and adequate safeguards provided against insider trading and manipulation in securities.

Apart from giving a fillip and boost to international trading in securities, these merged exchanges would also offer greater anonymity and opportunity to criminals to launder their proceeds in a relatively larger arena of securities trading. The seamless platform would also make money laundering a 24-hour industry.

THE TREND TOWARDS MEGA-CORPORATIONS AS A RESULT OF MERGERS

Huge business corporations are straddling the world scene today as a result of mergers of not only large companies but also large multinationals. In terms of their economic might, a number of these huge conglomerates are much stronger than the national economies of some countries. According to a study carried out by UNCTAD, 29 of the world's 100 leading economic entities were companies; this was determined by comparing profits and wages of countries to the economic output of the companies. According to this study, Exxon is bigger than Pakistan, General Motors is bigger than New Zealand, while Nigeria is a step lower than Chrysler and General Electric, the tobacco company Philip Morris is on a par with Slovakia, Tunisia and Guatemala.

The UNCTAD figures further revealed that the relative importance of the top 100 companies is on the rise because their activities accounted for 4.3 per cent of world GDP in 2000, compared to 3.3 per cent in 1990. According to the UNCTAD spokesman, one could state that in general the top companies are growing at a faster rate than countries.

The trend towards mega-mergers must once again be viewed against the backdrop of economic liberalization and the drive towards free markets which is now treated as an integral part of the trend towards globalization. There is also supposed to be a Washington consensus that also supports this 'new liberalism' – according to some this is a US-led initiative in a unipolar world wherein the US is the sole superpower. However, there is a kind of rethink under way in the world as to the efficacy and the usefulness of the Washington consensus. A number of economists feel that some regions need to be helped with special assistance programmes instead of being left to the mercies and vagaries of the free market.

Recent corporate bankruptcies in the US following accounting scandals are also leading many to question the enormous powers exercised by these mega-corporations and the need to discipline them. There is also always an inherent danger in this globalized world of mega-corporations passing into the hands of criminals and affording them the much-needed scope for almost limitless money laundering. The danger to countries from such criminalized mega-corporations becomes all the more sinister considering that quite a few of them have the capability to rival the national economies of some countries.

PART V

LAWS AND THE ROLE OF INTERNATIONAL/REGIONAL ORGANIZATIONS AND EXPERT BODIES

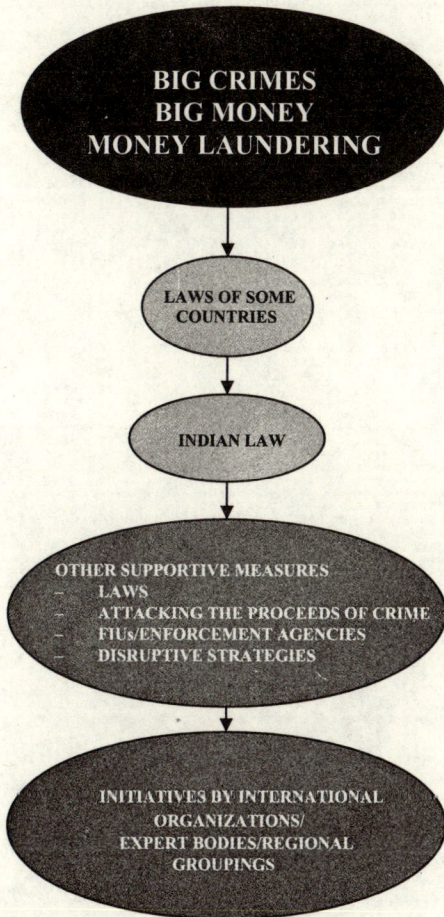

BIG CRIMES
BIG MONEY
MONEY LAUNDERING

LAWS OF SOME COUNTRIES

INDIAN LAW

OTHER SUPPORTIVE MEASURES
- **LAWS**
- **ATTACKING THE PROCEEDS OF CRIME**
- **FIUs/ENFORCEMENT AGENCIES**
- **DISRUPTIVE STRATEGIES**

INITIATIVES BY INTERNATIONAL ORGANIZATIONS/ EXPERT BODIES/REGIONAL GROUPINGS

CHAPTER XXI

MONEY LAUNDERING LAWS

BACKDROP TO THE LEGISLATIVE INITIATIVES TO COUNTER MONEY LAUNDERING

To counter any crime a legal framework has to be in place; since money laundering has only been perceived as a serious crime from 1970 onwards, most of the legislation to deal with it is subsequent to this period. While examining money laundering laws of several countries, it is noticeable that quite a few of the legal provisions to deal with it are scattered over several laws; this can be ascribed to the evolutionary process in the countries concerned as a response to the problem of money laundering. However, some countries who were late starters in perceiving the problem of money laundering have drawn up dedicated and comprehensive laws to deal with this crime: while enacting their anti-money laundering legislation they have drawn upon the experience of some of the countries that have pioneered the fight against money laundering. Today most of the countries who have not enacted money laundering legislation or who are in the process of enacting such legislation are drawing up a single dedicated comprehensive law to deal with it.

Several international organizations, special economic/expert groups and regional initiatives have seized the problem of money laundering and in their own way have been trying to devise ways and measures to deal with it effectively.[1] The initiative of these international organizations and economic/expert groupings has influenced the enactment of countries' legislation to counter money laundering; through constant pressure these organizations are also trying to ensure that most countries have an anti-money laundering regime in place.[2] Special attention has also been focused by these international forums on disciplining recalcitrant offshore jurisdictions which are also classified as financial havens.

Prior to an examination of the laws of countries to deal with money laundering, it is pertinent to point out that some countries have introduced very good legislation to deal with this problem; then there are other countries, especially recalcitrant jurisdictions, that have enacted inadequate laws to deal with it, which can only be described as 'shams'. In between these two types of laws described above have been half-hearted attempts by some countries to put an anti-money laundering law in place which again is not the right approach to deal with this problem because the laws enacted by these countries have several loopholes.

---

[1] The role of international organizations, economic/expert groups and regional initiatives vis-à-vis money laundering is dealt with in a subsequent chapter.

[2] Today 100 countries have anti-money laundering laws; see 'Enhancing Contributions to Combating Money Laundering' Policy Paper by the IMF and the World Bank, 26 April 2001, p. 13.

In this book it has not been possible to cover all of the anti-money laundering laws of all countries. However, an endeavour has been made to cover the laws of a fairly diverse group of countries, especially those that are pioneers in the legislative fight against money laundering. Most of the money laundering laws that are discussed during the course of this chapter can be categorized as good and effective laws. However, a couple of not-so-effective/diffused laws have also been examined.

While examining the anti-money laundering laws of various countries it will be noticed that some of them have unique provisions that have cropped up in the context of their socio-economic–legal evolution; some of these might be worth incorporating by other countries to make their laws more effective. The approach that has been followed while discussing the laws of various countries has been to define money laundering in the context of a particular law and then to go on to discuss salient features of that law.

LAWS OF SOME COUNTRIES

US law

The Money Laundering Control Act was enacted in the United States in 1986 to deal with the crime of money laundering. This Act was further amended by the Money Laundering Control Act 1988, which was passed as a part of the Anti-Drug Abuse Act 1988. Prior to these enactments, federal enforcement agencies in the United States had to rely on drug charges, racketeering charges and the Banking Secrecy Act 1970 to prosecute money launderers.

The Money Laundering Act Control 1986, as amended in 1988, has the following salient features:

(i) It creates a federal offence of criminal money laundering.
(ii) It deals with both domestic and international money laundering.
(iii) It provides for sting/undercover operations.
(iv) It defines both the domestic and international dimensions of money laundering under various circumstances, as well as money laundering in sting operations.
(v) The criminal law provisions under this Act include both fines and imprisonment.
(vi) Since money laundering is linked to specified unlawful activity under this Act, that term has also been defined.
(vii) It provides for forfeiture of proceeds of crime; it has provisions for both civil forfeiture and criminal forfeiture.
(viii) It has important provisions relating to asset sharing between domestic agencies and international authorities of the forfeited proceeds of crime.
(ix) It defines financial institutions and transactions of a financial nature.
(x) It lays down that monetary transactions in excess of US$10,000 linked to specified unlawful activity are subject to penal provisions of fine and imprisonment. Monetary transactions have also been clearly defined under the Act.
(xi) It prohibits the structuring of currency transactions in order to evade reporting requirements.

(xii) The concept of extra-territorial jurisdictions has been incorporated under this Act.

(xiii) It incorporates penalties for financial institutions and their employees in the case of non-compliance with the provisions of the Act.

According to this Act, domestic money laundering is defined as follows:

'Whoever, knowing that the property involved in a financial transaction represents the proceeds of crime from specified unlawful activity, conducts or attempts to conduct such a financial transaction which in fact involves the proceeds of specified unlawful activity:

(A) (i) With the intent to promote the carrying on of specified unlawful activity; or

(ii) With intent to engage in conduct constituting a violation of section 7201 or 7206 of the Internal Revenue Code of 1986; or

(B) Knowing that the transaction is designed in whole or in part:

(i) to conceal or disguise the nature, the location, the source, the ownership or the control of the proceeds of specified unlawful activity; or

(ii) to avoid a transaction reporting requirement under State or Federal law, shall be sentenced to a fine of not more that $500,000 or twice the value of the property involved in the transaction, whichever is greater, or imprisonment for not more than twenty years, or both.'

It defines international money laundering as:

'Whoever transports, transmits, or transfers, or attempts to transport, transmit, or transfer a monetary instrument or funds from a place in the United States to or through a place outside the United States or to a place in the United States from or through a place outside the United States:

(A) With the intent to promote the carrying on of specified unlawful activity; or

(B) Knowing that the monetary instrument or funds involved in the transportation, transmission, or transfer represent the proceeds of some form of unlawful activity and knowing that such transportation, transmission, or transfer is designed in whole or in part:

(i) to conceal or disguise the nature, the location, the source, the ownership, or the control of the proceeds of specified unlawful activity; or

(ii) to avoid a transaction reporting requirement under State or Federal law, shall be sentenced to a fine of not more that $500,000 or twice the value of the monetary instrument or funds involved in the transportation, transmission, or transfer whichever is greater, or imprisonment for not more than twenty years, or both. For the purpose of the offense described in subparagraph (B), the defendant's knowledge may be established by proof that a law enforcement officer represented the matter specified in subparagraph (B) as true, and the defendant's subsequent statements or actions indicate that the defendant believed such representations to be true.'

195

It provides for sting operations and money laundering offences through the following provisions:

'*(A) to promote the carrying on of specified unlawful activity;*

(B) to conceal or disguise the nature, location, source, ownership, or control of property believed to be the proceeds of specified unlawful activity; or

(C) to avoid a transaction reporting requirement under State or Federal law, conducts or attempts to conduct a financial transaction involving property represented to be the proceeds of specified unlawful activity, or property used to conduct or facilitate specified unlawful activity,

shall be fined under this title or imprisoned for not more than 20 years, or both. For purposes of this paragraph and paragraph (2), the term "represented" means any representation made by a law enforcement officer or by another person at the direction of, or with the approval of, a Federal Official authorised to investigate or prosecute violations of this section.'

The Banking Secrecy Act 1970 as amended in the 1990s also imposes an obligation on the financial institutions to report certain specified transactions and suspicious transactions. It also puts an obligation on the financial institutions to have internal regulations in place to ensure due diligence to guard against money laundering. Record-keeping requirements of financial institutions are also laid down in the amendments to the Banking Secrecy Act.

Federal agencies under the Department of Justice, Department of Treasury and Department of State are charged with enforcing various money laundering regulations. The principal agencies under the Department of Treasury include FinCEN, IRS-Criminal Investigative Division (IRS-CI), the US Customs Service (Customs), the United State Secret Service (USSS), and the Bureau of Alcohol, Tobacco and Firearms (ATF). The principal agencies under the Department of Justice are the Asset Forfeiture and Money Laundering Section (AFMLS) of the Criminal Division, the Special Operations Division (SOD), the Federal Bureau of Investigation (FBI), and the Drug Enforcement Agency (DEA). The Bureau for International Narcotics and Law Enforcement Affairs (INL) under the Department of State is also an important wing for dealing with money laundering.

In addition, the US postal service, Office of the National Drug Control Policy, Federal Banking Regulators under the Federal Reserve, The Security and the Exchange Commission and Commodities Future Trading Commission all have a role to play in countering money laundering. In the United States, local efforts to combat money laundering are also undertaken and form an important component in this fight. Thirty-three states have laws to deal with money laundering; these states have also set up specialized units for investigation.

The United States has also mandated that a national money laundering strategy is drawn up annually wherein tasks assigned to the various agencies are specified along with the targeted dates for carrying out the same. Thus the National Money Laundering Strategy Report for each year co-ordinates the role of the various agencies of the government both at the federal and state level.

UK law

The UK law dealing with money laundering is scattered over several statutes namely, the Criminal Justice Act 1993, the Drug Trafficking Act 1994, the Prevention of Terrorism Act 1989 and Money Laundering Regulations 1993. Following the Criminal Justice Act 1993, the law as it relates to drugs, terrorist crime, money laundering and other crimes is much the same.

Under the UK law money laundering relates to:

(a) Concealing or disguising property.
(b) Converting or transferring property or removing it from a jurisdiction.

To constitute an offence the money must be the proceeds of crime. The salient provisions pertaining to money laundering under the UK law are:

(i) Laundering another person's proceeds of crime, which means assisting another to retain proceeds of crime, acquiring, possessing or using another's proceeds of crime, or concealing, etc., another person's proceeds of crime; to constitute the offence of 'laundering another person's proceeds of crime', knowledge, suspicion or reasonable grounds to believe under varying circumstances are necessary conditions.

(ii) The offence of failure to disclose the knowledge or suspicion of money laundering extends only to drugs and terrorist offences.

(iii) The tipping-off offences, constitute 'tipping-off in connection with money laundering investigation', 'tip-off in connection with disclosures' and 'tip-offs in connection with production orders or warrants'.

(iv) Failure to install anti-money laundering systems are covered by the Money Laundering Regulations 1993 and apply to banks and other financial institutions. These regulations mandate that an internal regulatory system be put in place by banks and financial institutions for identification, record keeping and training of employees, so that the employees are aware of the same.

(v) The penal provisions for all the offences relating to money laundering extend from imprisonment to fine.

(vi) Asset sharing and confiscation of the proceeds of crime both domestically and internationally are also provided for in the UK law.

(vii) International co-operation amongst countries based upon reciprocity is another feature of the UK law on money laundering.

With regard to recovery of the proceeds of crime, the Financial Services Authority in the UK has also been charged with some functions. To recover the proceeds of crime under the Financial Services Act 2000, the Financial Services Authority has also been authorized to use civil as opposed to criminal proceedings. It is also proposed to set up a National Confiscation Authority in the UK to ensure that the proceeds of crime are forfeited/confiscated in a targeted and focused manner by the several agencies involved in this process.

Canadian law

Canadian law on money laundering is contained in part XII.2 of the Canadian Criminal Code. In the Code, the offence of laundering proceeds of crime is defined as follows:

> *'Every one commits an offence who uses, transfers the possession of, sends or delivers to any person or place, transports, transmits, alters, disposes of or otherwise deals with, in any manner and by any means, any property or any proceeds of any property with intent to conceal or convert that property or those proceeds and knowing that all or a part of that property or of those proceeds was obtained or derived directly or indirectly as a result of:*
>
> *(a) the commission in Canada of an enterprise crime offence or a designated drug offence; or*
>
> *(b) an act or omission anywhere that, if it had occurred in Canada, would have constituted an enterprise crime offence or a designated drug offence'*

and *inter alia* also defines money laundering. The criminal law provisions relating to laundering the proceeds of crime provide for imprisonment for a term not exceeding 10 years.

'Designated drug offence' and 'enterprise crime' offences have also been defined in the Canadian Criminal Code and amongst several others, cover offences such as bribery, frauds, breach of trust, extortion, murder, theft, forgery and counterfeiting. Both an attempt and a conspiracy to commit a crime are treated on a par with commission of enterprise crime under the Code.

Another interesting feature of Canadian law relates to the forfeiture of proceeds of crime. According to the Code, even if a person charged with an enterprise crime offence is discharged in connection with that offence, the court on the 'balance of probability' can still order the forfeiture of the proceeds of crime allegedly linked to the enterprise crime offence in question. The interesting feature of the Code relating to forfeiture is that even if the proceeds of crime are totally unrelated to the enterprise crime in question for which the person has been discharged, the court can still forfeit the same if it is satisfied 'beyond reasonable doubt' that the proceeds in question are those of crime.

Provisions also exist under Canadian law for imposing a fine in lieu of forfeiture, and imprisonment in default of fine. The Canadian Criminal Code also provides for an inference to be drawn about property being the proceeds of crime if the property, after the crime has been committed, exceeds that which the person had prior to commission of the crime.

German law

There are two laws in Germany to deal with money laundering, titled 'Act on the detection of proceeds from serious crimes (Money Laundering Act)' of 25 October 1993 and 'Money Laundering: Disguising of Illegally Acquired Assets' of 9 May 1998.

The law of 1998 *inter alia* defines money laundering in its criminal law sections and is reproduced below:

> *'From three months' up to five years' imprisonment shall be imposed on any person who conceals or disguises the origin of an item which derived from an illegal act named in the second sentence, or who prevents or places in jeopardy the detection of its origin, location, forfeiture, confiscation or seizure. Illegal acts in the meaning of the first sentence shall be:*
>
> *(i) Major crimes.*
> *(ii) Less serious crimes under "various provisions of law enumerated in this Act".'*

Aiding, abetting and attempt to commit the crime of money laundering are also made punishable under the law of 1998. This Act also provides for graded punishment whereby in particularly serious cases the punishment can be up to 10 years. A particularly serious case is defined as that in which the offender acts on a commercial basis or as a member of a gang formed for recurrent commission of money laundering. If a person does not take due caution regarding the criminal origin of the property he is again liable to punishment of up to 2 years' imprisonment or a fine. Proceeds of crime including laundered money are liable to confiscation under this Act whether they are the property of the offender or a third person.

The Act of 1993 deals primarily with financial transactions by financial institutions. It defines financial institutions and also lays down a regulatory framework to ensure due diligence by financial institutions. Reporting of certain transactions, including suspicious transactions, and maintenance of records for a specified period by financial institutions are also stipulated under this Act. Violations are punishable by fines. Federal police, local police and fiscal enforcement authorities are charged with responsibilities under the 1993 Act.

French law

The French law on money laundering is contained in 'Law No. 90-614 of 12 July 1990 relating to the participation of financial institutions in the prevention of laundering of capital originating from the drug traffic (I)' and 'Law No. 96-392 of 13 May 1996 relating to the prevention of laundering and the drug traffic, and international cooperation in the area of confiscation of the proceeds of crime (I)'.

The law of 1990 relates to financial institutions and their transactions. It provides for declarations by financial institutions of financial transactions and also suspicious transactions. It also requires financial institutions to put an internal regulatory mechanism in place to ensure due diligence in their transactions. Record-keeping requirements are also laid down under this law. Penal provisions extend to warning, reprimand and imposition of fines.

The law of 1996 defines money laundering under two headings – 'Simple Money Laundering' and 'Aggravated Money Laundering'. Simple money laundering corresponds to facilitating, by any means, the fraudulent justification of the origin of the assets or revenues of the perpetrator of a crime or offence having procured direct or indirect profit for said perpetrator. Assistance with the investment, dissimulation or conversion of the direct or indirect proceeds of a crime or offence also constitutes laundering. Laundering is punishable by imprisonment for a period of five years and a fine of FF 2,50,000. 'Aggravated' money laundering is punishable by imprisonment for a period of ten years and a fine of FF 5,000,000 (i) when committed on a regular basis or using the facilities provided in the exercise of a professional activity; or (ii) when committed by an organized group. Attempts to commit offences under this law attract the same penal provisions as the offences themselves.

However, this law also makes a distinction between natural persons and legal entities. It imposes certain other forms of punishment which are more in the nature of prohibition of certain privileges/facilities in the case of natural persons: the prohibition extends to refusal of the granting of a firearms licence or driving licence, restrictions on facilities for cheques and credit cards, etc. Legal entities convicted of money laundering are liable to fines and prohibition of the activity which enabled the offence to be committed.

This law also seeks to control the activities of currency dealers by imposing certain reporting requirements on them. Measures relating to international co-operation which extend to identification, search, seizure, forfeiture and confiscation of proceeds of crime are also provided in this Act. Another interesting feature of this French law is the provision of punishment and fine for persons who are unable to justify a financial resource corresponding to their lifestyle while keeping company with drug traffickers.

Swiss law

Switzerland is a recognized financial haven. According to the Swiss authorities, it is more liable to misuse in layering and integration of laundered money. Amendments were made in 1990 in the Swiss Penal Code to counter money laundering. Article 305 bis prohibits the laundering of money with an illegal origin; money laundering under this article is defined as 'an act intended to obstruct the identification, detection and confiscation of assets earned by criminal means'. Article 305 ter punishes the failure to exercise vigilance in financial dealings, in particular failure to verify the beneficial owner. It was further strengthened in 1999 and gave bankers the right to transmit to authorities information about activities which gave rise to suspicion that assets may derive from a crime.

A new law on money laundering was also enacted in 1998 which supplements the Swiss Penal Code provisions. This law relates to financial intermediaries, and under it financial entities are required to have internal regulations in place to exercise due diligence. Financial institutions are also required to maintain records and provide training to their personnel to comply with the law's provisions. Under this law, financial institutions must report all suspicious transactions relating to money laundering to the relevant authorities. Violations under the law of 1998 are punishable by fines. In addition, under the banking law the Federal Banking Commission can withdraw the licence of a bank if it finds that its conduct is not beyond reproach – which also means involvement of the bank in money laundering operations.

In Switzerland, self-regulation of the banks is ensured by an agreement between the Swiss Bankers' Association and the banks under a Code of Conduct with regard to exercise of due diligence. This self-regulation initiative in Switzerland dates back to 1977. The agreement on self-regulation is binding on the Swiss Bankers Association and the signatory banks and compliance with the same is an indicator of conduct being 'beyond reproach'. The para-banking sector and private insurance companies are also subject to supervision and self-regulation with regard to money laundering.

South African law

In South Africa the money laundering offence is dealt with under the Prevention of Organized Crime Act (POCA) 1998, with the promulgation of which all other laws which dealt with money laundering and other crimes were repealed. The Prevention of Organized Crime Act:

(i) criminalizes racketeering and creates offences relating to activities of criminal gangs;
(ii) criminalizes money laundering in general and also creates a number of serious offences in respect of laundering and racketeering;
(iii) contains a general reporting obligation for businesses coming into possession of suspicious property; and
(iv) contains mechanisms for confiscation of proceeds of crime under the criminal law and for forfeiture of proceeds and instrumentalities of offences under the civil law.

It also creates two sets of money laundering offences:

(i) offences involving proceeds of all forms of crime; and
(ii) offences involving proceeds of a pattern of racketeering.

Under the POCA, money laundering has been defined in three separate circumstances in the three main offences pertaining to it, which state:

First, a person who knows or ought to have known that property is or forms part of the proceeds of unlawful activities, commits an offence in terms of section 4 if he enters into any agreement, arrangement or transaction (whether legally enforceable or not) in connection with the property; or performs any other act in connection with the property, which has the effect or is likely to have the effect:

(i) of concealing or disguising the nature, source, location disposition or movement of the property or the ownership of the property or any interest in the property; or
(ii) of enabling or assisting any person who committed an offence to avoid prosecution or to remove or diminish any property acquired as a result of an offence.

201

Secondly, a person commits an offence in terms of section 5 if he knows or ought reasonably to have known that another person has obtained the proceeds of unlawful activities and enters into any transaction, agreement or arrangements in terms of which:

(i) the retention or control by or on behalf of that other person of the proceeds of unlawful activity is facilitated; or
(ii) the proceeds are used to make available to that person, to acquire property on his behalf, or to benefit him in any other way.

Thirdly, a person who acquires, uses or possesses property and who knows or ought reasonably to have known that it is or forms parts of the proceeds of unlawful activities of another person, commits an offence under section 6.

Severe penalties and fines are imposed on persons convicted for money laundering offences under the POCA and these range from imprisonment for up to 30 years and fines up to US$9 million.

The proceeds from the racketeering activities, if laundered, are also dealt with under the POCA, under which suspicious financial transactions relating to crime are also required to be reported. Tipping-off persons implicated in money laundering and other criminal offences is also an offence under the POCA.

Regarding financial institutions' internal regulations and.due diligence, record-keeping and reporting requirements, another Act has been enacted in South Africa, the Financial Intelligence Centre Act. This Act also creates a Financial Intelligence Centre to act as a clearing house for all intelligence relating to money laundering. It also creates a Money Laundering Advisory Council to evaluate the money laundering effort and ensure better co-ordination amongst the various government and enforcement agencies.

Money laundering from a South African perspective is not only confined to those acts that are committed with the intention of laundering the funds but extends, in principle, to every act that is committed in respect of the proceeds of unlawful activities. However, such acts will only constitute laundering offences if it can be proved that they were committed intentionally or by a person who negligently failed to appreciate the true nature of the property concerned.

Hong Kong law

In discussing the position with regard to Hong Kong, I think it will be helpful to quote the following extract on money laundering from a booklet entitled 'A Guideline for Remittance Agents and Money Changers' issued by the Joint Financial Intelligence Unit of Hong Kong:

'Many people think of "money laundering" as some form of complicated and sophisticated process by which proceeds of crime are hidden, disguised or made to appear as if they were generated by legitimate means. This can be termed the "traditional" definition of money laundering.

The definition of money laundering contained in Hong Kong law, the "legal" definition, is far simpler than the "traditional" definition. The legal definition is contained in Section 25 of the DTROP, and Section 25 of OSCO. In essence the legal definition of money laundering states that any transaction involving the proceeds of serious crime is money laundering. Anyone commits the offence of money laundering if they carry out a transaction involving property, including money, in circumstances in which a reasonable person would have believed that the property was the proceeds of serious crime. Whether or not there is any attempt to hide or disguise the source of the criminal proceeds is irrelevant. Money laundering is a serious criminal offence in Hong Kong.'

On the face of it, the stance of the Hong Kong authorities in not distinguishing between money laundering and proceeds of crime is nonsense because the proceeds of crime once laundered appear legitimate. It seems to be the intention of the Hong Kong authorities not to attack so-called 'legitimate proceeds'. As regards the contention of the Hong Kong authorities about striking at the proceeds of crime, that position holds with regard to law in all countries in the world and Hong Kong is no exception in this respect.

However, in Hong Kong the activities of remittance agents and money changers are licensed and regulated. They are required to have a regulatory mechanism in place to exercise due diligence; they are also required to keep records of their financial transactions and to report suspicious transactions. These measures with regard to remittance agents and money changers are meant to curtail illegal acts on their part.

Russian law

A law to counter money laundering became effective in Russia in February 2002. According to this law, money laundering is defined as 'attributing the legal form to the possession, enjoyment and disposal of cash and other assets gained as a result of crime'. It also defines financial institutions and lays down the regulatory mechanism for exercising due diligence. Under this law, financial organizations are required to keep records of financial transactions, report certain stipulated transactions and all suspicious transactions to the Central Agency to be authorized under the Money Laundering Act.

The Central Agency under the Money Laundering Act has been envisaged as having a supervisory and co-ordinating role with no investigatory powers; it is intended to be like an Intelligence Clearing House to ensure that appropriate agencies investigate money laundering offences. The Act also provides for international co operation in money laundering offences through the Central Agency; this co-operation extends to investigation, trial and confiscation of assets.

MODEL LEGISLATIONS ON MONEY LAUNDERING

There are also two international model legislations to counter money laundering; one is the United Nations Convention entitled 'Model Money Laundering and Proceeds of

Crime Bill 1998'[3] and the other is the Commonwealth Convention entitled 'Draft Model Law for the Prohibition of Money Laundering'. Both these conventions define money laundering and indicate penalties for the same.

UN Convention

According to the United Nations Convention a person commits the offence of money laundering if that person:

(a) acquires, possesses or uses property, knowing or having reason to believe that it is derived directly or indirectly from acts or omissions:
  (i) in (name of State) which constitute an offence against any law of (name of State) punishable by imprisonment for not less than (12 months);
  (ii) outside (name of State) which, had they occurred in (name of State), would have constituted an offence against the law of (name of State) punishable by imprisonment for not less than (12 months).
(b) renders assistance to another person for:
  (i) the conversion or transfer of property derived directly or indirectly from those acts or omissions, with the aim of concealing or disguising the illicit origin of that property, or of aiding any person involved in the commission of the offence to evade the legal consequences thereof;
  (ii) concealing or disguising the true nature, origin, location, disposition, movement or ownership of the property derived directly or indirectly from those acts or omissions.

Commonwealth Convention

According to the Commonwealth Convention money laundering means:

(a) (i) engaging, directly or indirectly, in a transaction that involves property that is the proceeds of crime; or
  (ii) receiving, possessing, concealing, disguising, transferring, converting, disposing of, removing from or bringing into the (territory) any property that is the proceeds of crime; and
(b) (i) knowing, or having reasonable grounds for suspecting that the property is derived or realized, directly or indirectly, from some form of unlawful activity; or
  (ii) where the conduct is of a natural person, failing without reasonable excuse to take reasonable steps to ascertain whether or not the property is derived or realized directly or indirectly, from some form of unlawful activity; or

---

[3] The UN model legislation is available both for common law and civil law systems.

(iii) where the conduct is of a financial institution, failing to implement or apply procedures and control to combat money laundering.

The role of financial institutions to control money laundering has also been outlined in these conventions. This entails putting in place an internal regulatory mechanism, keeping a record of all financial transactions and reporting certain specified financial transactions to the anti-money laundering authority. All financial institutions are expected to exercise due diligence in all of their transactions and also to report suspicious transactions to the anti-money laundering authority.

Targeting the proceeds of crime by tracing/search, freezing/seizure and confiscation/forfeiture is another feature of these two conventions; they also have provisions for international co-operation regarding various aspects of money laundering, including admissibility of evidence.

Both the conventions also provide for an anti-money laundering authority which would act as a financial intelligence unit, or clearing house, for intelligence. A co-ordinating and supervisory role is envisaged for the anti-money laundering authority under both of these conventions. It would not have investigatory powers, but would have powers of search and seizure; however, the anti-money laundering authority can pass on intelligence to enforcement authorities for investigation. It can also co-ordinate investigations amongst several authorities.

Disclosure statements made by financial institutions and their employees are protected under the Commonwealth Convention, which also provides for fairly comprehensive monitoring of currency movement across borders.

CONVENTIONS AND DIRECTIVES TO COUNTER MONEY LAUNDERING

United Nations Convention against Transnational Organized Crime

The United Nations Convention against Organized Crime, adopted by the General Assembly in 2000, also recognizes money laundering as one of the most serious transnational crimes. It defines money laundering as:

(a) (i) The conversion or transfer of property, knowing that such property is the proceeds of crime, for the purpose of concealing or disguising the illicit origin of the property or of helping any person who is involved in the commission of the predicate offence to evade the legal consequences of his or her action;

(ii) The concealment or disguise of the true nature, source, location, disposition, movement or ownership of or rights with respect to property, knowing that such property is the proceeds of crime.

(b) Subject to the basic concepts of its legal system:

(i) The acquisition, possession or use of property, knowing, at the time of receipt, that such property is the proceeds of crime;

(ii) Participation in, association with or conspiracy to commit and aiding, abetting, facilitating and counselling the commission of any of the offences established in accordance with the convention.

Among the measures to combat money laundering are:

(a) a regulatory and supervisory regime for banks and financial institutions which entails customer identification, record keeping and reporting of suspicious transactions;
(b) co-operation and exchange of information amongst administrative, regulatory, law enforcement and other authorities dedicated to money laundering both at the national and international level;
(c) monitoring of cash and other negotiable instruments across borders; and
(d) global, regional, sub-regional and bilateral co-operation.

European Council directives and other initiatives on money laundering

The Council of Europe issued a directive in June 1991 on the 'prevention of use of financial systems for the purpose of money laundering'. This directive was further amended in 1999 to cover 'proceeds of crime and money laundering offences'. The Council of Europe has also taken the initiative regarding the 'identification, tracing, freezing, seizing and confiscation of instrumentalities and the proceeds from crime' and improving mutual assistance in criminal matters, in particular, in the area of 'combating organized crime, laundering of the proceeds from crime and financial crime'.

CHAPTER XXII

MONEY LAUNDERING LAW IN INDIA

BACKDROP

The bill for the prevention of money laundering which had been pending before the Indian Parliament since 1998 was ultimately approved on 28 November 2002. This bill has now become law after receiving presidential assent. At the very outset it is worth mentioning that the passage of this law has had fairly a very chequered history; prior to its ratification it also faced tremendous opposition from various quarters.

The Prevention of Money Laundering Bill was first introduced in the Lok Sabha (Lower House of the Parliament) on 5 August 1998. The Lok Sabha referred the bill to a Joint Standing Committee of Parliament which submitted its report in March 1999; however, this bill lapsed due to the dissolution of the twelfth Lok Sabha. The bill was re-introduced in October 1999 in the thirteenth Lok Sabha after incorporating most of the recommendations of the Joint Standing Committee. The thirteenth Lok Sabha passed the bill in December 1999; when the bill went to the Upper House (Rajya Sabha), they referred it to a Select Committee for examination. The Select Committee of the Rajya Sabha, after examining the bill in detail, submitted a fairly comprehensive report on 24 July 2002. After deliberating at considerable length on the Joint Standing Committee Report, the government reintroduced the bill in Parliament and as mentioned, it was finally approved by the Parliament and has now become law.

One of the most unfortunate circumstances surrounding the Prevention of Money Laundering Law in its initial stages was to link its passage with the Foreign Exchange Management Bill (FEMA), which was designed to replace the much-maligned Foreign Exchange Regulation Act (FERA). The way FERA was implemented in India, by selectively targeting the top industrialists, around the time when the Prevention of Money Laundering Bill was introduced into Parliament, created tremendous apprehension in the minds of Indian business and industry that the money laundering law might also ultimately be targeted against them in the same draconian way. This linking of money laundering with FEMA/FERA was a most unfortunate development and the Indian policy-makers are to be blamed for this. This lack of perception on the part of policy-makers arose because they could not comprehend that one refrains from laundering money or going underground not only because of beneficial exchange rates; criminals have their own reasons to stay underground or launder money. Even in countries where there are no penalties for exchange control violations, such as the United States, Canada and countries in Western Europe, money laundering by criminals wishing to keep their activities underground does take place. Thus, in the very first instance, linking the passage of FEMA/repeal of FERA with the Prevention of Money Laundering Bill was quite unnecessary. The correct approach should have been to push both these bills as laws in their own right and independently of each other. However, following the dawn of some sense on policy-makers, FERA was finally repealed following the passage of FEMA, which sought to bring about a liberalized foreign exchange regime in the country; under FEMA, violation of foreign exchange regulations was to be treated as a civil, not a criminal offence. At that point, the passage of FEMA without its 'handmaiden', the Prevention of Money Laundering Bill, also led many people to think that the Money Laundering Bill might now never be able to muster enough support to go through the Indian Parliament.

Moreover, a policy of 'deliberate leaks' by the interested spokesmen of the government during the long suspension of this bill in parliament was also designed to generate fear in the minds of Indian business and industry. This fear led them to oppose the bill, which they did quite effectively through forums such as the Confederation of Indian Industry, Associated Chambers of Commerce and Industry, and Federation of Indian Chambers of Commerce and Industry.

The Prevention of Money Laundering Act is one of the few pieces of legislation that has been passed by the Indian Parliament pursuant to a United Nations Resolution. During its deferment in the Indian Parliament, India was under considerable pressure from various international forums and expert groups to enact a law to counter money laundering considering the seriousness of the problem it posed worldwide. Thus, the Indian law to prevent money laundering was long overdue. In fact, in the statement of objectives and reasons when the Money Laundering Bill was introduced in the Parliament on 25 October 1999, the Finance Minister had made mention of all the international initiatives pursuant to which the Money Laundering Bill was being introduced; the seriousness of the problem posed by money laundering was also highlighted in the statement of the Indian Finance Minister.

SALIENT FEATURES

Apart from defining the various terms used in it, the Prevention of Money Laundering Act as passed by the Indian Parliament has the following salient features. It first defines the offence of money laundering in the following provision:

> *'whosoever directly or indirectly attempts to indulge or knowingly assists or knowingly is a party or is actually involved in any process or activity connected with the proceeds of crime and projecting it as untainted property shall be guilty of offence of money laundering.'*

It also provides criminal sanctions for the offences of money laundering:

> *'Whoever commits the offence of money laundering shall be punishable with rigorous imprisonment for a term which shall not be less than three years but which may extend to seven years and shall also be liable to fine which may extend to five lacs INR.'*

In the case of drugs offences it provides for enhanced penal provisions.

The Act also contains a schedule of offences, in respect of which the offence of money laundering comes into operation. According to this Act, the proceeds of crime relate to the schedule of offences listed, which are further sub-divided into part A and part B. Offences under part A relate to offences against the State and offences under the Narcotics Act, whereas offences under part B are classified as those offences where the amount involved is INR 3 million or more.

The other provisions of this Act pertain to surveys, searches, seizures, attachment, confiscation and arrests, and list the various provisions of the law under which or according to which these are to be carried out. A detailed examination of these provisions is made below, in particular because of very serious flaws and procedural defects relating to searches, seizures and attachment.

The Act also provides for constitution of a Money Laundering Authority and authorities subordinate to the same. The powers of the Money Laundering Authority are also laid down; these extend to summoning of witnesses, production of documents, recording of evidence and searches, seizures and attachments under various provisions of the Act.

The Act also provides that financial institutions are to maintain records of certain transactions, furnish information regarding the same to the Money Laundering Authority and also exercise due diligence regarding the identity of clients. Non-compliance of reporting requirements by financial institutions is subject to a fine; however, disclosure is not liable to any legal proceedings. It also envisages a leading role for the RBI regarding reporting and record-keeping requirements of the banks.

The Money Laundering Act also provides for an Adjudicating Authority and an Appellate Authority. The basic functions of the Adjudicating Authority under this law are to be concerned with all matters pertaining to attachment and confiscation of property and the records seized under the various provisions of the Act. The Appellate Authority is a forum for appeals of the orders made by the Adjudicating Authority. However, an appeal against the orders of the Adjudicating and Appellate Authorities lies only to the High Court under the provisions of this Act. 'Special Courts' are the trial courts for offences under this Act. The High Court can designate Sessions Courts as Special Courts for certain jurisdictions, to try offences under the Act.

The Act also provides for certain presumptions which relate to records – that they are to be treated as true in the forms obtained or seized. It also provides for certain presumptions in the case of interconnected transactions in the sense that if a person is accused of money laundering in one transaction, then it will be presumed that the interconnected transaction also relates to money laundering. Perhaps the most revolutionary concept under the heading of presumption that has been introduced in this law relates to reversal of the burden of proof – i.e., the onus to prove that the proceeds are untainted property lies with the accused.

The Act also has provisions for appointment of special prosecutors and empowerment of officers belonging to certain government departments. It also lists the various departments whose officers are to assist in enforcing its provisions.

It also covers international co-operation in cases of money laundering. It has specific provisions pertaining to letters rogatory and the admissibility of the evidence so obtained. Attachment, seizure and confiscation of property abroad and vice versa is also dealt with.

It also has a proviso to deal with vexatious searches, furnishing false information and failure to give information. It also makes people controlling the companies, those acting on behalf of the companies and the representatives of companies, liable for offences committed by the companies under this Act. The Central Government has also been given the power to makes rules and to remove any difficulty arising with regard to implementation of the provisions of the Act.

CRITIQUE OF THE INDIAN LAW

The Money Laundering Act is subject to criticism on several counts. First, it introduces a revolutionary concept in defining money laundering, by adding the proviso that except in offences relating to the state or drugs, an offence can be classified as a money laundering offence only if the property involved is worth INR 3 million or more. No other country in the world has such a provision in their law pertaining to money laundering. In fact, such a provision would only encourage the technique known as 'smurfing' in the United States whereby, by keeping transactions below INR 3 million, one can avoid the so-called 'long arm of the law'.

Another area of criticism in relation to this Act pertains to the schedule of offences, which is deeply flawed. Many of the laws that should have been included have not been, and important provisions of some of laws that have been listed in the schedule have been left out. Since money laundering generally pertains to serious crimes such as organized crime, drugs and terrorism, it is the substantive laws enacted to deal with these serious crimes – in the present instance, The Prevention of Terrorism Act – that should have been included in the schedule of offences, and a substantive law to deal with organized crime could have been enacted by the Central Government, along the lines of the Maharashtra State Organized Crime Control Act, and the same could also have been included in the schedule of offences.[1] The way the Money Laundering Act proposes to deal with organized crime, terrorism, etc., is by listing offences under the Indian Penal Code such as robbery, dacoity and kidnapping in the schedule of offences; such an approach in dealing with serious crimes not only leads to lack of focus but is also liable to misuse – for instance, the Money Laundering Act could become applicable in cases of murders where the property involved is INR 3 million or more. Such apprehensions about the misuse of this Act are not misplaced in the Indian context, considering that 20,000 cases were registered under TADA[2] (Terrorist and Disruptive Activities Act) to deal with communal riots in Gujarat, whereas around 1,000 cases were registered under TADA in Punjab to deal with terrorists, which TADA was intended to target. Moreover, in the provisions of

---

[1] The Maharashtra State law to deal with organized crime has proved to be quite effective, because it provides for wire-tapping; it has resulted in some very successful prosecutions of organized criminals.
[2] TADA has now been repealed.

the Prevention of Corruption Act listed in part B of the schedule of offences, section 13 (which is the key section to countering corruption by making misuse of official position and having disproportionate assets indictable acts) has been excluded.

Since money laundering involves the use of instruments of trade and commerce, in most of the money laundering *modi operandi*, violations of the Income Tax Act, Customs Act and Foreign Exchange Act invariably take place. In fact the provisions of these Acts should have been incorporated in the schedule of offences, to counter money laundering more effectively; inclusion of FEMA in the schedule of offences would have the added advantage that in money laundering offences, foreign exchange violations would become criminalized instead of being civil offences.

Perhaps the most scathing criticism of the Money Laundering Act is in the sphere of procedural law. Regarding procedures to be followed in cases of search, seizure and attachment, the Act lays down that these can only be carried out by the Money Laundering Authority after charges have been filed in a court of law. Such a provision under the law shows ignorance of the investigatory process. It is only through searches and seizures (whether carried out *suo moto* or during the process of arrest and attachment) that material is built up as evidence to file charges; without sufficient back-up material no charges can be filed. By stipulating that search and seizure can only be carried out after filing of the charges amounts to putting the cart before the horse. In fact, the provisions on searches, seizures and attachments to tackle money laundering as given in this Act can all be termed as locking the stables after the horses have bolted.

Moreover, considering the difficulties imposed in carrying out searches and seizures, the provision for vexatious search under the Money Laundering Bill is a red herring; I mention this because a good deal of controversy had centred around vexatious searches in the media, when the fear surrounding the Money Laundering Act was being built up through deliberate leaks. While on the issue on vexatious search, it is also worth pointing out that such a provision even militates against the doctrine of good faith and no officer will carry out a search if such a provision exists in the law.

Another feature of this Act that again is the subject of controversy is that it provides two parallel avenues of adjudication. The provision of making the Special Courts trial courts for offences committed under this Act and having separate judicial channels for attachment and confiscations, might be considered by the trial courts as derogatory, in the sense that sufficient confidence has not been reposed in them. In the laws of all other countries, it is the trial courts which deal with all the matters pertaining to attachment and confiscation. The provisions relating to the Adjudicating Authority and the Appellate Authority seem to be an exercise in the proliferation of bureaucracy; a perusal of the provisions of this Act reveals that almost 50 per cent of its provisions deal with this proliferation of bureaucracy. Considering the statements of the Finance Minister of India about cutting the flab in bureaucracy, it is a strange coincidence that the Finance Minister who heads the department which piloted this bill in Parliament has chosen to pursue such a proliferation, ostensibly under the garb of experts dealing with matters of attachment and confiscation. A better approach to dealing with attachment and confiscation would have been to appoint chartered accountants and other financial experts to the Special Courts on a retainership basis to give the necessary inputs and expertise to them, which would enable them to decide an issue of attachment and confiscation, in conjunction with the trial of the money laundering offences.

Perhaps the biggest grey area in this Act is with regard to enforcement. Under the Act enforcement agencies have not been specified at all. The Act talks about searches, seizures, arrests, attachment, confiscation, public prosecutors and empowerment in general; in talking about empowerment, it tends to confuse it with providing assistance. It is nowhere specifically mentioned which are the agencies or authorities that can investigate cases and file charges in a court of law for offences committed under the Act.

Perhaps the most revolutionary concept that this Act introduces relates to the reversal of the burden of proof – that is, shifting the onus onto the accused to show that property has been legally acquired. But such a revolutionary and welcome concept in the Money Laundering Act – which exists in no other law in India –becomes totally pointless if one considers the various lacunae and laxities of this Act mentioned above.

As has been stated elsewhere in the book, if undercover operations and electronic surveillance had been made admissible evidence under this Act, it would have gone a long way to effectively counter money laundering. In the light of the restrictive approach adopted with regard to even basic functions of investigation such as searches and seizures, perhaps it was expecting too much from the 'mandarins' of the Finance Ministry and our lawmakers.

CHAPTER XXIII

OTHER INITIATIVES TO COUNTER
MONEY LAUNDERING

LEGISLATION

Supportive/substantive laws

Money laundering laws enacted by various countries can be a very effective tool to counter it if these laws are properly conceived and enacted in the first instance. Often it has been the experience that since money laundering is carried on in connection with other crimes, some substantive laws need to be enacted with regard to more serious crimes in order to deal with them effectively and thereby stem the flow of funds for laundering purposes. Even if the flow of funds from these serious crimes continues unabated, the substantive laws so enacted to deal with them should be linked to the money laundering statutes. For instance, substantive laws to deal with organized crime, drug trafficking, terrorism, corruption, economic scams, etc., could be incorporated in the schedule of offences of the Indian law on money laundering. By bringing these offences into the schedule of offences, money laundering provisions automatically become part of these crimes.

In general the tendency amongst countries is to have offences in criminal codes, such as murder, extortion and bribery, listed in the schedule of offences in their money laundering laws rather than substantive laws which may or may not be there to deal with serious crimes. Such an approach to dealing with serious crimes leads to diffused and unfocused efforts to counter money laundering. It could also result in the misuse of the provisions of the money laundering law by providing the temptation to make them applicable to all kinds of murders, frauds, forgeries, etc.

The schedule of offences of a money laundering law would also need to be tightened, or in other words made more comprehensive, in order to deal with money laundering. Since it is through the instruments of trade and commerce that money laundering takes place, the laws relating to the violation of the Income Tax Act, and the Customs Act should also figure in the schedule of offences of money laundering laws in order to counter it more effectively. The inclusion of provisions of the Income Tax Act and Customs Act in the schedule of offences is being suggested because their violations are invariably noted in the various *modi operandi* of money laundering.

Since economic scams and international economic crimes are surfacing all over the world, substantive laws to deal with them or the provisions relating to criminal misappropriation, cheating, fraud or forgery should always figure in the schedule of offences of a money laundering law. In view of the rapid advances being made in the field of information technology and other related technologies such as broadcasting and telecommunication, a form of convergence law incorporating provisions to deal with all three technologies should also figure in the schedule of offences of money laundering laws of countries.

With economic liberalization being the trend worldwide, countries are opting for abolition of foreign exchange controls. Even if some form of exchange controls are retained, contraventions of these are being dealt with as civil offences. In cases where these exchange control violations are inserted in the schedule of offences of money laundering laws, especially in the context of developing economies in order to deal with them more effectively, they would become criminalized; this criminalization of exchange control violations would result in tackling them more effectively wherever they are linked to serious crimes or money laundering.

It has already been mentioned in an earlier chapter that a substantive law to counter underground banking is also needed by many countries, in view of the fact that this system is becoming more prevalent and widespread and is increasingly being used to launder money, in conjunction with conventional money laundering.

Procedural/evidentiary laws

Alongside substantive laws, procedural and evidentiary laws would need to be amended to tighten the anti-money laundering effort. As regards procedural laws, they would need to be simplified and also aligned with the laws of other countries, considering the international dimension of money laundering. For instance, a provision could be incorporated that a magistrate could endorse a warrant for execution in the home country, even if a warrant is issued by another country; such a step would go a long way toward tackling transnational criminals and their money laundering activities. The procedural laws would also have to cater for the new developments in information technology, broadcasting and the telecom sector.

Coming to the evidentiary laws, certain provisions which are considered either too drastic or too radical by sizeable sections of lawmakers and enforcement officers would need to be incorporated to ensure conviction of serious offenders and confiscation of their proceeds. The first radical provision under the law of evidence would relate to making electronic surveillance and undercover operations admissible evidence, which is not the case in most countries at present. Moreover, considering the highly complex nature of the financial transactions involved in money laundering and other economic offences, the concept of reversal of the burden of proof would need to be introduced in evidentiary law.

Providing for presumptions against the accused is another provision that needs to be introduced in evidentiary law, particularly to deal effectively with the mafia dons who are so far removed from the crime that it is very difficult to connect them with it in any way in most of the cases. Such presumptions are provided for in the Racketeer Influenced and Corrupt Organizations Act in the United States.

Witness protection laws

Another major law that would need to be enacted, and perhaps the most important one, would be in the sphere of providing protection to witnesses. The best way to provide such protection to witnesses is to have a witness protection programme in place which provides for a change of identity and relocation of witnesses. Although witness protection programmes are quite expensive to implement, these would need to be introduced, at least on a selective basis, in some of the important cases, to make the fight against criminals an equal battle instead of an unequal one. If the witness cannot be won over, intimidated or eliminated, the criminals would know for sure that the 'long arm of the law' will finally catch up with them and their proceeds.

While on the issue of laws, one pertinent observation that needs to be made is that laws are not able to keep pace with the fast-moving developments in the field of trade, commerce and technology; this lag would have to be tightened and lawmakers would need to be sensitized on all issues calling for their attention.

TAKING THE PROFIT OUT OF CRIMES

Civil remedies versus criminal remedies to tackle the proceeds of crime

In the field of confiscation of proceeds of crime, civil procedure is generally a preferred option. The reason civil proceedings are preferred to criminal proceedings for confiscating the proceeds of crime is that the level of proof required in civil proceedings is less rigorous than in criminal proceedings. According to the principles of jurisprudence, whereas the requirement of civil law is preponderance of probability, the requirement in criminal law is beyond reasonable doubt. Thus, in a particular case, on the basis of certain data, it is possible to construct a sliding scale of proof, whereby the requirements of civil law can be more easily met than those of criminal law. The provision for civil forfeiture is a feature of the money laundering laws of several countries; this also comes across very clearly in Chapter XXI.

However, using civil law for the forfeiture of the proceeds of crime is an easier option, and quite a few regard it as an infringement of one's human rights. In fact, a fairly agitated debate took place in the UK before civil forfeiture proceedings were incorporated in their Financial Services Act 2000, because it was argued that they were in violation of the European Convention on Human Rights. To ensure that civil forfeiture proceedings are not misused in a routine manner and also to safeguard the human rights of individuals, certain guidelines for implementing civil forfeiture proceedings in the UK that have been laid down are that the proceedings would not apply to amounts falling below 'certain threshold limits', that the onus would lie on the prosecution to prove that the proceeds are proceeds of crime, and that the proceedings will be used on a selective basis and only after the chances of forfeiture under criminal confiscation options are found to be negligible.

Taxing the proceeds of crimes

Since attaching the proceeds of crime, whether laundered or unlaundered, is a vital component for taking the incentive out of the crime, all options are being explored by lawmakers and enforcement agencies to target these proceeds. Apart from the criminal and civil forfeiture provisions that have been discussed, the option that is being increasingly used is to tax these proceeds, in cases where one cannot get at them in any other way. Taxing the proceeds of crime is a legitimate weapon in the armoury of enforcement, because for the purposes of taxation there is no difference between legal income and illegal income according to the taxation laws of most countries.

Confiscation strategy

In practically every country in the world there are a number of enforcement agencies and other arms of the government involved in the confiscation of the proceeds of crime. However, experience shows that such a confiscation effort is not subject to any direction and in the ultimate analysis the confiscation results are highly unsatisfactory. To make confiscation a principal tool in the fight against crime, a number of countries are proposing a centralized confiscating authority that would bring about a multidisciplinary and co-ordinated approach to confiscation proceedings being initiated by the various agencies. Such a national confiscation authority, proposed in the UK, would decide on the form of confiscation proceedings that are to be initiated, the best agency to initiate the same, the inputs that are required for success in confiscation proceedings and the agencies that are in a position to provide additional inputs for the confiscation process.

Asset sharing

In general, enforcement agencies worldwide are starved of funds. Another welcome trend now is to transfer the confiscated proceeds to these enforcement agencies. Often a number of agencies are involved in a particular case, each claiming its share of the confiscated proceeds. Asset sharing of the confiscated proceeds at the domestic level amongst enforcement agencies, according to certain norms, is a well-established practice. Some countries have even enacted regulations and laws relating to asset sharing at the international level.

THE CRITICAL ROLE OF FINANCIAL INTELLIGENCE UNITS AND ENFORCEMENT AGENCIES

Financial Intelligence Units

The roles of intelligence and enforcement are critical for success in the fight against money laundering. As regards intelligence, most of the countries that are in the forefront in the fight against money laundering have set up Financial Intelligence Units (FIU). In several countries, the FIU is like the apex body, co-ordinating the overall anti-money laundering effort. In many of the countries, these FIUs have been set up because the anti-money laundering laws mandated the same.

While setting up an FIU, a multi-disciplinary approach is generally adopted, in the sense that experts from various government agencies are co-opted to these units: these experts are chartered accountants, lawyers, bankers, other financial experts and officers from various enforcement agencies. Constituting an FIU as a multidisciplinary body obviously has an advantage in terms of expertise to deal with practically all the facets of money laundering.

In their capacity as the co-ordinating agency in the overall anti-money laundering efforts in the country, the FIUs are also assigned some regulatory and supervisory functions. In most countries, these regulatory and supervisory functions relate to ensuring that financial institutions are reporting all financial transactions, including suspicious transactions, as per the requirements of law, that they have an adequate internal regulatory framework to ensure due diligence in their functioning and that they maintain records as per the requirements of the law.

These FIUs also act as clearing houses for all the intelligence that flows to them. Based upon the intelligence inputs, the FIUs decide which enforcement agency should take charge of a certain case. At times FIUs also constitute joint task forces of enforcement agencies to tackle a case in the best possible manner by bringing in the expertise and the adequate legal back-up to bear upon that particular case.

Based upon their experience and expertise, FIUs are also able to indicate the most effective approach to tackle money laundering cases. Another area in which FIUs are performing a very useful role is that of training. Indeed FIUs in most countries have set up training modules for financial institutions and enforcement agencies to ensure that people in the field have adequate skills to tackle a case. The help of FIUs is also sought and is generally forthcoming in the setting up of specialized units in the various enforcement agencies to deal exclusively with cases of money laundering.

It has also been the experience of several countries that international co-operation if channelled through the FIUs leads to more effective and expeditious action with regard to all aspects of international co-operation such as searches, seizures, confiscation, extradition, asset sharing, and production and admissibility of documentary and oral evidence.

Enforcement agencies

For effective enforcement each country has to draw up an enforcement strategy. These strategies first of all deal with identifying the existing agencies that have the charter and capabilities to deal with money laundering cases. Sometimes specialized units have to be created within the enforcement agencies to deal with cases of money laundering. At times, countries have even gone to the extreme of setting up entirely new agencies to deal with money laundering cases. Since money laundering calls for a good deal of expertise and skill, these specialized units/agencies set up exclusively to deal with it are absolutely essential for proper investigation, prosecution and trial of cases.

Another point to be borne in mind with regard to these specialized units is that they should be staffed by skilled personnel having the relevant education and background, especially in the field of financial investigations. The skills of personnel could be considerably enhanced by providing in-house training for them.

There is a tendency amongst enforcement agencies to project their output in terms of resources devoted. Since financial/money laundering investigations can consume a sizeable proportion of their resources without any guaranteed success, the enforcement agencies generally shy away from devoting sufficient resources to such investigations. In fact, such an attitude on the part of enforcement agencies needs to be corrected, and adequate resources should be devoted to tackling money laundering cases.

For effective enforcement, agencies would also need to ensure better co-operation with other enforcement units and financial entities; they would also need to have a sound and adequate legal framework in which to operate. If such a legal back-up is not there, the same should be ensured by bringing in the necessary amendments in law or by enacting suitable laws.

To be successful in their anti-money laundering drives the enforcement agencies would also have to keep abreast with the latest technologies and also equip themselves for sound undercover operations and effective electronic surveillance.

DISRUPTIVE STRATEGIES

A number of experts in the field of countering money laundering feel that traditional law enforcement has by and large failed to tackle it and the proceeds of crime; to buttress their argument they cite statistics which cannot easily be discounted. For instance, an investigation and trial in a money laundering case might cost a few million dollars whereas the proceeds (whether laundered or unlaundered) that are confiscated might be derisory.

Nevertheless, even though traditional law enforcement might be a losing battle, efforts are afoot worldwide to further tighten and strengthen these traditional methods, because they at least operate within the bounds of law as laid down by civil society. In the context of this failure of the traditional law enforcement effort, a number of enforcement chiefs nowadays are even advocating the concept of 'audacious law enforcement' which according to them amounts to 'sabre-rattling' within the confines of law.

Realizing that traditional law enforcement has not been equal to the task of countering serious crime and money laundering, it is being openly suggested by several experts that drastic steps should be adopted to counter the same. When talking about drastic steps one is obviously referring to the strategies or the methods used by intelligence agencies in their operations. With the end of the cold war and the changing focus, and the lack of work on defence-related matters worldwide, intelligence agencies have been turning their attention to countering transnational crimes and the proceeds of such crimes. To tackle the laundered or unlaundered proceeds of crime is considered to be a particularly challenging task by these intelligence agencies. The advantage that they have is that they are not bound by the constraints of law. They can use the same set of rules or code as the criminals and they have various intelligence tools to thwart criminal enterprises.

The intelligence tools that could be used to deadly effect by these intelligence agencies include intrigue, deception, inducement, blackmail, honey traps and ideological brain-washing. Intelligence agencies generally also have considerable resources and gadgets with which to gather information and intelligence on criminal enterprises. In fact, intelligence modules could be prepared to disrupt certain forms of crime and to seize their proceeds. For instance, in the case of drug trafficking, the dynamics of a drug market could be studied and then the intelligence agency could hit its weak spots in markets, thereby making the whole enterprise unprofitable or less profitable for the traffickers. Likewise, through intrigue intelligence agencies could ensure that two rival criminal groups destroy each other: this happens quite often in connection with terrorist operations.

CHAPTER XXIV

THE ROLE OF INTERNATIONAL ORGANIZATIONS, EXPERT GROUPINGS AND REGIONAL BODIES

There are a number of international/regional organizations, specialized/expert groups and regional economic bodies that are dealing with or are concerned with money laundering in one way or another. Let us first consider international organizations dealing with money laundering.

INTERNATIONAL ORGANIZATIONS

International Monetary Fund

The International Monetary Fund (IMF) is acutely aware of the problems posed by money laundering. In order to analyse these problems it has embarked upon special studies. Some of the macro-economic implications of a serious nature which these studies have revealed are the misallocation of resources, corruption of markets and consequent destabilization of economies, fluctuation in economic growth rates due to significant amounts of illicit-gotten/laundered proceeds and the contaminating effects on legal transactions based on their perceived association with crime. The managing director of the IMF also emphasized the magnitude of the problem of money laundering by stating in a speech to the Financial Action Task Force (FATF) in 1989, that 2 to 5 per cent of the global GDP constitutes transactions involving money laundering.

The IMF endeavours to counter money laundering in several indirect ways. First, it relies upon publicity to highlight the problems posed by money laundering. It also provides technical assistance to countries, especially offshore financial centres, to put a credible anti-money laundering regime into place. Since one of the primary functions of the IMF is to assess some of the economic parameters of a country, it is in a position to collect a large amount of data and information relating to money laundering; as such, the IMF can be a major source for data on money laundering which can ultimately be honed to strategic and tactical intelligence. The IMF also collaborates with other international organizations, specialized/expert groups and regional bodies in the fight against money laundering. The principal collaboration of the IMF is with the FATF: the IMF has made implementation of the 40 recommendations of the FATF the primary plank in its drive against money laundering. Following the 11 September 2001 terrorist attacks in the USA, the IMF has also adopted eight recommendations formulated by the FATF to curb financing of terrorism, as another equally important focus area. It has also embarked upon certain assessments in collaboration with the FATF and the World Bank to assess the success of anti-money laundering measures worldwide.

World Bank

The World Bank like the IMF, also endeavours to counter money laundering in an indirect way. By creating awareness amongst member countries the World Bank seeks to ensure that the countries concerned take steps to counter it. It alo extends co-operation to other international/regional organizations and specialized/experts groups to counter money laundering; the nature of this co-operation is not clearly defined and depends primarily upon the needs of the organizations seeking the co-operation. Since the World Bank is very active on the anti-corruption front, especially in countries where it is disbursing loans, it indirectly helps to counter money laundering as a result of its anti-corruption drive. It recognizes that emerging markets are increasingly vulnerable to money laundering operations, and is also aware that in order to prevent money laundering, the focus has to extend beyond the banks to securities markets, insurance and the money-changing businesses.

United Nations

In order to counter money laundering, the United Nations has devised a global programme against money laundering, known as GPML. Under GPML the United Nations provides technical assistance, undertakes research on money laundering issues and pioneers special study projects for affected regions in the world.

Under the technical assistance programme as envisaged by GPML, the needs of various states/jurisdictions are identified and a review of the legal framework to counter money laundering is ensured. The UN has a model legislation entitled the Model Money Laundering and Proceeds of Crime Bill 1998, which enables countries to enact a suitable anti-money laundering law; this model legislation is periodically updated and has versions to suit both civil and common law systems.

Under its technical assistance component the United Nations also helps countries to put in place mechanisms and institutions to counter money laundering; the GPML focuses in particular on the development of financial intelligence units. As part of technical assistance, the UN also organizes training workshops and seminars for various bodies – such as enforcement agencies, banks, businesses and financial sectors – involved in the fight against money laundering.

The GPML technical assistance programme also strives to foster awareness, understanding and implementation of prudent practices in the regulation of financial services. Following a conference in the Cayman Islands in March 2000, the United Nations also launched a GPML Forum of the participating countries. This forum has set up minimum performance standards to counter money laundering, and 75 per cent of the countries from the forum have entered into a commitment to ensure the same.

Under GPML the United Nations also collaborates with other international organizations. It has a strong collaboration with the FATF, Interpol and the Commonwealth Secretariat. Under GPML the United Nations has also undertaken a mentoring exercise to provide greater assistance to needy states to fight money laundering; under these mentoring exercises, experts are located in the states concerned to oversee the effectiveness of their anti-money laundering programmes and suggest corrective measures.

As already mentioned, under GPML the United Nations also undertakes research activities; for enabling research, the GPML gathers and analyses crime data. It also fosters research by carrying out specialized studies and publishing the same. The research activities of GPML are geared to tackle the rapid developments in the field of money laundering. At present the focus areas of research by the United Nations under GPML includes states' vulnerability to money laundering, corruption and money laundering, the political economy of international financial centres, money laundering typologies, drugs and money laundering, the national legislative response and the development of Financial Intelligence Units (FIUs). At present, the United Nations under GPML is also carrying out a special study in the Central Asian region to ensure adequate measures to counter money laundering.

The United Nations GPML also co-ordinates an international money laundering information network, also known as IMoLIN; the participating organizations in this network are the United Nations, the Financial Action Task Force, Interpol, the Council of Europe, the Commonwealth Secretariat, the Caribbean Financial Action Task Force, the World Customs Organization and the Asia Pacific Group on Money Laundering.

In 2000 the United Nations also adopted a Convention against Transnational Organized Crime. This Convention recognizes money laundering as one of the principal offences that needs to be combated at the international level. This Convention has now come into force, since it has been ratified by 40 countries. All the members of the United Nations are expected to ratify this Convention and are urged to implement its provisions.

Commonwealth Secretariat

The Commonwealth has also been actively engaged in the fight against money laundering ever since it set up the commercial crime unit in the Commonwealth Secretariat in the early 1980s. The commercial crime unit, ever since its inception, has adopted a highly proactive approach to countering economic crimes and money laundering. The proactive approach of the commercial crime unit entailed passing on hard intelligence to the relevant countries, and giving active assistance in the investigation process, which would generally involve several countries. This proactive approach was also prompted to a very large extent by the fact that a number of countries in the Commonwealth were fairly underdeveloped and needed outside help to effectively counter international criminals.

The commercial crime unit of the Commonwealth Secretariat has also drafted a model law to combat money laundering. This law is entitled 'Draft Model Law for the Prohibition of Money Laundering' and several countries have relied upon it to draft their anti-money laundering legislation. A number of studies on various facets of money laundering have also been undertaken and published by the commercial crime unit of the Commonwealth Secretariat.

ICPO-Interpol

The International Criminal Police Organization, also known as ICPO-Interpol, is one of the pioneers in the fight against money laundering. It set up the FOPAC (Fonds Provenant d'Activités Criminelles) group to counter money laundering in the early 1980s. The FOPAC group co-ordinates money laundering investigations amongst various countries wherever requests to do so are received. It also carries out special studies on various facets of money laundering and publishes the same. It publishes an information bulletin which lists the important cases, developments and typologies in the field of money laundering. The FOPAC group has also compiled an encyclopedia listing the laws and provisions of various countries to counter money laundering. It organizes working group meetings to address problems in certain critical areas pertaining to money laundering and thereby find effective ways to counter the same by way of co-ordination and other suitable measures.

SPECIALIZED/EXPERT GROUPS

There are numerous specialized/expert groups that are trying to counter the problem of money laundering on a worldwide scale.

Financial Action Task Force

The Financial Action Task Force (FATF) is the principal organ that is spearheading the fight against money laundering on a global scale. Most of the other international/regional initiatives are complementary and supportive of its efforts.

The FATF was set up following the concerns about money laundering expressed by the G-7 summit in 1989. The FATF operates out of the OECD office in Paris but is not a part of it. It does not have an unlimited life span and according to the present understanding it will continue its work until 2004; only if the member governments consider its work necessary will it continue beyond 2004. Originally, the membership of FATF comprised 20 countries, but by 1992 it had expanded to 28 member countries. Certain organizations also have observer status with the FATF.

The FATF is charged with the responsibility of examining money laundering techniques and trends, reviewing the action taken at national and international level to counter it and also spelling out further measures needed to combat it. Within a year of its formation, the FATF produced a set of recommendations to combat money laundering, known as the

'40 recommendations' because they are 40 in number. These recommendations cover the criminal justice systems including law enforcement, the financial system and its regulation and international co-operation. These recommendations are the main plank not only for the FATF but also for other regional bodies in combating money laundering; the 40 recommendations were first revised in 1996 in the light of developments that had taken place in the fast-moving world of money laundering. At present these 40 recommendations are again being reviewed in the light of the latest developments in the field of money laundering. Some of the main features of the 40 recommendations are:

– The criminalization of the laundering of the proceeds of serious crimes and the enactment of laws to seize and confiscate the proceeds of crime.
– Obligations for financial institutions to identify all clients, including any beneficial owners of property, and to keep appropriate records.
– A requirement for financial institutions to report suspicious transactions to the competent national authorities, and to implement a comprehensive range of internal control measures.
– Adequate systems for the control and supervision of financial institutions.
– The need to enter into international treaties or agreements and to pass national legislation which will allow countries to provide prompt and effective international co-operation at all levels.

In order to ensure effective global action on the money laundering front, the member countries of the FATF carry out self-assessment exercises based upon the 40 recommendations. The member countries are also subject to a mutual evaluation process based on the 40 recommendations; in this mutual evaluation process (also known as the peer group review) experts from the other member countries of the FATF comprise the evaluation team. The FATF is actively engaged in spreading the anti-money laundering message to all continents and regions in the world: it also carries out a review of money laundering trends and produces a money laundering typologies report on an annual basis. Following the 11 September 2001 terrorist incidents in the United States, the FATF has also been charged with the task of countering financial terrorism. In order to counter global terrorist financing the FATF has proposed eight special recommendations which cover the following points:

– Take immediate steps to ratify and implement the relevant United Nations instruments.
– Criminalize the financing of terrorism, terrorist acts and terrorist organizations.
– Freeze and confiscate terrorist assets.
– Report suspicious transactions linked to terrorism.
– Provide the widest possible range of assistance to other countries' law enforcement and regulatory authorities for terrorist-financing investigations.
– Impose anti-money laundering requirements on alternative remittance systems.
– Strengthen customer identification measures in international and domestic wire transfers.
– Ensure that entities, in particular non-profit organizations, cannot be misused to finance terrorism.

The FATF has also drawn up an action plan to ensure effective implementation of these recommendations; this action plan involves a time limit for self-assessment by all FATF members as per these eight recommendations. Other countries of the world are also encouraged to participate in these assessment exercises. In order to effectively combat funding of terrorism the FATF is also expected to publish additional guidelines for financial institutions. The FATF has also initiated a process to identify jurisdictions that lack appropriate measures to combat financing of terrorism and to suggest measures to plug loopholes in these jurisdictions. In order to make the fight against financing of terrorism more broad-based, the FATF members would also provide technical assistance to vulnerable centres/jurisdictions for the implementation of these eight recommendations. The FATF also proposes to intensify co-operation with other international bodies, specialized groups and regional groupings to effectively combat financing of terrorism; in this context the co-operation with the IMF and the Egmont Group needs special mention.

In order to counter money laundering effectively on a global scale and not just within the FATF member countries, the FATF has lately (i.e., from 2000 onward) also embarked upon a process of identifying non-co-operative countries and territories which encourage money laundering or hamper countermeasures against money laundering. The FATF has also drawn up a 25-point plan to classify non-co-operative countries and territories. This policy of the FATF of classifying non-co-operative countries and territories is known as a 'name and shame' policy. By this name and shame policy, the FATF hopes that countries will fall into line and enact suitable measures to counter money laundering. As a further extension of the name and shame policy, the FATF is also contemplating imposition of sanctions against countries that do not fall into line and enact counter measures against money laundering.

The Basel Committee on Banking Supervision

Following the financial crises that had occurred in the aftermath of the Bretton Woods system, an international standing committee of banking supervisors was formed in late 1974 with headquarters at Basel in Switzerland. This committee was composed of the Banking Supervisors and Central Bank Governors of the G-10 countries. Though initially called the Committee on Banking Supervision and Supervisory Practices, it later came to be known as the Basel Committee on Banking Supervision. The International Bank for Settlements at Basel serves as the administrative office for the Basel Committee. The Committee has played a major role in establishing voluntary principles and standards of best practice to regulate the international operation of banking institutions.

In 1997 the Basel Committee issued 25 core principles for an effective supervisory system to regulate international banking. These 25 core principles serve to counter money laundering by way of various provisions such as know your customer, reporting of suspicious transactions, effective supervision of bank branches in the home country, monitoring supervision of bank branches located outside home country jurisdictions, and plugging of supervisory gaps wherever they come to light in the corporate structuring of banks.

Egmont Group

During the last decade, a number of countries have set up specialized units, known as Financial Intelligence Units, to counter money laundering – these are dealt with in considerable detail in Chapter XXIII. Realizing that it is possible to exchange highly useful information and hard intelligence on money laundering, the FIUs of some countries came together in 1995 to form an informal organization, known as the Egmont Group, because its first meeting was held in the Egmont-Arenberg Palace in Brussels. At present, membership of the Egmont Group comprises FIUs of 69 countries. Apart from exchange of information and intelligence, the Egmont Group also strives to improve the expertise and capabilities of the personnel manning the FIUs of the member countries.

Offshore Group of Banking Supervisors

The Offshore Group of Banking Supervisors operates in collaboration with the FATF. It follows the same principles as the FATF to evaluate the effectiveness of the money laundering laws and policies of its members. However, the activities and effectiveness of the Offshore Group of Banking Supervisors has been considerably curtailed because half of the offshore banking centres are not members of this expert body.

International Organization of Securities Commissions

This body is concerned with countering money laundering in securities markets and futures trading; it encourages self-regulatory measures by its members to fight money laundering.

International Association of Insurance Supervisors

This body has issued a set of principles to curb money laundering in the insurance sector.

International Banking Security Association

The International Banking Security Association is another body that is concerned with money laundering and strives to curb it in collaboration with other organizations.

World Customs Organization

The World Customs Organization (WCO), based in Brussels, is a collaborative effort on an international scale by the customs authorities of various countries worldwide. The WCO is also concerned with countering money laundering. By its very nature the WCO plays a fairly proactive role in curbing money laundering by way of investigation and disseminating information on money laundering techniques and trends throughout the world.

REGIONAL GROUPINGS

Regional groupings are also fairly active in curbing money laundering in their respective regions. The following are the regional groupings engaged in the fight against money laundering.

Caribbean Financial Action Task Force

The Caribbean region has a number of offshore jurisdictions. Several of them have been fairly active in facilitating money laundering, therefore this region has become an area of concern as far as money laundering is concerned. In a meeting of the ministers of the region held in Jamaica in 1992, a communiqué was issued, known as the Kingston Declaration, which lays down the framework for the countries of the Caribbean region to counter money laundering, as a result of which the Caribbean Financial Action Task Force (CFATF) was constituted. This task force works on the basis of the 40 recommendations of the FATF. In addition to these recommendations, considering the peculiarities of this region, 19 other recommendations have been developed by the nations concerned to effectively counter money laundering; these 19 recommendations were revised in 1996, in which year 21 member countries of the CFATF adopted a Memorandum of Understanding to adopt measures to counter money laundering. These measures are the same as those of the FATF, being self-assessment exercises by the countries of the region and mutual evaluations by the expert groups from member countries. The countries of the region also participate in training and technical assistance programmes; proper co-ordination is sought to be ensured in implementation of these technical assistance programmes.

Asia Pacific Group on Money Laundering

The Asia Pacific Group (APG) was set up in 1997, its headquarters being in Sydney, Australia. At present its membership comprises 19 countries; there are also seven observer jurisdictions and 13 international/regional observers. The APG also works on the basis of the 40 recommendations of the FATF. It provides technical assistance and training expertise to the countries in the Asia/Pacific region on measures to counter money laundering. It also studies typologies of money laundering on the basis of workshops, and produces a typologies report on a regular basis. It carries out mutual evaluation of the member countries by expert groups on the same lines as the FATF, and facilitates information exchange between member countries for effective action against money laundering. It also co-operates with other international organizations, expert groupings and regional bodies for effective co-ordination of anti-money laundering measures.

227

GAFISUD

GAFISUD is the Financial Action Task Force for South America and it performs more or less the same functions as the FATF in this region.

CICAD

CICAD is the Inter-American Drug Abuse Control Commission, which is an offshoot of the Organization of American States. CICAD strives to counter money laundering in the North- and South-American regions.

ESAAMLG

This stands for Eastern and Southern African Anti-Money Laundering Group and works on the same lines as the FATF.

MONEYVAL Committee

This is a select committee of experts from the Council of Europe on anti-money laundering measures. This committee works on the same lines as the FATF.

Europol

Europol is a regional police organization in Europe. Its membership comprises police forces in the European Union. Europol is also active in countering money laundering by way of co-ordination of investigation.

Efforts are afoot to develop effective regional groupings in Africa and Latin America to counter money laundering.

REGIONAL ECONOMIC GROUPINGS

Regional Economic Groupings such as the European Economic Community, the ASEAN and SAARC are also fairly active in the fight against money laundering. All of these economic groupings have expressed their firm resolve to counter money laundering. Perhaps the most active Regional Economic Groupings are the European Economic Community and the European Union. Through the European Council the EEC has issued directives to counter money laundering and these directives are binding on the member countries, requiring them to enact suitable domestic legislation to ensure the implementation of the European Council directives. In 1990 the European Union also adopted a Convention to counter money laundering, the scope of which extends to all crimes; the Convention lays down a common definition of money laundering and lists measures to deal with it.

The Asian Development Bank is also seeking to play a meaningful role in the fight against money laundering in collaboration with other international/regional organizations and expert groupings.

TOWARDS A WORLD FINANCIAL AUTHORITY

The world economy today is vulnerable to systemic risks because of differing economic systems and non-uniform financial regulatory mechanisms which are operating in different countries. Quite a few have argued that since the IMF and the World Bank are not in a position to counter this systemic risk, a World Financial Authority with far-reaching powers should be constituted to do so. Such a World Financial Authority, by the very nature of its function, would also counter money laundering in direct and indirect ways.

Note:
1. For the text of the 40 recommendations of the FATF, the 8 recommendations of the FATF for combating terrorism, the 25 criteria of the FATF for judging non-cooperative jurisdictions, the membership of the FATF and organizations having observer status, see www1.oecd.org/fatf/index.htm.
2. For the 19 recommendations specific to CFATF, the membership of CFATF and the organizations having observer status, see www.cfatf.org.
3. For membership of the APG and those having observer status with it, see www.apgml.org/content/index.jsp.
4. For membership of the Egmont Group and those having observer status, see www1.oecd.org/fatf/Ctry-orgpages/org-egmont_en.htm.

SELECT BIBLIOGRAPHY

CHAPTER I

Compendium of Recommendations of the Police Commissions of India (National Crime Records Bureau, Ministry of Home Affairs, New Delhi).

Crime in India (annual publication) 1994 to 2000 (National Crime Records Bureau, Ministry of Home Affairs, New Delhi).

Encyclopedia of Crime and Justice, 4 Vols (ed. S.H. Cadish) (Macmillan Free Press, London, 1983).

Manual of Central Acts and Important Rules in India (A Compilation of Central Bare Acts — pertaining to Civil, Criminal, Labour, Taxation and Commercial matters) 17 Vols (5th edn) (R.G. Sagar for Law Publishers India Pvt. Ltd., Allahabad, 1994).

CHAPTER II

Abadinsky, H., *Organized Crime* (Allyn & Bacon, Boston, 1980).

Achari, G., *Note on Organized Crime & Criminal Intelligence*, presented at the Conference on Organized Crime, New Delhi, 22 and 23 February 2000.

Albini, J.L., *The American Mafia: Genesis of a Legend* (Irvinton, New York, 1979 (reprint)).

Alexander, H.E. and Caden, G.E., *The Politics and Economics of Organised Crime*.

Bresler, F., *The Chinese Mafia* (Stein & Day, New York, 1981).

Caputo, D.A., *Organized Crime and American Politics* (General Learning Press, Morristown, NJ, 1974).

Chu, Y.-K., 'International Triad Movements: The Threat of Chinese Organized Crime'.

Federal Bureau of Investigation, *International Organized Crime and the Enterprise Theory of Investigation* (US Department of Justice, Washington, DC,).

Fiorentini, G. and Peltman, S., *The Economics of Organized Crime* (Cambridge University Press, Cambridge, 1997).

Ghosh, S.K., *The Indian Mafia* (Ashish Pub. House, New Delhi, 1991).

Gressey, D.R., *Theft of the Nation: The Structure and Operations of Organized Crime in America* (Harpers & Row, New York, 1969).

Hess, H., *Mafia and Mafiosi: The Structure of Power* (trans. E. Osers) (Lexington Books, Heath, 1973).

Ianni, F.A.J., *Black Mafia: Ethnic Succession in Organized Crime* (Simon & Schuster, New York, 1974).

Jamieson, A., *The Antimafia* (Macmillan Press Ltd., London, 2000).

Kefauver, E., *Crime in America* [1951] (ed. S. Shalett) (Greenwood Press, Westport, Conn., 1968).

Kennedy, R.F., *The Enemy Within* (Popular Library, New York, 1960).

Landesco, J., *Organized Crime in Chicago* [1929] (intro. M.H. Haller) (University of Chicago Press, 1968).

Maas, P., *The Valachi Papers* (Putnam, New York, 1968).

Mill, J., *The Underground Empire* (Sidgwick & Jackson, London, 1987).

Nelli, H.S., *The Business of Crime: Italians and Syndicate Crime in the United States* (Oxford University Press, New York, 1976).

New York Police Department, *Profiles of the New York Mafia, Russian Organized Crime Groups, Asian Organized Crime Groups*.

Pace, D.F. and Styles, J.C., *Organized Crime: Concept and Control*.

Pantaleone, M., *The Mafia and Politics* (Coward-McCann, New York, 1966).

Rao, V.S., *Criminal Justice: Problems and Perspectives*.

'Report on Japanese Organized Crime', *Australian Customs Service Information Bulletin*, No. 3/91.

Rider, B.K., 'The Promotion and Development of International Co-operation to Combat Commercial and Economic Crime', 'The Enterprise of Crime' and 'The Policing and Control of Syndicated and Organized Crime Activity in Britain', papers presented at seminar on Organized Crime and Terrorism, Midrand, South Africa, July 2001.

Salerno, R. and Tompkins, J.S., *The Crime Confederation: Cosa Nostra and Allied Operations in Organized Crime* (Doubleday, Garden City, NY, 1969).

Saraf, V.K., 'Formation of Criminal Gangs in Big Cities' (unpublished study sponsored by the Government of India).

Schiavo, G., *The Truth about the Mafia and Organized Crime in America* (Vigo Press, New York, 1962).

Sharma, M.L., 'Organized Crime in India – Problems and Perspectives, part I', *Bulletin of the Central Bureau of Investigation*, India, July 1998.

——, 'Organized Crime in India – Problems and Perspectives, part II', *Bulletin of the Central Bureau of Investigation*, India, August 1998.

Singh, M.N., *Growth of Gangsterism in Bombay City – A Report* (following the serial bomb blasts in Mumoai in 1993).

Sterling, C., *The Mafia* (Hamish Hamilton, London, 1990).

Trehan, J., 'Transnational Crimes: Some Traits' in Singh, J. (ed.), *Peace in the New Millennium* (Knowledge World, New Delhi, 2002), pp. 83–89.

United Nations Convention on Transnational Organized Crime 2000.

United Nations, *Problems and Dangers Posed by Organized Transnational Crime in the Various Regions of the World*, UN Document E/CN.15/1993/3, 11 January 1993.

US Department of Justice, *Report of the Task Force on Organized Crime* (1976).

Willams, P. (ed.), *Russian Organized Crime: The New Threat* (Frank Cass, 1997).

CHAPTER III

Andhra Pradesh Police, Intelligence Wing, *Note on the Peoples War Group*.

Aram, M., *Peace in Nagaland: Eight Year Story: 1964–72* (Arnold-Heinemann, New Delhi, 1974).

Baruah, S., *India Against Itself: Assam and the Politics of Nationality* (Oxford University Press, New Delhi, 1999).

Bhattacharjea, A., *Kashmir, the Wounded Valley* (UBSPD, New Delhi, 1994).

Bhaumik, S., *Insurgent Crossfire: North-East India* (Lancer Publishers Pvt. Ltd., New Delhi,).

Bhuyan, B.C. (ed.), *Political Development of the North-East* (Omsons Publications, New Delhi, 1992).

Central Bureau of Investigation, India, *Confidential Note on Serial Bomb Blasts in Bombay (1993)*.

Chalk, P., *West European Terrorism and Counter-Terrorism: The Evolving Dynamic* (Macmillan, Houndmills, 1996).

——, *Technology and Terrorism* (Frank Cass, London, 1993).

Das, A.K., *Assam's Agony: A Socio-Economic and Political Analysis* (Lancers Publishers, New Delhi, 1982).

Fernandes, S.G., 'The Global Fight against Terrorism; Where to Begin and How to End', paper presented at the International Seminar on 'The Global Threat of Terror: Ideological, Material and Political Linkages', New Delhi, 29–31 October 2001.

Filler, A.L., 'The Abu Sayyaf Group: A Growing Menace to Civil Society', paper presented at the International Seminar on 'The Global Threat of Terror: Ideological, Material and Political Linkages', New Delhi, 29–31 October 2001.

Gill, K.P.S., *Punjab: The Knights of Falsehood* (Har-Anand Publications Pvt. Ltd., New Delhi, 1997).

Gill, K.P.S. and Ajai, S. (eds), *Faultlines: Writings on Conflict & Resolution* (a quarterly journal); published by Institute for Conflict Management, New Delhi.

Gunaratna, R., *International & Regional Security Implications of the Sri Lankan Tamil Insurgency* (Alumni Association of the Bandaranaike Centre for International Studies, Sri Lanka, 1997).

Gundevia, Y.D., *War and Peace in Nagaland* (Palit and Palit, Dehradun, 1975).

Hazarika, S., *Strangers of the Mist* (Viking, Penguin Books India Pvt. Ltd., New Delhi, 1994).

Husain, N., 'Menace of Small Arms and its Mitigation: Bangladesh Perspective', paper presented at workshop on 'Curb on Small Arms and Human Security', New Delhi, 17–18 April 2000.

Jafa, V.S., *Insurgency and the Problem of Integration*, circulated in the Lal Bahadur Shastri, National Academy of Administration, Mussoorie.

Jagmohan, *My Frozen Turbulence in Kashmir* (Allied Publishers Ltd., New Delhi, 1991).

Karim Afsir (ed.). *Aakrosh: Asian Journal on Terrorism and Internal Conflicts* (a quarterly publication) by Forum for Strategic and Security Studies, New Delhi,

Kartha, T., 'The Spread of Small Arms and Light Weapons: The Dynamics of Trafficking and Impact on the State', paper presented at workshop on 'Curb on Small Arms and Human Security', New Delhi, 17–18 April 2000.

Kozhokin, E., 'The Problem of Terrorism in the Post-Soviet Era', paper presented at the International Seminar on 'The Global Threat of Terror: Ideological, Material and Political Linkages', New Delhi, 29–31 October 2001.

Kumawat, M., 'The Left Extremism in India – Naxalism, its Recent Growth and Prospect', *National Defence College Journal*, No. 103.

Kurz, A. (ed.), *Contemporary Trends in World Terrorism* (Mansell Publishing Ltd., London, 1987).

Maley, W., 'Messianism and Political Action: Some Contextual Characteristics', paper presented at the International Seminar on 'The Global Threat of Terror: Ideological, Material and Political Linkages', New Delhi, 29–31 October 2001.

Marwah, V., *Uncivil Wars: Pathology of Terrorism in India* (HarperCollins Publishers India Pvt. Ltd., New Delhi, 1995).

Mourad, M., 'Terrorism & Politics; Relation of Time & Place', paper presented at the International Seminar on 'The Global Threat of Terror: Ideological, Material and Political Linkages', New Delhi, 29–31 October 2001.

Nepram, B.L., 'Small Arms, Narcotics and Insurgency in India's North East', paper presented at workshop on 'Curb on Small Arms and Human Security', New Delhi, 17–18 April 2000.

Paz, R., 'The Brotherhood of Global Jihad', paper presented at the International Seminar on 'The Global Threat of Terror: Ideological, Material and Political Linkages', New Delhi, 29–31 October 2001.

Peiris, G.H., 'Secessionist War and Terrorism in Sri Lanka: Transnational Impulses', paper presented at the International Seminar on 'The Global Threat of Terror: Ideological, Material and Political Linkages', New Delhi, 29–31 October 2001.

Prevention of Terrorism Act, India.

Raha, M.K. and Ghosh, A.K. (eds), *North-East India: The Human Interface* (Gyan Publication House, New Delhi, 1998).

Rubin, B. (ed.), *Terrorism and Politics* (Macmillan, London, 1991).

Saikal, A., 'The Taliban: Pakistan's Geopolitical Instrument and America's Problem', paper presented at the International Seminar on 'The Global Threat of Terror: Ideological, Material and Political Linkages', New Delhi, 29–31 October 2001.

Salahuddin, G., 'Human Security and Curb on Small Arms: The Pakistan Perspective', paper presented at workshop on 'Curb on Small Arms and Human Security', New Delhi, 17–18 April 2000.

Singh, J. (ed.), *Pakistan-Occupied Kashmir: Under the Jackboot* (Siddhi Books, New Delhi, 1995).

Strategic Analysis (monthly journal), published by Institute for Defence Studies and Analysis, New Delhi.

Strategic Digest (monthly journal), published by Institute for Defence Studies and Analysis, New Delhi.

Trehan, J., 'Terrorism and the Funding of Terrorism in Kashmir', *Journal of Financial Crime*, Vol. 9 No. 3.

U.S.I. Journal (a quarterly), published by the United Services Institute of India, New Delhi.

Verghese, B.G., *India's Northeast Resurgent* (Konark Publishers Pvt. Ltd., Delhi, 1996).

Wilkinson, P. (ed.), *Terrorism: British Perspectives* (Dartmouth Publications, Aldershot, 1993).

CHAPTER IV

Andelman, D., 'The Drug Money Maze', *Foreign Affairs* Vol. 73 (No. 4), July/August, 1994.

Annual Assessment of Cocaine Movement 2000, February 2001, ONDCP-01-01.

Bagley, B.M. and Walker, W.P. (eds), *Drug Trafficking in the Americas* (Lynne Rienner Publications, Boulder, 1996).

Bentham, M., *The Politics of Drug Control* (Macmillan, London, St. Martin's Press, New York, 1998).

Broadbent, R., 'Combating Illegal Trade', paper presented at Conference on 'The Global Economy of Illegal Drugs', London, UK, 25–26 June 2001.

Bureau for International Narcotics and Law Enforcement Affairs, *International Narcotics Control & Strategy Report, 2001* (US Department of State, Washington, DC, 2002).

Clawson, P.L. and Lee, R.W., *Andean Cocaine Industry* (Macmillan, Houndmills, 1996).

Clutterbuck, R., *Drugs, Crime and Corruption: Thinking the Unthinkable* (Macmillan, Houndmills, 1995).

Cocaine, Opium, Marijuana: Global Problem, Global Response (summary by D. Willoughby), May 1988.

Drugs Enforcement Administration, *Drugs of Abuse* (1989 edn.) (US Department of Justice, Washington).

Goldberg, T., *Demystifying Drugs: A Psychosocial Perspective* (Macmillan, London, 1999).

Griffith, I.L., 'Drugs in the Caribbean: A Political Reality Check', paper presented at Conference on 'The Global Economy of Illegal Drugs', London, UK, 25–26 June 2001.

——, 'The Political Economy of Drugs in the Caribbean: Problems without Passports', paper presented at Conference on 'The Global Economy of Illegal Drugs', London, UK, 25–26 June 2001.

ICPO-Interpol General Secretariat, *Reports on International Illicit Drug Traffic.*

——, *National Statistics on Illicit Drug Production, Traffic and Use.*

Jalalzai, K.M., *Drug War in South Asia* (Institute of Current Affairs, Lahore, 1992).

Jayasuriya, D.C., Nayak, R.K. and Wells, A. (eds), *Global Drugs Law* (Har-Anand Publication Pvt. Ltd., New Delhi).

Jordan, D.C., *Drug Politics: Dirty Money and Democracies* (University of Oklahoma Press, 1999).

Keelty, M., 'The Global Economy of Illegal Drugs', paper presented at Conference on 'The Global Economy of Illegal Drugs', London, UK, 25–26 June 2001.

Keh, D.I., *Drug Money in A Changing World: Economic Reform and Criminal Finance* (United Nations International Drug Control Programme).

Koerbel, C.H., 'Impact of the Illicit Crops on the Rainforest', paper presented at Conference on 'The Global Economy of Illegal Drugs', London, UK, 25–26 June 2001.

Messmer, F., 'The Fight Against Drug Trafficking in Bolivia', paper presented at Conference on 'The Global Economy of Illegal Drugs', London, UK, 25–26 June 2001.

Miller, R.L., *Drugs Warriors and Their Prey: From Police Power to Police State* (Praeger, Westport, 1996).

Narcotics Control Bureau of India, *Annual Report 1998.*

——, *Annual Report 1999.*

——, *Annual Report 2000.*

——, *Annual Report 2001.*

Narcotics News Bulletin (a monthly journal), published by DEA, Country attache for India, 2000–02.

Office on Drugs and Crime, *The Opium Economy in Afghanistan: An International Problem* (United Nations, Vienna, 2003).

Phongpaichit, P., Piriyarangsan, S. and Treerat, N., *Guns, Girls, Gambling, Ganja: Thailand's Illegal Economy and Public Policy* (Silkworm Books, Chiang Mai, 1998).

Raman, B., *Heroinisation of the Pak Economy.*

Reuter, P., 'Do Middle Markets for Drugs Constitute an Attractive Target for Enforcement?', paper presented at Conference on 'The Global Economy of Illegal Drugs', London, UK, 25–26 June 2001.

SAARC Convention on Narcotic Drugs and Psychotropic Substances which came into force on 15 September 1993.

Storbeck, J., 'Middle Markets', paper presented at Conference on 'The Global Economy of Illegal Drugs', London, UK, 25–26 June 2001.

Szendrel, K., 'Synthetic Drugs: Many Dilemmas', paper presented at Conference on 'The Global Economy of Illegal Drugs', London, UK, 25–26 June 2001.

Thoumi, F.E., 'Illegal Drugs in Colombia: From Illegal Economic Boom to Social Crisis', paper presented at Conference on 'The Global Economy of Illegal Drugs', London, UK, 25–26 June 2001.

UNDCP Regional Office for South Asia, *South Asia Drug Demand Reduction Report.*

United Nations Convention against Illicit Traffic in Narcotics Drugs and Psychotropic Substances, 1988.

United Nations Convention on Psychotropic Substances, 1971.

United Nations International Drug Control Programme, *World Drug Report 1997* (Oxford University Press, New York, 1997).

——, *World Drug Report 2000* (Oxford University Press, New York, 2000).

United Nations Single Convention on Narcotics Drugs, 1961 as amended by the 1972 protocol.

United Nations, *Report of the International Narcotics Control Board for 1999* (2000).

United Nations, *Report of the International Narcotics Control Board for 2000* (2001).

United Nations, *The United Nations and Drug Control* (1982).

US Office of National Drug Control Policy, *Estimation of Cocaine Availability 1996–1999*, 2000.

——, US Information Agency, *National Drug Control Strategy 2001 Annual Report.*

Wong, J.Y., *Deadly Dreams: Opium and the Arrow War in China* (Cambridge University Press, Cambridge, 1998).

CHAPTER V

Burkill, N., 'The Civil Law Consequences of Laundering or Receiving the Proceeds of Corruption'.

Clarke, M. (ed.), *Corruption: Causes, Consequences and Control* (Frances Pinter Publishers Ltd., London, 1983).

Elliot, K.A., *Corruption and the Global Economy* (Institute for International Economics, 1997).

Gill, S.S., *The Pathology of Corruption* (HarperCollins Publishers India Pvt. Ltd., New Delhi, 1998).

Graham, T.S., 'Civil and Criminal Liability of those that Pay Bribes to Win Contracts'.

——, 'Criminal Liability of Banks and Others that Handle the Proceeds of Grand Corruption'.

Independent Commission Against Corruption, *Annual Report 1999*, Special Administrative Region, Hong Kong, Government.

——, *2000: Policy Address – Fighting Corruption*, Special Administrative Region, Hong Kong, Government.

Lal, B., *Corruption: Functional Anarchy in Governance* (Siddharth Publications, New Delhi, 2002).

Reddy, D.N., *Crime, Corruption and Development* (Deep & Deep Publications Pvt. Ltd., New Delhi).

Rider, B.A.K. (ed.), *Corruption: The Enemy Within* (Kluwer Law International, The Hague – London – Boston, 1997).

Rose-Ackerman, S., *Corruption and Government: Causes, Consequences and Reform* (Cambridge University Press, London, 1999).

Saighal, V., *Model for Restoration of Good Government*, Movement for Restoration of Good Government, New Delhi.

Singh, N., *The World of Bribery and Corruption* (Mittal Publications, New Delhi, 1998).

Singh, N.K., *The Politics of Crime and Corruption* (HarperCollins Publication India, New Delhi, 1999).

Sutherland, E.H. and Cressey, D.R., *Criminology* (10th edn) (Lippincott, Philadelphia, 1978).

United Nations, *Action against Corruption and Bribery* (1997).

Vittal, N. and Mahalingam, Dr. S., *Fighting Corruption and Restructuring Government* (Manas Publications, New Delhi, 2000).

Vittal, N., *Towards Effective Governance*, text of talk delivered at India International Centre, New Delhi, 16 June 2000.

CHAPTERS VI, VII AND IX

Adler, P., *Wheeling and Dealing* (2nd edn), (Columbia University Press, New York, 1993).

Central Bureau of Investigation, India, in collaboration with Reserve Bank of India, *Large Value Frauds in Banks* (a Confidential Paper).

Davis, L.J., *Bad Money* (St. Martin's Press, New York, 1982).

Directorate of Revenue Intelligence, *Annual Report 1998–99* (Department of Revenue, Ministry of Finance, Government of India).

——, *Annual Report 1999–2000* (Department of Revenue, Ministry of Finance, Government of India).

——, *Annual Report 2000–01* (Department of Revenue, Ministry of Finance, Government of India).

Friedrichs, D.O., *Trusted Criminals: White Collar Crime in Contemporary Society* (Wadsworth Publishing Company, Belmont, Calif, 1996).

Joint Committee of the Indian Parliament (Vols. I–III) Report of Enquiry into Irregularities in Securities and Banking Transactions 1993.

Koker, L. de, Rider, B.A.K. and Henning, J.J. (eds), *Victims of Economic Crime*, UOVS/UOFS 31 Med SOR/31 Tran CBL Bloemfontein, 1999.

Levi, M. (ed.), *Fraud, Organization, Motivation and Control* (Aldershot, Brokfield, Vt., Ashgate, 1999).

Ministry of Home Affairs (North Eastern Council), *Basic Statistics of the North Eastern Region* (2000), Government of India, Shillong.

Reuvid, J. (consultant ed.), *The Regulation and Prevention of Economic Crime Internationally* (Kogan Page Ltd., London, 1995).

Securities and Exchange Board of India (Collective Investment Scheme) Regulations, 1999.

Securities and Exchange Board of India, *Annual Report 1997–98.*

——, *Annual Report 1998–99.*

——, *Annual Report 1999–2000.*

Tamil Nadu Protection of Interests of Depositors Act, 1997.

World Gold Council, *Gold Demand Trends* (quarterly publication).

Zdanowicz, J.S., Welch, W.W., and Pak, S.J., 'Capital Flight from India to the United States through Abnormal Pricing in International Trade', *Finance India* (1995) Vol. IX, No. 3, pp. 609–627.

CHAPTER VIII

Acharya, S.N. *et al.* (with contribs by Chelliah, R.J.) *Aspects of the Black Economy in India* (Ministry of Finance, Government of India, 1985, repr. 1986 National Institute of Public Finance and Policy, New Delhi).

Associated Chambers of Commerce and Industry of India, *Report on Black Money* (New Delhi, 1991).

Bagai, S.S., *Black Money in India* (Bagai Tax Law Services Pvt. Ltd., Bombay, 1991).

Chattopadhyay, S., *Macroeconomic Disequilibrium and the Black Economy in the Context of Stabilization Policy in India*, Ph.D. thesis, Jawahar Lal Nehru University, New Delhi, May 2000.

Chugh, R.L. and Uppal, J.S., *Black Economy in India* (Tata McGraw-Hill Publication Company Ltd., New Delhi, 1986).

Gupta, S.B., *Black Income in India* (Sage Publications, New Delhi, 1992).

Kabra, K.N., *The Black Economy in India – Problems and Policies* (Chanakya Publications, New Delhi, 1982).

Kumar, A., *The Black Economy in India* (Penguin Books India Pvt. Ltd., New Delhi, 1999).

Lok Sabha (Lower House, Indian Parliament) Answer to Starred Question No. 281 (08-12-2000) regarding Black Money in the Country.

CHAPTER X

Ali, S.A., 'Offshore Trusts – Trusted Friend or Sinister Enemy?', paper presented at 18th International Symposium on Economic Crime held at Jesus College, Cambridge, UK.

Australian Transaction Reports and Analysis Centre, *Estimates of the Extent of Money Laundering in and through Australia* (1995).

Baily, M.N., Farrell, D. and Lund, S., 'The Color of Hot Money', *Foreign Affairs*, March/April 2000.

Baldwin, F.N. and Munro, R.J., *Money Laundering, Asset Forfeiture and International Financial Crimes* (Oceana Publications, New York, 1992).

Birks, P., *Laundering and Tracing* (Clarendon Press, New York: Oxford University, 1995).

Blum, J.A., Levi, M.R., Naylor, T. and Williams, P., *Financial Havens, Banking Secrecy and Money Laundering*: a study prepared on behalf of the United Nations under the auspices of the Global Programme against Money Laundering (Office for Drug Control and Crime Prevention, Vienna, 1998).

Chaikin, D.A., *Investigating Criminal and Corporate Money Trails*.

Correspondent Banking: A Gateway for Money Laundering, Report by Minority Staff of the Permanent Subcommittee on Investigations, US, 5 February 2001.

Doggart, C., *Tax Havens and Their Uses*, Special Report No. 1084, The Economist Intelligence Unit, London, 1987.

Ehrenfeld, R., *Evil Money: Encounters Along the Money Trail* (HarperCollins Publishers, New York, 1992).

Financial Crimes Enforcement Network (FinCEN), *Wire Transfer Systems: CHIPS and SWIFT: A Reference Guide* (United States Department of the Treasury, Washington, DC, 1992).

——, *An Assessment of Narcotics-Related Money Laundering* (United States Department of the Treasury, Washington, DC, 1992).

Fisse, B., Fraser, D. and Coss, G. (eds), *The Money Trail* (Law Book Co., Sydney, 1992).

Gaylord, M.S., 'The Chinese Laundry: International Drug Trafficking and Hong Kong's Banking Industry', Department of Applied Studies, City Polytechnic of Hong Kong.

Glover, J., 'Taxing the Proceeds of Crime', *Journal of Money Laundering Control*.

Graycar, A. and Grabosky, P. (eds), *Money-Laundering in the Twenty-First Century: Risks and Countermeasures* (Australian Institute of Criminology, Canberra, 1996).

Hopton, D., 'Prevention of Money Laundering: The Practical Day-to-Day Problems and Some Solutions', *Journal of Money Laundering Control*.

Johnson, L.B., 'The Law and Practice Relating to Offshore Financial Institutions', paper presented at 8th Commonwealth Law Conference, Jamaica, 7–13 September 1986.

Karchmer, C., *Illegal Money Laundering – A Strategy & Resource Guide for Law Enforcement Agencies* (Police Executive Resources, Washington, DC, 1998).

Levi, M., 'New Frontiers of Criminal Liability: Money Laundering and Proceeds of Crime', *Journal of Money Laundering Control*.

McCusker, R., 'Money-Laundering Control: Elusive Dream or Achievable Reality?, *Journal of Money Laundering Control*.

Naylor, R.T., 'Drug Money, Hot Money, and Debt', *European Journal of International Affairs*, Winter, 1989.

Office of Technology Assessment, Congress of the United States, *Information Technologies for the Control of Money Laundering*.

Possamai, M., *Money on the Run* (Penguin, Toronto, 1992).

Powis, R., *The Money Launderers: Lessons from the Drug Wars – How Billions of Illegal Dollars are Washed Through Banks and Businesses* (Probus Publishing, Chicago, 1992).

Private Banking and Money Laundering: A Case Study of Opportunities and Vulnerabilities, US Senate Hearing.

Rider, B.A.K. and Ashe, M. (eds.), *Money Laundering Control* (Round Hall/Sweet & Maxwell, Dublin, 1996).

Rider, B.K., 'The Crusade Against Money Laundering – Time to Think!', *European Journal of Law Reform*.

——, 'The Control of Money Laundering – A Bridge too Far?', *European Journal of Law Reform*.

Robinson, J., *The Laundrymen* (Simon & Schuster Ltd., London, 1994).

United States Department of State Bureau for International Narcotics and Law Enforcement Affairs, *International Narcotics Control Strategy Report – Executive Summary, March 2000*.

237

Walter, I., *Secret Money Market: Inside the Dark World of Tax Evasion. Financial Fraud, Insider Trading, Money Laundering, and Capital Flight* (Harper & Row, Ballinger Division, New York, 1990).

Willoughby, P., 'The Law and Practice of Tax Havens: Uses and Abuses', paper presented at 8th Commonwealth Law Conference, Jamaica, 7–13 September 1986.

CHAPTER XI

Adams, J.R. and Frantz, D., *A Full Service Bank: How BCCI Stole Millions Around the World* (Simon & Schuster Inc., New York, 1992).

Baxter, T.C., 'Breaking the Billion Dollar Barrier – Learning the Lessons of BNL, Daiwa and BCCI', *Journal of Money Laundering Control*, Vol. 1, June 1997.

Financial Action Task Force, *1998–1999 Report on Money Laundering Typologies.*

——, *1999–2000 Report on Money Laundering Typologies.*

Mitchell, A., Sikka, P. and Willmott, H., *The Accountants' Laundromat* (University of Essex, Essex, 1998).

Money Laundering Methodologies and International and Regional Counter Measures – paper prepared for CSCAP Study Group on Transnational Crime Meeting in Bangkok (10/11 October 1997).

Naylor, R.T., *Bankers, Bagmen and Bandits* (Black Rose, New York, 1990).

Potts, M., Kochan, N. and Whittington, R., *Dirty Money* (National Press, Washington, DC).

Richardson, L.D., 'The Urgency of Detergence (Or How Money Laundering is Carried out)', *TVI Journal*, Winter 1986.

Trehan, J., 'And quiet flows the cash', *Hindustan Times*, 5 May 2001.

US Customs for the Financial Action Task Force, *Typology of Money Laundering* (Washington DC).

Woolner, A., *Washed in Gold: The Story Behind the Biggest Money Laundering Investigation in U.S. History* (American Lawyer Books, Simon & Schuster, New York, 1994).

CHAPTER XII

Bruton, W.F., 'Money Laundering: Is it Now A Corporate Problem?', *Journal of Money Laundering Control*, Vol. 3, No.1.

Cassidy, W.L., *Fei-Ch'ien Flying Money: A Study of Chinese Underground Banking*, annotated text of address to 12th Annual International Asian Organized Crime Conference, Ft. Lauderdale, Florida, 26 June 1990.

ICPO-Interpol General Secretariat, *Report No. 14 on System of Illegal International Financial Transactions: Underground or Parallel Banking* submitted to 60th General Assembly Session, Interpol, 4–8 November 1991, Punta Del Este. This report was compiled by Jyoti Trehan and its Appendix 2 has an extensive bibliography dealing with the subject matter of the report.

——, *The Hawala Alternative Remittance System and its Role in Money Laundering* (Lyon, 2000).

Kapoor, S., *Bad Money, Bad Politics: The Untold Hawala Story* (Har-Anand Publications, New Delhi, 1996).

Passas, N., *Informal Value Transfer Systems and Criminal Organizations – A Study into So-called Underground Banking Networks* (conducted for The Netherlands), No. 1999/4.

Rider, B.A.K., 'Fei Ch'ien Laundries – The Pursuit of Flying Money', *Journal of International Planning*, August 1992.
Trehan, J., 'Underground and Parallel Banking Systems', *Journal of Financial Crime*, July 2002.
US Customs Service, Handout, *Black Market Peso Exchange*.

CHAPTER XIII

Brown, H., *Thinking About National Security: Defense and Foreign Policy in a Dangerous World* (Westview Press, Boulder, Colo., 1983).
Brzezinski, Z., *In Quest of National Security* (Westview Press, Boulder, Colo., 1988).
Cable, V., 'What is International Economic Security?', *International Affairs* 71/2 (1995).
Cimbala, S.J. (ed.), *National Security Strategy: Choices and Limits* (Prager Publishers, New York).
Clark, J.J., *The New Economics of National Defense* (Random House, New York).
Datta, N.P., 'Towards a National Security Council', *Indian Defence Review*.
Deger, S. and Sen, S., *Military Expenditure: The Political Economy of International Security* (SIPRI) (Oxford University Press, 1990).
Freedman, R.O., *Economic Warfare in the Communist Bloc: A Study of Soviet Pressure Against Yugoslavia, Albania and China* (Praeger Publishers, New York).
From Surprise to Reckoning: The Kargil Review Committee Report (Sage Publications, New Delhi, 1999).
Garg Usha, V.J., *Poverty of Nations and the New Economic Order* (UDH Publishers, New Delhi, 1985).
Hagerty, D.T., 'India's Regional Security Doctrine', *Asian Survey* Vol. XXXI (No. 4), April 1991.
Hartley, K., *The Economics of Defence Policy* (Brassey's, London 1991).
Hazari, K.K., 'National Security: Future Threat & Challenges', *Studies in International Strategic Issues*, Vol. 2, No. 1, 1996.
Hosey, W.J., 'Economics, National Policy, and Military Strategy: The Growing Linkage in the 1990s', *Naval War College Review*.
Kaufmann, W.W., *McNamara Strategy* (Harper & Row Publishers, New York, 1964).
Mohan, R., 'The Economy and National Security Strategy', *Strategic Analysis* (February 1995).
Moran, T.H., 'International Economics and National Security', *Foreign Affairs*.
Rao, R.R., 'National Security Perspectives', *USI Journal of the United Services Institute of India*.
Ray, A.K., 'Political Economy of the National Security Council', *Economic and Political Weekly*, 3 March 1990.
Samuels, W.J. (ed.), *Research in the History of Economic Thought and Methodology*, Vol. 17 (Jai Press, London, 1999).
Shorey, A., 'Proliferation of Internal Security and Allied Agencies in India: A Fresh Look', *Strategic Analysis* (July 1989).
Singh, J., 'A National Security Council for India', *Indian Defence Review*.
——, 'Indian Security: A Framework for National Strategy', *Strategic Analysis* (November 1987).
Sorensen, T.C., 'Rethinking National Security', *Foreign Affairs*.
Sperling, J. and Kirchner, E., 'Economic Security and the Problem of Cooperation in Post-Cold War Europe', *Review of International Studies*.

Transnational Crime as a Security Issue – presentation to third meeting, Council for Security Cooperation in the Asia-Pacific, 23–24 May 1998, Manila, The Philippines.

USA, Panel on the Impact of National Security Controls on International Technology Transfer (National Academy Press, Washington DC).

Venkateswaran, A.P., 'What Role for a National Security Council?', *Indian Defence Review*.

Verma, A.K., 'National Security: Decision Making', *Indian Defence Review*.

Viano, E.C. (ed.), *Global Organised Crime and International Security* (Ashgate, Aldershot, 1999).

Williams, P., 'Transnational Criminal Organisations and International Security', *Survival*, Vol. 36, No. 1, Spring 1994.

Zakheim, D.S., 'Economic Security after a Settlement: The Prospects for Israel'

CHAPTER XIV

Acharya, S., 'Managing External Economic Challenges in the Nineties: Lessons for the Future', 18th Anniversary Lecture of the Centre for Banking Studies, Occasional Papers Number 33-1999.

Baker, R.W., 'The Biggest Loophole in the Free-Market System', *The Washington Quarterly*, Autumn 1999.

Bhagwati, J. and Srinivasan, T.N., *India's Economic Reforms* (Ministry of Finance, Government of India, 1993).

Das, T.K., 'Structural Reforms and Stabilization Policies in India: Rationale and Medium-Term Outlook', in *Liberalization: Its Impact on the Indian Economy* (SG Wasani for Macmillan India Limited, New Delhi, 1993).

Finance Ministers of India Budget Speeches for the financial years 1989–90, 1990–91, 1991–92, 1992–93, 1993–94, 1994–95, 1995–96, 1996–97, 1997–98, 1998–99, 1999–2000, 2000–01, 2001–02 and 2002–03.

Gupta, S.P., 'Recent Economic Reforms and Their Impact' in *Liberalization: Its Impact on the Indian Economy* (SG Wasani for Macmillan India Limited, New Delhi, 1993).

Jalan, B. (ed.), *The Indian Economy Problems and Prospects* (Penguin Books India (P) Ltd., New Delhi, 1993).

Ministry of Finance, India, *Economic Survey* (annual publication) for the financial years 1988–89, 1990–91, 1992–93, 1994–95, 1996–97, 1997–98, 1998–99, 1999–2000, 2000–01, 2001–02, 2002–03 (Ministry of Finance, Government of India).

——, *Government Subsidies in India – Discussion Paper* (Government of India, Department of Economic Affairs, 1997).

——, *India's External Debt – A Status Report* (Government of India, Department of Economic Affairs, 2000).

Mohan, R., 'Economic Reforms: The Next Wave', Lalit Doshi Memorial Lecture, Mumbai, 1999.

Naylor, R.T., *Hot Money and the Politics of Debt* (The Linden Press/Simon & Schuster, New York, 1987).

Reserve Bank of India, *Handbook of Statistics on Indian Economy* (1999).

Samuelson, P.A. and Nordhaus, W.D., *Economics* (International Fifteenth Edition) (McGraw-Hill, Inc., New York).

Tarapore Committee, *Report on Capital Account Convertibility* (Reserve Bank of India, Mumbai, 1997).

CHAPTERS XV, XVI AND XVII

Alexander, R., *Emerging Markets – Inherent Risks* (Institute of Advanced Legal Studies, London).

Camdessus, M., 'Money Laundering: The Importance of International Countermeasures', address to Plenary Meeting of the IMF Financial Action Task Force on Money Laundering, Paris, 10 February 1998.

Global Programme Against Money Laundering, *Russian Capitalism and Money Laundering: A Study* (Office for Drug Control and Crime Prevention, Vienna).

Money Laundering and Related Issues in Turkmenistan; Money Laundering and Related Issues in Uzbekistan; Global Programme Against Money Laundering, *Money Laundering and Related Issues in Kazakhstan*, Central Asia Briefings, Central Asia Study Project, United Nations.

Quirk, P.J., *Macroeconomic Implications of Money Laundering*, IMF Working Paper, June 1996.

——, 'Money Laundering: Muddying the Macro-economy', 1997.

Rider, B.A.K., 'Combating International Commercial Crime' (unpublished paper).

——, 'The Price of Probity', *Journal of Financial Crime*, Vol. 7, No. 2 – Analysis.

Savona, E.U., 'Economic Crime in the Financial Markets – The Case of Eastern European Countries: Analysis and Remedies', paper presented at the 18th Cambridge International Symposium on Economic Crime.

Shelley, L.L., 'The Criminal–Political Nexus: A Russian Case Study', paper presented at the Institute for Contemporary Studies and NSIC Conference on 'Confronting the Challenge of the Political–Criminal Nexus', Mexico, March 1997.

Tanzi, V., *Money Laundering and the International Financial System*, IMF Working Paper, May 1996.

Varese, F., *Pervasive Corruption and Economic Crime in Russia* (Kluwer Law International, London, 1999).

Verwoerd, L., 'Money Laundering and Economic and Financial Development: Five Popular Economic Fallacies', paper presented at the Asian Money Laundering Symposium, Kuala Lumpur, 29 November–1 December 1994.

CHAPTERS XVIII, XIX AND XX

APG Standard Mutual Evaluation Questionnaire.

Australian Federal Police, *Inquiry into the Law Enforcements Implication of New Technology –* Report to Parliamentary Joint Committee on the National Crime Authority.

Basel Committee on Banking Supervision Consultative Document – Customer Due Diligence for Banks.

Carroll, W.J., 'Market Manipulation: An International Comparison'.

Council of Europe Procedures for Mutual Evaluations.

Draft Convention on Cyber-Crimes, Secretariat, Directorate General (Legal Affairs), European Committee.

Draft Convergence Bill (India) relating to Information Technology, Communication and Broadcasting.

FATF Report on Non-Cooperative Countries and Territories (NCCT).

FATF Review of Anti-Money Laundering Systems and Mutual Evaluation Procedures 1992–1999.

Figge, V.B., *Panama's Experience in the Fight Against Money Laundering.*

Graycar, A., *Speeches and Papers by the Australian Institute of Criminology about Nine Types of Cyber Crime.*

Hampton, M., *The Offshore Interface: Tax Havens in the Global Economy* (Macmillan, Basingstoke, 1996).

Hampton, M., *Microstates and Offshore Finance: The Political Economy of Vulnerability* (University of Portsmouth, Department of Economics, Southsea, 1999).

Hutchins, G., 'The Electronic Dimension to Money Laundering – The Investigator's Perspective', *Journal of Money Laundering Control*, Vol. 3, No. 3.

Information Technology Act.

Johnstone, P., 'Financial Crime: Prevention and Regulation in the Intangible Environment', *Journal of Money Laundering Control*, Vol. 2, No. 3.

Jones, R. and Keasey, K., 'Money Laundering and the Internet: A Challenge for Regulation', *Journal of Money Laundering Control*, Vol. 8, No. 1.

Langevoort, D.C., 'Cross-Border Insider Trading', paper presented at 18th International Symposium on Economic Crime, Jesus College, Cambridge, UK.

London School of Economics (Computer Security Research Centre), *Comely: Control of Money Laundering in the Electronic Years* (Ufficio Italiano dei Cambi and RAND).

Musalem, E. L. and A., *Offshore Banking: An Analysis of Micro-and Macro-Prudential Issues* (IMF, Washington, DC, 1999).

Mussington, D.A., Wilson, P.A. and Molander, R.C., *Exploring Money Laundering Vulnerabilities Through Emerging Cyberspace Technologies: A Caribbean-Based Exercise* (RAND, Washington, DC, 1998).

Nardo, M., 'Electronic Financial Transactions and Money Laundering', paper presented at 18th International Symposium on Economic Crime, Jesus College, Cambridge, UK.

Offshore Group of Banking Supervisors Procedures for Mutual Evaluations.

Pocica, R.S., 'The Fight against Cybercrime', paper presented at 18th International Symposium on Economic Crime, Jesus College, Cambridge, UK.

Retledge, G.P., 'Electronic Markets: Risks and Rewards', paper presented at 18th International Symposium on Economic Crime, Jesus College, Cambridge, UK.

Richards, J.R., *Transnational Criminal Organization, Cybercrime and Money Laundering: A Handbook for Law Enforcement Officers, Auditors and Financial Investigators* (CRC Press, Boca Raton, Flo., 1999).

Tan, S.T., 'Economic and Financial Crime Trends and New Threats', paper presented at 18th International Symposium on Economic Crime, Jesus College, Cambridge, UK.

United States General Accounting Office, *Money Laundering:Rapid Growth of Casinos Makes them Vulnerable* (Washington, DC, 1996).

US Department of Justice Drug Enforcement Administration, *Financial Investigative Methods* (Instructor's Manual).

Wilson, P. and Mussington, D., 'Money Laundering and Financial Crime: Exploiting Cyberpayments and Ecommerce Technologies', paper presented at 18th International Symposium on Economic Crime, Jesus College, Cambridge, UK.

Winer, J.M., 'The Coming Wave of Transparency Reforms: A Tidal Shift', keynote address, 17th Cambridge International Symposium on Economic Crime, Jesus College, Cambridge University, UK, 13 September 1999.

Wittelsberger, H., 'Protecting the Euro against Counterfeiting: A Case for EC Regulation'.

CHAPTER XXI

FinCEN Overview & Mission – Information for Law Enforcement Customer, US Department of Treasury.

2nd Review of the Suspicious Activity Reporting System, US Department of Treasury.

Home Office Organized and International Crime Directorate, *Confiscation and Money Laundering: Law and Practice – A Guide for Enforcement Authorities* (HMSO, London, 1997).

Koker, L. de, *Money Laundering Trends in South Africa*.
Koker, L. de and Henning, J.J., *Money Laundering Control in South Africa*.
Nakajima, C. and Rider, B.A.K., *Anti Money Laundering Guide* (CCH Editions, Bicester, 1999).
National Crime Squad (UK), *Annual Report 1999/2000*.
Organized and Serious Crime Ordinance and Drug Trafficking (Recovery of Proceeds) Ordinance of Hong Kong.
US Departments of Treasury and Justice, *National Money Laundering Strategy for 2000*.

CHAPTER XXII

Conservation of Foreign Exchange and Prevention of Smuggling Activities Act 1974 (as amended 1996).
Foreign Exchange Management Act 1999.
Prevention of Money Laundering Act 2002.
Prevention of Money Laundering Bill 1999.
Report of the Select Committee on the Prevention of Money Laundering Bill 1999.
Smugglers and Foreign Exchange Manipulators (Forfeiture of Property) Act 1976.
Trehan, J., 'Money Talks', *Hindustan Times*, 4 June 2001.

CHAPTER XXIII

An Introduction to International Forfeiture (Asset Forfeiture Office and Office of International Affairs, US Department of Justice, Washington).
Bhala, R., *Legal Aspects of Money Laundering*.
Introduction to Asset Removal Investigations (Drug Enforcement Administration, Office of Training, Quantico, Virginia).
Jayasuriya, D.C., *Money Laundering: The Role of Legislation in Developing Economies*.
Mitchell, A., Hinton, N. and Taylor, S., *Confiscation* (2nd edn) (Sweet and Maxwell, London, 1996).
Mitchell, A., Taylor, S.M.E. and Talbot, K.V., *Mitchell, Taylor & Talbot on Confiscation and the Proceeds of Crime* (2nd edn) (Sweet and Maxwell, London, 1997).
Parlour, R., *Butterworths International Guide to Money Laundering: Law and Practice* (Butterworths, London, 1995).
Performance and Innovation Unit, *Recovering the Proceeds of Crime – a Summary*, Cabinet Office, UK.
——, *Recovering the Proceeds of Crime*, Cabinet Office, UK, June 2000.
Rider, B.K. 'The Limits of the Law: An Analysis of the Interrelationship of the Criminal and Civil Law in the Control of Money Laundering', *Journal of Money Laundering Control*, Vol. 2, No. 3.
United Nations, *Control of the Proceeds of Crime*, Report of the Secretary General, UN Document E/CN.15/1996/3, 3 April 1996.
United Nations, *Investigators Manual on Financial Investigations and Money Laundering*.

CHAPTER XXIV

Alexander, K., *Threat to the Stability and Integrity of the Economic Order and the Good Governance of the Financial Markets*, paper presented at the 18th Cambridge International Symposium on Economic Crime.

Commonwealth Model Law for the Prohibition of Money Laundering.

Edwards, A., *Review of Financial Regulation in the Crown Dependencies* (A Report on Jersey, Guernsey and the Isle of Man).

European Council Directive 91/308/EEC of 10 June 1991 on *Prevention of the Use of the Financial System for the Purpose of Money Laundering*.

European Parliament amending Council Directive 91/308/EEC of 10 June 1991 on *Prevention of the Use of the Financial Systems for the Purpose of Money Laundering*.

European Parliament and Council Directive amending Council Directive 91/308/EEC of 10 June 1991 on *Prevention of the Use of the Financial System For the Purpose of Money Laundering*.

European Parliament Report on the initiative of the French Republic with a view to adopting a *Convention on Improving Mutual Assistance in Criminal matters*, particularly in the area of *Combating Organized Crime, Laundering of the Proceeds from Crime and Financial Crime*.

European Parliament Report on the initiative of the French Republic with a view to adopting a Council Framework Decision on *Money Laundering, the Identification, Tracing, Freezing, Seizing and Confiscation of Instrumentalities and the Proceeds from Crime*.

Garcia, J., 'International Measures to Fight Money Laundering', *Journal of Money Laundering Control*, Vol. 3, No. 1.

Gillmore, W.C., *Dirty Money* (Council of Europe Press, 1995).

Gillmore, W., *The International Perspective to Money Laundering – International and Regional Initiatives* (International Tracing of Assets, Rel, 1997).

Gilmore, W.C., University of Cambridge, Research Centre for International Law. Commonwealth Secretariat, *International Efforts to Combat Money Laundering* (Grotius Publications, Cambridge, 1992).

Savona, E. (ed.), *Responding to Money Laundering: International Perspective* (Harwood Academic Publishers, Amsterdam, 1997).

Stessens, G., *Money Laundering: A New International Law Enforcement Model* (Cambridge University Press, New York, 2000).

The World Financial Authority, a paper by Lord Eatwell for the Ford Foundation.

United Nations Model Bill on Money Laundering and Proceeds of Crime 2000 (Common Law Systems).

United Nations Model Legislation on Laundering, Confiscation and International Cooperation in Relation to the Proceeds of Crime 1999 (Civil Law Systems).

United Nations Model Mutual Assistance in Criminal Matters Bill 1998 (Common Law Systems).

US Customs Service, *Financial Intelligence Project: The European Community: 1992 and Money Laundering* (New York, 1990).

Index

Omnibus Crime Control and Safe Streets Act (US)
13–14, 20
online securities trading   171–2, 174
onshore banking   179, 182–3
open general licences (OGLs)   82–3
Operation Casablanca   116
organized crime   8–28, 205–6
organized-crime groups   8–12, 17–18, 19–20

Pacific islands   160, 182
   see also Asia-Pacific
Pakistan   18, 31, 35, 39, 41, 86
Panama   183
paper trails   99, 121, 123
parallel banking   112, 115–16
   see also underground banking
parallel economy   5, 51
perceptions of terrorism   29
peso exchange *see* black market peso exchange
physical placement of money   110–12
Pindari   9–10
plantation companies   60
police   25, 26, 27, 28, 228
political corruption   49, 50–1
political economy model   138
polity   141, 144
population   141, 144–5
poverty alleviation   28
power brokers   164
Presidential Commission on Law Enforcement and
   Administration of Justice   13
presumptive tax   79
Prevention of Irregularities by Gangsters (Japan)   14
Prevention of Money Laundering Act (India)
   207–12
Prevention of Organized Crime Act (South Africa)
   201–2
Prevention of Terrorism Act (India)   33, 210
preventive detention   23
primary teacher scams   63
privacy   175–6
private sector   53–4
proactive intelligence   165
procedural laws   24, 214
proceeds of crime   44, 51, 163, 185–9, 215–16
professionals role   166
profiling   19–20
property   105–6
protocols, wire money transfers   97–8
public-sector reform   156–7
Punjab   31, 35

racecourses   105
Racketeer Influenced and Corrupt Organizations
   (RICO) Act (US)   14, 20–1, 214
Rajasthan   64
Rao, Narasimha   53
Ray, Aswin   138
Red Army, Japan   36
reforms   154, 157–8
   see also combating measures
regional economic groupings   228–9
regional organizations, underground banking
   control   132
regular banking   132
regulatory bodies   166
Reserve Bank of India   61, 132, 152
retail sector   48–9, 103–4
RICO Act *see* Racketeer Influenced...
rights   175–6, 215
routes   39, 42, 80–1, 85
Russia
   Euro-dollar market   185
   KGB   181
   money laundering laws   203
   offshore   93, 160, 181–2
   Russian Organized Crime Groups   10, 19
   second economy   76
   terrorism   36
   transition problems   160–1

sales tax   62
scams   59–65, 150, 164
Scandinavia   55
Schmoller, Gustav   138
secrecy in banking   94, 180, 184, 194, 196
securities market
   conversions   97, 111
   frauds   71–2
   international trading   155–6
   money laundering   106–7
   online trading   171–2, 174
September 11 2001   32–3, 128, 150, 224
services sector   155
shell entities   94, 95, 113, 180–1
short-term certificates of deposit   186
Shourie, Arun   64
shroffs   120
silver   84
simple money laundering   199–200
Singapore   117, 118, 182, 184
Single Convention on Narcotic Drugs   44
smart cash   172